Cost–Benefit Analysis

THEORY AND PRACTICE

Other Macmillan books by the same authors:

Ajit K. Dasgupta and A. J. Hagger:
THE OBJECTIVES OF MACRO-ECONOMIC POLICY

C. J. Hawkins and D. W. Pearce:
CAPITAL INVESTMENT APPRAISAL

D. W. Pearce: COST−BENEFIT ANALYSIS

Cost–Benefit Analysis

THEORY AND PRACTICE

Ajit K. Dasgupta

PROFESSOR OF ECONOMICS,
SIR GEORGE WILLIAMS UNIVERSITY, MONTREAL

AND

D. W. Pearce

LECTURER IN ECONOMICS,
UNIVERSITY OF SOUTHAMPTON

MACMILLAN

First published 1972 by
THE MACMILLAN PRESS LTD
London and Basingstoke
Associated companies in New York Toronto
Dublin Melbourne Johannesburg and Madras

SBN 333 11395 0 (hard cover)
333 11397 7 (paper cover)

Printed in Great Britain by
RICHARD CLAY (THE CHAUCER PRESS) LTD
Bungay, Suffolk

Contents

Preface

T HIS book has been divided into four Parts. The first, on 'objective functions', deals with the cost–benefit objective of maximising gains to social welfare. Chapters 1 and 2 discuss the welfare foundations of cost–benefit and Chapter 3 is devoted to the problems of defining and deriving a social welfare function in terms of individual preferences. The second Part deals with 'accounting' or 'shadow' prices, beginning with a general chapter, Chapter 4, on the meaning and derivation of accounting prices in the context of Pareto optimality. Chapter 5 discusses the important phenomenon of externalities and raises some of the problems of finding accounting prices for non-marketed goods. Chapter 6 looks at the social discount rate as the accounting price which reflects society's intertemporal preferences.

Part 3 completes the theoretical analysis of cost–benefit with a discussion of the appropriate 'normalisation' techniques – net present value, internal rate of return and so on – while Chapter 8 looks at the complex problem of risk and uncertainty.

Part 4 details two applications of cost–benefit, one to a project in an advanced economy, and one which, while applicable to many advanced economies, is used to illustrate the relevance of cost–benefit for underdeveloped economies. We have deliberately chosen to discuss only two applications. This choice obviously risks giving the impression that cost–benefit is not a widely applicable approach to decision-making, when the very opposite is true. On the other hand, we felt that highly superficial outlines of the possible applications of CBA would not provide the reader with a proper insight into the many problems which arise when cost–benefit is actually applied.

Bibliographies are grouped at the back of the book. These are necessarily select, but we hope that they will act as a guide to the reader who wishes to investigate the subject in more depth.

Lastly, we have done our best to avoid complex discussions and to avoid mathematics beyond that which can reasonably be expected of the general undergraduate.

A. K. D.
D. W. P.

Acknowledgements

WE should like to thank Dr Jaleel Ahmad for reading the complete manuscript and for making helpful suggestions for improvement. Christopher Chapman and Professor John Wise provided useful comments on Chapter 9, enabling several errors of fact and interpretation to be corrected. Sanjoy K. Das and Tancredi Zollo checked the typescript for consistent notation and typographical errors: we are indebted to their patient work. Thanks are due to Professor James Mirrlees for discussions with one of the authors over a number of years on the methodology of project evaluation, and to Professor John Wise who afforded a similar role for the other author. Dr E. J. Mishan drew our attention to an error of interpretation relating to his normalisation procedure, described in Chapter 7.

The ideas outlined in section 5 of Chapter 6 on the relationship between the shadow price of savings and the social discount rate are developed from an earlier formulation in Ajit Dasgupta's Ph.D. thesis on 'The Theory and Application of Optimum Investment Decisions with Special Reference to the Indian Fertiliser Industry' (Cambridge University, mimeo). A grant from the United Kingdom Ministry of Overseas Development from 1967 to 1969 financed much of the research upon which the ideas presented in Chapter 10, on the Damodar Valley scheme, are based. Especial thanks are due to Richard C. Cornes for research assistance relating to this chapter which was read in an earlier version to the Annual Meeting of the Canadian Economic Association in Winnipeg, 1970. Chapter 9, on the location of London's Third Airport, partly reflects the written and oral evidence presented to the Roskill Commission by Professor John Wise, Christopher Chapman and David Pearce in 1970.

Miss Lise Brault, Mrs Mary Mundye, Mrs Trish Bloxham and Mrs P. Dunn typed the manuscript, and bore with infinite patience the task of retyping some chapters several times. We owe them a considerable debt of thanks.

Despite this wealth of assistance and advice, errors must surely remain. These are our responsibility alone.

AJIT K. DASGUPTA
D. W. PEARCE

Introduction

THE idea of measuring the net advantages of a capital investment project in terms of society's net utility gains originated with Dupuit's famous paper 'On the Measurement of the Utility of Public Works', published in 1844 [1].[1] In this work, Dupuit pointed out that 'political economy has not yet defined in any precise manner the conditions which these [public] works must fulfil in order to be really useful' ([1] p. 83), and proceeded to develop his definition of what we now call consumers' surplus, the excess of consumers' willingness to pay for a good or service over and above its market price, as a measure of the net welfare gain from a project. Despite refinements to the concept and theory of consumers' surplus by Marshall, Hotelling and Hicks, the *practical* application of the theory to public investments which had been recognised by Dupuit was not resurrected until the 1950s, with the formal advent of cost–benefit analysis.

Consumers' surplus theory suggested a way of measuring the social return to a capital project. The flow of services from the project, multiplied by their prices, merely defined the minimum social benefit. Since some purchasers would have been willing to pay more, they obtained something for nothing, an excess of utility which constituted consumers' surplus. This aspect of the definition of net social benefit is fundamental to cost–benefit analysis (CBA), and is readily extended to cases where persons who are not direct beneficiaries of a project obtain some 'overspill' benefit. They obtain some utility from a good or service for which they have not paid – a consumers' surplus in a context where the market price, to them, is zero. It follows that the measurement of net *social* benefits requires the estimation of all the consumers' surpluses, to whomsoever they accrue. This link between surplus theory and the indirect third-party losses and gains from capital projects was again not made until the 1950s. However, the idea of adding up *all* the benefits had achieved formal recognition in the United States in the 1930s, even if no guidance was given at that time about how benefits were to be measured.

[1] References in square brackets are to the Bibliography at the back of the book.

The United States Flood Control Act of 1936 enunciated the principle that a project be declared 'feasible' (desirable) if 'the benefits, *to whomsoever they may accrue*, are in excess of the estimated costs'. But the precise meaning of a 'benefit' remained obscure, and the individual agencies responsible for capital projects in the field of water resources (the only area of public investment in the United States covered at that time by 'benefit–cost' criteria) – the Army Corps of Engineers, the Bureau of Reclamation, the Tennessee Valley Authority, the Department of Agriculture, etc. – often approached similar projects from different standpoints. It was not until the Federal Inter-Agency River Basin Committee's Subcommittee on Benefits and Costs reported in 1950 that any real attempt was made to formalise the procedures for valuing costs and benefits. The resulting publication, usually known as the *Green Book* [2], was notable at least for using some of the language of welfare economics, and thus merging for the first time the separate developments in practical project analysis and welfare economics. The *Green Book* was quickly superseded by the Bureau of the Budget's 1952 *Budget Circular A-47* [3], which produced a further attempt at the formalisation of valuation procedures, the Bureau being the financial overseer of the agencies in respect of their requests for capital funds. Both the 1950 and 1952 documents talked of social gains in terms of the national product, ignoring the fact that some social gains and losses are not expressible in terms of recorded national product, and that governments might have aims other than maximising gains to the national product.

In the meantime, academic interest in appraisal techniques had grown. The agencies' methods had been commented on since the early 1950s, but it seems fair to identify 1958 as a turning-point. This year saw the publication of Otto Eckstein's *Water Research Development* [4], Roland McKean's *Efficiency in Government through System Analysis* [5] and John Krutilla and Otto Eckstein's *Multiple Purpose River Development* [6]. All three works attempted to lay down fairly clear benefit–cost criteria as they related to water resource projects. In 1955 the Harvard University Water Program had brought together a group of economists, engineers and systems analysts interested in appraisal techniques. The result was the further development of a reasonably integrated theory of cost–benefit analysis, with costs and benefits being related more clearly to welfare losses and gains, so that the substantial body of welfare theory could be brought to bear on the issue. One of the major works on project appraisal in the water resource field remains the volume produced by the Harvard Program in 1962 [7]. Many of the contributors to this volume had also helped to produce the 1962 Consultants' Report [8] requested by President Kennedy which, in turn, stimulated a new inter-agency committee to formalise further the appraisal rules for government use, in 1962.

That cost–benefit analysis should have begun life in the United States is not surprising. The United States has a tradition of federal control of water resource projects, investment in which, even in the early years, was on a substantial scale. More important, however, is the fact that academic economists had secured links with government earlier in the United States than in, say, the United Kingdom. The influence of the Harvard Water Program is the supreme case in point. It was not until the very late 1950s that economists were recruited on a significant scale into the civil service in the United Kingdom. It is significant that water resource projects, which in the United Kingdom are smaller in scale compared to the United States and are also under the control of a number of diverse authorities, were not the first projects to be subjected to cost–benefit analysis in the United Kingdom. The earliest application was to Britain's first motorway, the M1, the study being carried out by the Road Research Laboratory in 1960 [9]. Since then, the main application has been to transport projects – road bridges over the river Tay and the river Severn, the withdrawal of railway services, 'validation' studies of motorways and initial studies of new motorways and road links, the proposed Third London Airport and so on. Some advances have been made in measuring the benefits of higher education expenditures, and 'modified' studies, which do not always quite fit the general framework of CBA, have been carried out on urban renewal and expansion schemes and on aspects of the health services. It was not until 1967 that official government directives were given to the nationalised industries to adopt cost–benefit procedures, although in very limited contexts [10].

Cost–benefit analysis has also been widely applied in underdeveloped countries to irrigation, hydroelectricity and transport investments. The 'rules' of applications in these particular contexts were felt to be sufficiently well defined for the publication by O.E.C.D. of a *Manual of Industrial Project Analysis* [11] in 1969.

How is the prevailing and expanding interest in CBA to be explained?

Firstly, public expenditure in the United States and the United Kingdom has risen substantially since the last war. In underdeveloped countries, the need to build an infrastructure of social capital has necessitated large expenditures, and procedures designed to reduce the risk of waste have become essential. In short, the scales of capital expenditure have become so large in both developed and underdeveloped countries that they have virtually forced themselves on to the attention of economists.

Secondly, appraisal techniques were already fairly well developed for *private* investment decisions where the outcomes – profits or sales – were well defined. The idea of discounting future cash flows and of making allowances for risk and uncertainty were well known, even if DCF (discounted cash flow) techniques remained (and still remain) unadopted by large numbers of businessmen. It seemed an anomaly that private investment techniques should be so well developed, even though disputes over the theory remained, while the ever-expanding public sectors should be devoid of efficiency criteria.

These reasons acted as an impetus to the definition of social output as the objective of agencies acting 'in the public interest'. Once translated into these terms, the language of welfare economics became appropriate and this at a time when many of the theorems of general equilibrium were being restated with the techniques of mathematical programming. In short, what cost–benefit analysis has done is to extend the idea of efficiency to public expenditures at a time when efficiency has become more a byword than ever before, and at a time when these expenditures had grown so much that they demanded the application of some techniques for improving productivity.

It is tempting to think that after some fifteen or twenty years of development, cost–benefit analysis must have reached the stage where a clear consensus of opinion exists about the 'proper' procedures to be followed. This would be a mistake. It is as well to note briefly the fundamentals of the disputes. The diverse applications of CBA have served to show that theory and practice are, often necessarily, divorced from one another. Further, the procedures followed in one application are not necessarily relevant to another application. Indeed, 'cost–benefit' has become a generic term, covering a large range of evaluation procedures which frequently differ in what they include and omit as benefits and costs, and in the way outcomes are valued. There is also frequently little or no relationship between practical applications and the welfare theory which, one supposes, should underlie the practice.

In particular, some problems appear insuperable. If a project involves an amenity loss, how is that loss to be valued? If a motorway reduces the risk of deaths in road accidents, how is a life saved to be valued? If a project totally destroys a species of wildlife, how is such an irreversible loss to be valued? It is precisely because cost–

benefit analysts have either ignored these problems, or because they have made bold attempts to value such gains and losses (and boldness is not necessarily a virtue here), that many people have become disenchanted with the procedure. To omit certain gains and losses is to fail to meet the all-encompassing definition of social costs and benefits. To include them is to stand charged with 'arbitrariness' or valuing that which cannot be valued. One commentator has referred to cost–benefit as 'a comfortable corner of overheated speculation, mutual academic congratulation, and overspending of public money in painstaking cost and benefit appraisals of elusive significance' [12]. Others are upset by the links between CBA and welfare economics, the latter discipline having been thought by many academics to be well dead by the 1950s under the final attacks of Baumol [13] and Graaff [14]. Precisely the same problems that faced welfare economics face cost–benefit analysis, particularly in respect of the distributional consequences of projects (see below, Chapter 2). In addition, others argue that there are too many unknowns and assumptions, and that a discipline based upon such a shaky structure is being elevated to unwarranted heights. Still others had sought to establish economics as a 'positive science', resting only upon propositions the truth of which is testable directly or indirectly. Since welfare economics is unashamedly 'normative' – its whole purpose being to give guidance in 'recommending' change – and since normative statements are not testable, welfare economics appears to have no place in the new scientific era. *Ergo*, cost–benefit analysis belongs to the same unscientific field. Further, like welfare economics, the theory of CBA rests upon a philosophy of *as if*: values are derived as if a particular hypothetical configuration of the economy existed, lending what many feel to be a fanciful aspect to the study. Lastly, disputes exist, as they always will, over the theory. On one issue alone, the selection of a social discount rate, a huge literature has built up, although there are signs of the disputants forming clearly defined camps, even if they remain in disagreement.

Even this brief list of the causes of dissent would be sufficient to deter many from taking a further, serious look at cost–benefit analysis. But it remains true that the alternatives to CBA are just as vulnerable to charges of arbitrariness, indeed often more so. The town planner, for example, is frequently without any systematic criteria, save his own paternalistic preferences. Cost–benefit analysis does at least make the attempt to refer to individuals' preferences and to place them on a comparable basis for measurement. The objections to the manner in which these preferences are recorded can be partly overcome by suitable adjustments to the valuation procedures – by explicit attempts to incorporate distributional or social need considerations into the concept of social benefit, for example. The 'weights' so obtained might be subject to criticism, but they at least possess the virtue of being observable and explicit. And the positivist argument is always open to the danger of degeneration: criteria for policy changes must, after all, exist. It is difficult to see how anyone can quarrel with the requirement that these criteria should be explicit. In short, criticisms of cost–benefit analysis are only admissible if they can demonstrate that alternative prescriptive procedures are in some way superior. To this end, there must be criteria of 'superiority' – e.g. whether the procedure is objective, whether it records society's preferences, whether it safeguards minority interests, gives adequate weight to the heritage passed on to future generations and so on. Failure to agree on the criteria for what constitutes an acceptable procedure will of course account for much of the failure to agree on the desirability of using one particular prescriptive model such as CBA. But whatever criteria are chosen, however, it has yet to be shown that cost–benefit analysis compares unfavourably with either the political or the planning process.

Nonetheless, it would be wrong to suggest that cost–benefit analysis is devoid of serious faults: the problems of defining and deriving a social welfare function, the complexities raised by 'second best' arguments, the proper choice of a discount rate, all of these loom large in any honest discussion of cost–benefit analysis. Whether these problems constitute insuperable objections to the use of CBA, bearing in mind the objections which can easily be raised against the alternative decision procedures, is for the reader to judge.

Part One

The Objective Function in Cost–Benefit Analysis

1 Utility, Costs and Benefits

1.1 SOCIAL PREFERENCES AS THE OBJECTIVE FUNCTION

The basic idea of cost–benefit analysis is simple. To decide on the worth of a project involving public expenditure (or, more extensively, public policy) it is necessary to weigh up the advantages and disadvantages. The province of cost–benefit is usually confined to public projects because the advantages and disadvantages are defined in terms of *social* gains and losses. It is assumed, correctly one suspects, that most private decisions are not concerned with the wider social effects, but with the effects on profits, sales or producer status.

The idea of weighing up the pros and cons appears well founded in 'rationality' since it would seem odd deliberately to choose a policy which is known to have harmful net effects. It is of course possible to disagree over what are 'good' and 'bad' effects and it is precisely because such disagreement is possible that cost–benefit analysis is a somewhat tendentious subject. The next sections show that cost–benefit is consistent with the assumption that social objectives can be defined in terms of individuals' preferences, even though the process of aggregating individual preferences to obtain total social preference presents some serious difficulties.

Essentially, *cost–benefit analysis purports to be a way of deciding what society prefers. Where only one option can be chosen from a series of options, CBA should inform the decision-maker as to which option is socially most preferred.*

The implicit judgement is that individual preferences *should count*. In a sense this is very 'democratic': it is equivalent to obeying the maxim of consumers' sovereignty. CBA is a way of recording these preferences, either as they are revealed directly in the market, or, where no market exists, as the cost–benefit analyst sees them revealed indirectly through other means, and of reducing all these preferences and 'dispreferences' to a unique overall figure, which gives the *net* benefit to society. Two questions are pertinent.

Firstly, should individual preferences always count? There are frequent occasions when 'democratic' societies do not allow individuals' preferences to determine outcomes. In the United

Kingdom the abolition of capital punishment was secured despite a probable majority of the general public being in favour of its retention. Governments frequently adopt a 'paternalistic' attitude to individuals, arguing that, in some cases at least, they know best what is 'good' for them. Appeal is made to the judgement of 'informed opinion'. Is there any reason to allow this appeal in some cases but not in others? Why prevent the public deciding on capital punishment, but allow them to record their (implicit) preference for a new road which might equally well involve extra accidents and deaths? Possibly, the beneficiaries of an investment may not have an understanding of the benefits, as is the case with some categories of mental health patients. On other occasions an innocent myopia might prevent the beneficiary appreciating the benefits, as perhaps with education, where the benefits tend to accrue well into the individual's future. Wherever the dividing line between 'merit wants' and other wants exists, indeed *if* it exists, CBA would claim to come down on the side of simple democracy. It aims to record the preferences of the community and recommends on that basis.

Secondly, what role should CBA play in the decision-making process? This question is important because the overall normative content of CBA depends on whether CBA acts as a guide to, or a substitute for, 'political' decisions. If it is regarded as a total substitute for assessment on the part of the decision-maker, then CBA becomes heavily value-loaded – it implies that the maximisation of 'society's preferences' (however defined) is a good thing and that such a rule *should* govern policy decisions. If, on the other hand, the decision-maker is aware of the underlying value premise, he should be able to view CBA as an *aid* to decision-making. That is, in so far as he is interested in what the aggregate of individuals *want*, CBA will enable him to look at those preferences in a convenient form, hopefully in the form of a single real number expressing the net benefits of the policy.

But it is always open to the decision-maker to 'weigh up' the results of a CBA against other objectives. A recorded preference pattern might be heavily weighted in favour of the preferences of the wealthy, or those in a certain social class or even a geographical region. The possible sources of 'bias' in cost–benefit are discussed later. For the moment it is only necessary to note that the decision-maker may wish to use the results of CBA to provide *one element* in guiding his overall decision, possibly adjusting the results to reflect some concept of fairness or 'equity', or simply subjectively weighing up the relative importance of the preferences recorded by cost–benefit compared to other social objectives. The role which CBA plays in decision-making will depend in part upon the extent to which its objective function coincides with that of the decision-making body.

Perhaps, too, all the gains and losses of a policy cannot be measured. Loss of amenity frequently falls into this category, although heroic attempts are made to value these aspects. Once again, the decision-maker must be careful to observe the inventory of costs and benefits to see if they have all been valued. If any are omitted, the decision-maker must decide what weights he is to attach to the excluded objectives and effects.

Lastly, the decision-maker should observe the *way* in which costs and benefits are valued. It would be grossly misleading to suggest that any CBA measures gains and losses with precision: there are errors attached to each item, errors which arise from inadequate information, the nature of the data, uncertainty – especially about projected values over time – and errors in the models used for 'simulating' behaviour in non-market contexts.

It is difficult to avoid the impression that CBA is frequently treated as the decision-maker's dream – a golden rule which actually substitutes a simple figure for the judgement he might otherwise have to express. CBA meets a desire for certitude and simplicity, but to treat it this way is to venture on to dangerous ground. It is a *guide*, an aid to decision-making. It gives an approximation (no more than that) of what 'society' prefers. It does not follow that what 'society' wants is good for society – we can all continue to argue about that – nor that CBA has valued all the factors the decision-maker wishes to take into account.

The decision-maker, then, is assumed to have an *objective function*, an entity which he aims to *maximise*. This objective function may be profits, or income, or net social benefits defined in a way so as to incorporate things other than income. CBA works with an objective function defined in terms of some concept of net benefits. Of course, it is possible that the decision-maker wishes only to achieve some given level of net benefits. If several policies meet that aim it is conceivable that he will be indifferent between the policies. In general, however, it would seem odd if he did not try to *rank* the alternatives in terms of his objective function, choosing the alternative with the highest value of this function. It is assumed that the decision-maker aims to maximise the difference between social benefits and social costs.[1]

[1] We shall speak of the 'decision-maker' as though he is always readily identifiable. Actual decisions frequently emerge from more complex political situations, usually situations of conflict even within a one-party

In addition to his objective function, the decision-maker will be faced with *constraints*, frequently of the kind noted earlier – concern for a 'regional balance', equity considerations and perhaps balance of payments restrictions. Sometimes the constraints can be 'built in' to the objective function, as with income distribution for example. On other occasions the decision-maker will have to aim at the maximisation of his objective function subject to the various constraints which remain.

1.2 PREFERENCE AND UTILITY

The previous section argued that the aim of cost–benefit analysis is to aid the decision-maker in assessing the advantages and disadvantages of a policy, where the expected gains and losses are looked at from the point of view of society's preferences. It was seen that identification of gains and losses (benefits and costs), their measurement, and the decision rule itself were derivative of the decision-maker's objective function. It was further assumed that the decision-maker aimed to maximise net social gain, so that the choice rule is one of selecting policies which have the largest difference between social benefits and social costs. The crucial problem that arises is the definition of 'social gain' – a problem which has absorbed considerable attention in cost–benefit analysis and in welfare economics before it. Benefits and costs cannot be measured until it is known what it is that is being measured.

This section outlines what is best described as the 'dominant' view of the philosophical foundations of cost–benefit analysis. This view is amply expounded in the literature of welfare economics, but it tends to be implicit rather than explicit in cost–benefit analysis. At the end of this section, some issues are raised concerning the logic of the dominant view.

For a systematic language to exist at all there must be 'primitive notions' or 'basic concepts'. The meaning of these concepts is known intuitively: they may be analysed in detail and their relationships with other concepts may be shown, but such analysis, it is argued, would add little or nothing to our understanding of the

---

or majority-party context. Some writers have taken exception to the mention of decision-makers as if these persons have an entity separate from the whole political process. For our purposes, however, this character, mythical or otherwise, is a useful and fairly harmless construct. See P. D. Henderson, 'Some Unsettled Issues in Cost–Benefit Analysis', in P. Streeten (ed.), *Unfashionable Economics* (London, 1970).

concepts. The economist adopts as a basic concept the notion of 'preference'. We all know what it is to prefer x to y, so that a search for the meaning of the sentence 'individual 1 prefers x to y' is not worth while. Others would perhaps argue that the notion of preferring is not basic, since preferences reflect 'wants' or 'tastes' and it is the wants that are basic. It would seem reasonable to argue that preferring logically entails wanting, so that '1 prefers x to y' can always be translated into '1 wants x more than y'. Since preferences dictate the choices we make, the basic notion of a preference underlies any theory of choice.

The objects of preferences or wants are 'states of nature', or, more strictly for economic problems, 'states of the economy'. These states will involve various combinations of goods and services, or 'commodities' to use the collective term. In cost–benefit analysis it is necessary to widen the definition of commodities a little to include any activity or event the outcome of which affects the preferences of individuals. Thus, commodities which are not sold or bought on the market must be considered. The beauty of a landscape may be enhanced by a particular policy, affecting the preferences of individuals for that policy. Alternatively, the landscape may be reduced in beauty – a 'disgood' or 'bad', to borrow what is perhaps slightly clumsy terminology from recent economic literature – and preferences may again be affected.

In general, preferences are assumed to be 'selfish', that is, individuals behave such that they choose on the basis of the outcome of a policy as it affects them and not as it affects others. This point is raised again at the end of this section.

Given the existence of preferences, individuals must be able to *rank* the alternative states facing them. A ranking involves two types of preference – a 'strict' preference and the relationship of 'indifference'. To say '1 strictly prefers x to y' implies that x will be chosen by 1. To say '1 is indifferent between x and y' implies that 1 finds x and y equally preferable. To aid exposition, it is convenient to introduce some simple notation. For the individual 1, 'x is strictly preferred to y' can be written

$$xPy.$$

If 1 is indifferent between x and y, this is written

$$xIy$$

and the symbol R will be used to denote a general, or 'weak', ranking, so that

$$xRy$$

means 1 is at least indifferent between x and y, and might prefer x to y. The process of ranking is logically entailed by the concept of a preference. Ranking is frequently referred to as 'ordering'.

In the face of several alternatives, the individual is assumed to order those alternatives so that his final choice will be for the *most preferred* state. Indeed, this defines *rational* choice. If the individual orders (ranks) several states in terms of his preferences and then chooses the least preferred state, he will be acting irrationally within the context of economic choice theory.

At this stage it is possible to indicate the relationship between cost–benefit analysis and the logic of preference. Suppose society consisted of only one individual. The maximisation of net social gains is tantamount to letting our individual reach the most preferred state. A 'benefit' becomes an outcome for which the individual exhibits a preference, and a 'cost' is an outcome for which the individual exhibits a negative preference, a sort of 'dispreference'. The essential links between preferences and *social* gains in the (more realistic!) case where society consists of more than one individual cannot be demonstrated until section 1.4, but the link between preference and gain should now be clear.

Instead of the word 'gain' the word 'utility' or 'welfare' can be used. Having laid the foundations of preference theory, the meaning of the word 'utility' becomes evident. To say '1 has a higher utility in state x than in state y' is to say xPy by 1, so that 'has more utility' *means* 'prefers'. Looked at in this way, most of the problems of defining utility disappear. As long as a preference is thought of as a basic concept, there is no need to become involved in any discussion about the relationship between the concept of utility and concepts such as 'satisfaction', 'pleasure' and 'happiness'. If we write $U(x)$ as the utility derived from x, $U(y)$ as the utility derived from y, then the possible relationships discussed earlier are all expressible in terms of utility. Thus

$$xPy \text{ entails } U(x) > U(y)$$
$$xIy \text{ entails } U(x) = U(y)$$
$$xRy \text{ entails } U(x) \geqslant U(y).$$

With these definitions in mind it is possible to define a *utility function* as a scale which will reflect the preference relationships of the individual. The utility function is sometimes called a 'representation' of the relationship R.

Certain axioms (conditions) must hold for the individual to have a definable utility function. These axioms arise from reflection about the concept of preference. They are most usually described as:

Axiom I: *Connectedness.* This tells us quite simply that given two alternatives x and y, the individual must be at least indifferent between x and y. In other words, xRy or yRx.

Axiom II: *Transitivity.* If 1 prefers x to y and y to z, he must prefer x to z. Symbolically: xPy and yPz entails xPz.

Axiom III: *Reflexivity.* This says simply that any state x must stand in a relationship R to itself, so that xRx.

Axiom IV: *Continuity.* This axiom is a little more complicated. Roughly, it means that if xPy and z is any state which is very close to x, then zRy. An example where the continuity property does not hold is the case where someone chooses between alternative states on the basis of the size of one element out of the many elements in each state. Thus, state x might be preferred to state y simply because x has more of one particular good, regardless of the amounts of other goods in the two states. The result of an ordering of this kind (a 'lexicographic' ordering) is that it is impossible to derive an indifference curve as we know it in micro-economics. Essentially, this is because the lexicographic ordering is not continuous. The reader will find a useful discussion of the continuity axiom in Newman [1].

1.3 ORDINAL AND CARDINAL UTILITY

It is necessary to distinguish two possible aspects of a utility function. No mention has been made of the *intensity of preference* which an individual may have for x over y. We speak of wanting things 'very much' or 'badly', or of being 'just in favour' of other things. This language seems to suggest that preference logic could be extended to account for different intensities of preference. Psychometricians (psychologists interested in the measurement of psychological variables) certainly use measures of this kind. In the nineteenth century, economists assumed that utility was measurable to the extent of indicating different intensities of preference – they assumed a *cardinal* measure of utility. While cardinalists still exist (e.g. Armstrong [2]), the 'dominant' view is that utility is not capable of cardinal measurement. Rather it is susceptible only to *ordinal* measures, such that we can say that utility is greater or less in one situation than in another, but we cannot say by how much. Ordinalism is clearly entailed by preference logic. To establish cardinalism, however, some further means are required for saying by how much 1 prefers x to y. Some approaches are discussed shortly, but it is important to make the ordinal–cardinal distinction clear.

The distinction between ordinalism and cardinalism is best shown by the introduction of some simple mathematical concepts. If it were possible only to rank states in terms of 'greater' or 'less' utility, the scale obtained would be *ordinal*. Thus it would be possible to say that

$$U(x_1) > U(x_2) > U(x_3) > \ldots > U(x_n)$$

where x_1 is the first state of nature and x_n is the nth state. Ordinal rankings of this kind tell us nothing about the absolute size of the states, and hence nothing about the 'distance' between them. If we

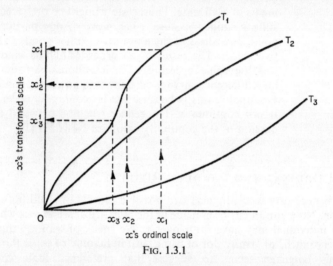

Fig. 1.3.1

knew that $U(x_1)$ was 20 units and $U(x_2)$ 8 units, we would know the *size* of $U(x_1)$ and $U(x_2)$ and the *distance* between them – i.e. 12 units. But ordinal scales do not provide this information. It is, of course, logical to conclude that x_1 is preferred to x_3 more intensely than x_1 is preferred to x_2, since clearly $U(x_1) - U(x_3) > U(x_1) - U(x_2)$. It is not possible, however, to say anything about the intensity of preference for x_1 over x_2 compared to x_2 over x_3. An ordinal scale simply does not provide this information.

In more technical language, we say that an ordinal scale is *invariant over a monotonic transformation*. The meaning of this statement is best seen with reference to Fig. 1.3.1. The rankings of the *x*s are shown along the horizontal scale. The vertical scale shows what would happen if the rankings were transformed on to a new scale, the transformation being made through any of the curves shown (T_1, T_2, T_3). Thus, the relationship between x_1, x_2, x_3 is preserved on the new scale, and this is so as long as the curves through which the transformation is made are *monotonic* – i.e. rise (or fall) in one direction. A non-monotonic curve would, say, slope upwards and then downwards. If the transformation of an ordinal scale were made through a non-monotonic curve the rankings on the horizontal axis would not be preserved. Note that it does not matter what the precise shape of the transformation curve is, as long as it is monotonic.

To say that utility is capable only of ordinal measurement is therefore to say that it is capable of being ranked only in the fashion just described. To say that utility is 'cardinally' measurable, on the other hand, is to suggest that utility can be measured rather like temperature, height and weight are measured. Unfortunately, the meaning of 'cardinal' is not altogether clear and the fact that it is possible to put at least two interpretations on its meaning has been a source of confusion in the literature, particularly in respect of the recent attempts to revive cardinal indicators of utility. One approach is to distinguish 'interval' scales from what economists tend to call 'cardinal' scales.

For an interval scale to be established, the ordinal rankings of states must be known, and the distance between the states must also be known. But it is not necessary for the absolute magnitude of the states to be known. Notice the logical relationship between distance and absolute size. If size is known, so is distance; but the converse is not necessarily true. Thus, we could know that x_1 is greater than x_2 by 12 units, x_2 exceeds x_3 by 10 units, x_3 exceeds x_4 by 28 units, and so on. This information is sufficient to establish the interval scale shown below. But it is not sufficient to attach absolute magnitudes

to the *x*s. We could of course assign an arbitrary number to any one of the *x*s, and this would enable us to assign numbers to the others. Thus, if x_1 is called 100, x_2 becomes 88, x_3 78 and x_4 50. Interval scales clearly carry much more information than do ordinal scales. They are said to be *invariant over any linear transformation*. This is shown in Fig. 1.3.2. T_1 and T_2 are linear functions, T_2 having the equation

$$x^1 = a + bx.$$

If $a = 5$ and $b = 0.5$, and x_1 is assigned the arbitrary number 100, x_1 would be transformed through T_1 to $5 + 0.5(100) = 55$. x_2 would be transformed through T_1 to $5 + 0.5(88) = 49$. The ranking of x_1 and x_2 has been preserved and so has the relationship between the intervals. That this is so can be seen by considering x_4 which, on the

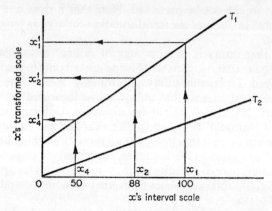

FIG. 1.3.2

original scale, equals 50. On the transformed scale, through T_1, it becomes $5 + 0.5(50) = 30$. Similarly, on the original scale $x_1 - x_2 = 12$, while on the new scale it equals 6. In other words, the new scale is proportionate to the old in that the intervals on the new scale are proportions of the intervals of the old scale. In this particular case the new intervals are half the old ones. Note, however, that x_1 was twice x_4 on the old scale, but it is less than twice x_4 on the new scale (55/30). In other words, it is not possible to use the elementary operations of multiplication and division on the arbitrarily assigned *absolute magnitudes* of an interval scale, but it is possible to use these operations on the *intervals themselves*.

Putting numbers on an interval scale, therefore, seems to be a somewhat arbitrary procedure. However, once numbers are assigned it does not matter which state is chosen as the 'origin', nor whether the origin is changed, which is effectively what happened in the linear transformation in Fig. 1.3.2.

The final scale of interest (and there are many variants of the interval scale, for example) is the one which we call 'strictly cardinal'. The strictly cardinal scale possesses all the properties of the interval scale except that it relates to a 'real' origin. Height, weight and distance are examples of cardinal scales. Fig. 1.3.3 shows the significance of the 'real' origin attribute. Any transformation of a cardinal scale must preserve the origin and it must be linear. Thus T_1 in Fig. 1.3.3 has the equation

$$x^1 = bx$$

which is linear and does not permit a change of origin. Cardinal scales are therefore invariant to linear transformations which do not

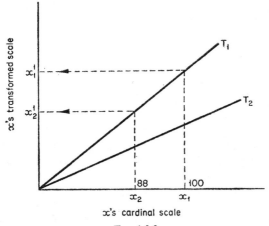

Fɪɢ. 1.3.3

alter the origin. If b in the above equation is taken to be 0·5, and the same magnitudes are assigned to x_1 and x_2 – i.e. 100 and 88 – the transformed values become 50 and 44. In this case it *is* possible to carry out all mathematical operations on the actual magnitudes, which contrasts the 'cardinal' scale with the interval scale.

To what extent the distinction between interval and cardinal scales is unambiguous is a matter of dispute. The assignment of an arbitrary origin to an interval scale seems to differ little from calling some point on a cardinal scale the 'real' origin. The choice of origin could therefore be regarded as a matter of convention, and the establishment of origins for the interval scale simply becomes equivalent to introducing a convention for that scale.

The details of this debate need not concern us here, but the contrast between the two types of utility measure is important. Firstly, it will be shown that what generally underlies cost–benefit analysis is the ordinal utility concept. Secondly, cardinal utility concepts figure prominently in some of the controversies over the integration of 'distributional' and 'efficiency' benefits. Essentially, the argument reduces to one of deciding whether the appropriate objective function is some concept of social utility in a cardinal sense, or of social utility in the ordinal sense. Thirdly, Chapter 3 shows that there are problems in aggregating individuals' preferences, problems which many economists would consider as precluding any possibility of securing a well-defined concept of social utility in the ordinal sense. The possibility of a cardinal measure, however, offers a possible escape from this problem. For all these reasons, it is appropriate to spend a little time investigating some of the recent claims for the establishment of a cardinal utility measure.

1.4 SOME APPROACHES TO CARDINAL UTILITY MEASUREMENT

The first route to cardinalisation, which has been explored notably by Armstrong [2], starts from the observation that the individual's ability to discriminate between alternatives is limited. The concept of a 'utility perception threshold' – i.e. a range of difference in utility beyond, but not within, which preference can be said to exist – follows. This difference has been variously described in the literature as a 'barely noticeable difference', a 'bare preference' or a 'preference threshold'. One obvious consequence of this for utility theory is that while preference is a transitive relation, indifference need not be.

In the context of the present discussion, the more important point is that on Armstrong's approach the distance between any two alternatives on an individual's preference scale can be naturally interpreted as being equal to the number of 'bare preferences' that lie between them. Taking this bare preference as our unit of measurement of utility it is possible to construct an interval scale as described earlier.

To do this, start with some particular alternative x, label other alternatives y, z, w, . . ., so that y is *barely* preferred by the given individual to x, z is *barely* preferred to y, w is *barely* preferred to z, and so on. With the utility of x being taken as the origin 0 and the interval of 'bare preference' as the scaling unit ($=1$), the utility numbers for y, z, w, . . ., for this individual become 1, 2, 3, . . ., respectively. The choice of the zero point and the scale (the number taken to represent the common unit) are arbitrary, a property of interval scales in general.

The concept of 'bare preference' is given some support by current research on the psychology of perception. While a number of theoretical problems remain (for example, since the number of discrimination levels must depend on the number of alternatives available, the introduction of a new good could change the index), these do not appear to be insuperable.

The Armstrong approach therefore establishes an interval scale for any one individual, and, since it was argued that interval scales may suffice for cardinal measures, it follows that the approach establishes a 'cardinal' scale in the less strict sense of the word. Now, if the concept of a 'barely noticeable difference' (BND) is the *same* for all individuals, there can be no objection to adding individual utilities to secure a measure of social utility. Armstrong's approach does indeed assert that a BND is the same for all persons: hence utilities can be aggregated.

While this approach to utility measurement is clearly useful in experimental, small group situations, it has obvious operational defects in terms of its possible application to problems on the social scale. It is unlikely, at least in the foreseeable future, that any such measure could be developed in an operational fashion. Nor, of course, will everyone be satisfied that every individual means the same thing by a 'barely noticeable difference'. While it is intriguing, therefore, we conclude that this approach could not be developed for social policy purposes.

The second approach to cardinalisation derives from the von Neumann–Morgenstern theory of rational behaviour under 'risk' [3], only situations to which the theory of probability applies being considered for this purpose.

On this approach, the individual is regarded as being faced with the choice not merely between simple alternatives $x, y, z, \ldots$, as has been the case so far, but also between different *probability combinations* of $x, y, z, \ldots$. Thus, if there is a probability p of securing x, and a probability $1-p$ of securing y, then the probability combination p, $1-p$ of x, y (where $0 < p < 1$) is defined to be a *prospect* of a p, $1-p$ chance of getting x, y respectively. A probability combination of 0.4, 0.6 of x, y means that there is a $40:60$ chance of winning either x or y respectively. A probability combination of 0.5, 0.5 means an even chance, and so on. Now, each probability combination, or prospect, can itself be regarded as an alternative to something else, where the 'something else' might also be a prospect. Where the alternative is another prospect and there is a probability attached to each prospect the choice is called a 'compound prospect' – e.g. an even chance of winning either a 40 : 40 chance or a 50 : 50 chance of x, y.

Individual choice under conditions of risk is held to be governed by certain axioms of preference similar to those introduced in section 1.2.

It can then be shown that as between any two prospects an individual will choose that with a higher mathematical expectation of utility. Further, the utility indices applied to the outcomes (the probability combinations of which constitute various prospects) are unique up to a positive linear transformation, i.e. are unique except for scale and origin.[1]

It has been suggested by Robertson [5], Baumol [6] and others that the 'utility' measured by the von Neumann–Morgenstern index is fundamentally different from the concept of utility which occurs in economic theory. Baumol bases his argument on the admission by von Neumann and Morgenstern ([3] p. 28) that in practice they define utility 'as being that thing for which the calculus of mathematical expectations is legitimate'. This argument does not appear to be well founded. Von Neumann–Morgenstern utility must indeed be different from traditional utility simply because their analysis takes as its point of departure the principles of rational behaviour under risk, which the traditional theory ignores. However, this does not in itself invalidate the generalised approach to choice represented by the von Neumann–Morgenstern theory. This must depend on the validity of the axioms of preference to which the expected utility hypothesis is logically equivalent. If these are accepted, utility is in effect being defined as that for which 'the calculus of mathematical expectations is legitimate'. Hence the question really turns on the acceptability of the axioms themselves.

For this purpose, it is convenient to consider the system of axioms proposed by Marschak rather than the original von Neumann and Morgenstern presentation, as Marschak's axioms are easier to interpret.

Marschak's system consists of four axioms.

1. *The Axiom of Complete Ordering*
This states that the ordering over alternatives (prospects) is (*a*) *connected* – i.e. the relationships of preference or indifference must exist

---

[1] The mathematical expectation of utility of a prospect of outcomes $x_1, x_2, \ldots, x_n$ with respective utility indices $u_1, u_2, \ldots, u_n$ and probabilities $p_1, p_2, \ldots, p_n$ is defined to be $p_1u_1 + p_2u_2 + \ldots + p_nu_n$. The proof is given in Neumann and Morgenstern [3] and in Marschak [4].

between any two states – and (*b*) *transitive*. The two conditions together comprise the axiom of 'completeness'.

2. *The Axiom of Continuity*
Suppose there are three prospects, *x*, *y* and *z*, such that *x* is preferred to *y* and *y* is preferred to *z*. Then there exists some probability combination of *x* and *z* such that the individual is indifferent between it and *y*. Again, this axiom is similar to the continuity assumption underlying the ordinary (riskless) theory of utility and choice.

3. *The Strong Independence Axiom*
If prospects *x* and *y* are indifferent, then for any prospect *z* a given probability combination of *x* and *z* must be indifferent to the same probability combination of *y* and *z*.

What this axiom states is that as long as the probability in which *z* is combined with *x* and with *y* respectively is the same, the original indifference relation choice between *x* and *y* should not be 'contaminated' by *z*.

4. *The Axiom of a Sufficient Number of Non-indifferent Prospects*
There must be at least four non-indifferent prospects. This is a relatively trivial assumption. Marschak includes it simply because it is needed for the proof of the Expected Utility Theorem.[1]

The first assumption, that of complete ordering of prospects, is acceptable to most. Assumption 4, that there are no less than four distinct prospects, will also readily be granted. Assumptions 2 and 3 have been the subject of some discussion.

On the face of it, axiom 2 seems relatively harmless. In economics as in the natural sciences, the assumption that the phenomena under study vary continuously provides a convenient first approximation to reality.

The nature of the objections raised against this axiom can be understood more easily if we start from a specific example. Rothenberg [7] cites the following as a counter-example to axiom 2. Let *x* consist of receiving five safety pins and *y* consist of receiving three safety pins and *z* consist of being executed at dawn. The individual

---

[1] For the proof itself, which involves some mathematics, the reader is referred to Marschak [4].

B

concerned prefers x to y and y to z. But there may not exist any probability p which will make the individual concerned indifferent between y and the prospect of x, z with probabilities p, $1-p$ respectively.

This is essentially because the consequences of the outcome z (being executed) are so extremely unpleasant that *any* probability combination including it is likely to be rejected.

Other counter-examples to the continuity axiom that are found in the literature also involve such 'extremely unpleasant' outcomes as starvation, serious illness, etc. They involve the same principle.

Whether or not one finds this criticism persuasive turns, then, on whether or not one finds it reasonable to include outcomes with 'extreme' consequences among the feasible alternatives.

In practice, economists have generally confined their attention to more 'routine' situations. Formally, this is expressed by saying that the utility function is assumed to be 'bounded'. The assumption of bounded utility automatically excludes choice among alternatives involving consequences incommensurably worse – or better – than those of others.

The point is not that such situations cannot exist but rather that they cannot easily be tackled by means of the analytical tools that the economist can command. Fortunately for the economist, they also appear to be rare.

It is axiom 3, the Strong Independence Axiom, which has been most strongly attacked. However, some at least of these attacks appear to be based on a misinterpretation of the axiom itself.

Thus, the axiom has nothing to do with the presence or absence of substitution or complementarity between goods the probability combination of which forms a prospect. This follows from the definition of a probability combination which refers to a combination between mutually exclusive events. Thus, in talking about a probability combination p, $1-p$ of outcomes x, y, it is necessarily implied that the outcomes x, y cannot occur simultaneously. Hence if x, y, z are as defined in axiom 3, the question of substitution or complementarity between x, z or between y, z cannot arise.

What then is the correct economic interpretation of the Strong Independence Axiom? Economists are still divided on the question.[1] However, the following implication of the axiom, which has been pointed out by Rothenberg ([7] pp. 239–40), seems to be important. In our example, suppose the individual is indifferent between x, y

[1] A useful discussion is to be found in Rothenberg [7] and in Samuelson [8].

regarded as sure outcomes. Suppose further that the attractiveness of x is *increased* by being placed in a risky context: viz. the prospect of getting x, z with probabilities p, $1-p$ respectively. Suppose also that the attractiveness of y is *reduced* by being placed in a similar risky context. Then the individual concerned may prefer the prospect $p(x)$, $(1-p)(z)$, to the prospect $p(y)$, $(1-p)(z)$ even though he is indifferent between x and y. Such behaviour is excluded by the axiom in question.

This example is related to a more general consideration. It has often been pointed out that the von Neumann–Morgenstern (or Marschak) axioms exclude the love or hatred of gambling as such. The precise meaning of the expression 'love or hatred of gambling' in the language of economics, as opposed to its meaning in ordinary language, is far from clear.[1] However, one possible interpretation of it is that a lover of gambling gets more satisfaction the greater the number of lotteries he participates in. Similarly, one who hates gambling is worse off the greater the number of lotteries involved.

It can be shown that either case contradicts the Strong Independence Axiom which implies that only the overall probabilities matter and hence that 'compounding' probabilities of a series of successive gambles is permissible.[2]

There is yet another sense in which the axioms described may be said to exclude 'love of gambling'. Marschak [4] has shown that the axioms 1–4 together imply the following monotonicity rule for rational choice between prospects. Suppose that a person obeys the axioms and that between alternatives x and y he prefers x. Then, in choosing between prospects, i.e. probability combinations of x and y, he will always choose a prospect offering a higher probability of x to one offering a lower probability.

On the other hand, somebody who loves gambling in the sense that he derives an added zest from the possibility of loss might well prefer a prospect offering a 90 per cent probability of x and a 10 per cent probability of y to one offering x with certainty (100 per cent probability). Such behaviour contradicts the monotonicity rule and hence the axioms.

To sum up, it was the contention of von Neumann and Morgenstern that their approach involved 'very little extra effort' by way of additional assumptions on preferences as compared to the standard indifference curve analysis. Economists still appear to be divided in their opinions whether this is so. On the other hand, few

[1] This was pointed out by von Neumann and Morgenstern ([3] p. 28).
[2] A simple proof of this is given in Samuelson, Dorfman and Solow [9].

would contend that the von Neumann–Morgenstern axioms are excessively restrictive.

So far the discussion has been concerned with the axioms as such. An alternative approach would be to test whether people faced with the choice between uncertain prospects do in fact behave as if they were guided by the von Neumann–Morgenstern axioms. Such tests have been carried out by Mosteller and Nogee [10], and others. However, there is considerable difference among economists in interpreting the experimental evidence. All that one can say safely is that the theory has not been clearly disproved.

It remains a slightly controversial question, then, as to whether the possibility of a cardinal measure of utility has been established. This section has been directed towards a very brief outline of some of the ways in which 'modern' cardinal measures have been justified.

It was said earlier that the dominant viewpoint rejected cardinalism. The reasons for this are twofold. Firstly, it is argued that preferences are not capable of measurement in the cardinal sense. This point is debatable. There is nothing logically odd about measuring the intensity of a want, and psychologists do use such measures. Nonetheless, the consensus among economists is that utility is not capable of cardinal measurement in all the choice situations in which we are interested. Secondly, and perhaps more important, economists have demonstrated convincingly that, in most of the contexts to which modern choice theory has been applied, cardinalism adds nothing. The theorems of the neoclassical economists (Jevons, Menger, Walras, Marshall), who relied on the idea of cardinal utility indicators, although to varying extents, are all provable in terms of modern ordinal preference logic. The proviso about 'most contexts' is important, however. Once preferences are aggregated to the social level the maximisation of utility measured in ordinal terms need not produce the same results as the maximisation of utility in cardinal terms. This problem is raised in section 1.8.

Some comments about the 'dominant' view are perhaps in order. Firstly, philosophers might be slightly surprised to find the economist treating all wants as selfish. It makes sense to think of wanting something *for* others, as might be the case if we act out of an altruistic motive. If we choose to stay at home to look after an aged grandmother, rather than go out to the theatre, we might be acting out of a sense of duty. If wants are capable of being unselfish in this way, in what sense is the economist's theory of choice behaviour a general one? The answer might be that it is not general, for although preferences can be thought of as logically entailing wants, it is not the case that all choices logically entail preferences. That is, some actions are executed out of a sense of duty or altruism which does not fit easily into the economist's use of the term 'preference'. However, to go further with this point is to venture into areas peripheral to the main concern. Suffice it to say that the economist is not propounding, as some of his forebears did (Edgeworth for example), a universal theory of choice explanation based on selfish wants.

Secondly, the concept of utility has been introduced without raising the issue of 'value judgements'. A value judgement is a statement which is ultimately reducible to the form 'X is good (bad)'. Nothing that has so far been said implies anything good or bad about preferences. Preferences are observable activities, they are 'revealed' in the market place. Frequently it is difficult to observe preferences, or to find out what people *really* want. Anyone who has compiled a questionnaire will know that individuals sometimes give answers which they believe reflect the questioner's preferences, simply to please the person asking the question. Other preferences may be difficult to discover, especially where there is no market place. The 'surrogate questionnaire' approach might be used here – asking persons who are not directly involved what their preferences would be, and then inferring that the affected persons will have the same preferences. This approach is often necessary in cost–benefit analysis where a policy will involve loss of utility to persons who, if they knew the purpose of the questionnaire, might overstate the harm suffered in order to 'put their case'. Problems of observation apart, however, utility is not, in its present context, a 'value word'; it describes the ranking of wants. When translated to the social level, however, it is possible for it to assume some 'emotive' content which would imply that it is a 'good thing' to undertake policies which are socially preferred. Problematical terms such as 'democracy' impinge upon the argument. Of course, an individual may reveal different preferences when acting in his self-interest compared to his preferences when acting 'in the community's interest': i.e. the individual adopts different roles in different contexts. The question is: which preference is the relevant one for CBA? Since CBA purports to act 'in the public interest' it should perhaps record the preferences of persons thinking of the community's best interest. In practice it does not do this; it records preferences in the selfish category.

Thirdly, just as it was seen that some choices do not involve preferences in the sense defined here, so it is possible that individuals do not aim to reach the most preferred state, to maximise utility. Some experiments suggest that people are frequently 'satisficers', aiming to reach a reasonable level of utility but not aiming any further. The interested reader is referred to the stimulating work of H. A. Simon [11] on this possibility.

Fourthly, many philosophers would be unhappy with the economist's treatment of preferences or wants as 'primitive notions'. He would almost certainly wish to refer to the substantial literature which denies that any empirical science, which economics purports to be, can be built upon foundations which necessarily require the existence of unanalysable notions. The troubled reader is referred to C. W. Churchman's essay [12] if he wishes to open this particular Pandora's box.

1.5 Market Votes and Political Votes

The preferences which CBA *in its standard form* attempts to measure and aggregate are 'market' preferences: a vote recorded in a competitive market place, or the vote which the cost–benefit analyst infers (as best he can) *would* be expressed *if* there was a competitive market place. Clearly, these votes are not equally allocated between individuals: those with larger incomes have more market votes compared to those with smaller incomes. Compare this to a democratic political voting system in which each man has one vote, regardless of his income. Ethical arguments can be adduced for either system. 'One man, one vote' appears to serve the principle of equity, of 'distributive justice'. If, on the other hand, it could be argued that each individual is paid according to his marginal social product, and that he *deserves* to receive the value of his marginal product, then the market voting system has some ethical force. In its 'standard' form, CBA adopts the market voting system, so that the value judgement underlying its use is really a compound of two independent value judgements: (*a*) a judgement that *preferences* should count, and (*b*) a judgement that preferences *should* be weighted by market power – i.e. by income – because the existing distribution of income is, in some sense, optimal. These arguments are discussed in more detail in Chapter 2.

1.6 UTILITY AND BENEFIT

Having defined utility in terms of preferences, it is possible to define the link between utility and the idea of a 'benefit'.

Leaving many qualifications aside, it can be assumed that the preference of an individual for a given state is indicated by the price he is willing to pay for that state. This statement is the logical outcome of the consumer seeking equilibrium – i.e. of seeking to maximise his own utility (reach his highest level of preference) subject to the limitations of his income. This is easily shown in the simple indifference curve diagram, Fig. 1.6.1 below.

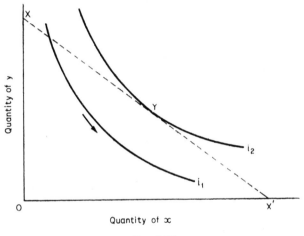

FIG. 1.6.1

x and y are commodities, and the curve i_1 shows the combinations of x and y between which the consumer is indifferent. As the consumer moves down i_1 in the direction of the arrow, in order to have the same total utility he requires more of good x to compensate for the loss of good y: there is a diminishing marginal rate of substitution between x and y. The slope of i_1 reflects the ratio of the utility of an extra unit of y compared to the utility of an extra unit of x, i.e.

$$\text{slope } i_1 = \frac{\text{MU}_x}{\text{MU}_y}.$$

The line XX' defines the consumer's income so that he is unable to reach any point outside the triangle OXX'. Now i_2 is a higher indifference curve, indicating a higher level of utility compared to i_1.

In this case, the consumer is able to reach i_2 at Y, which constitutes his highest utility level. Given that the consumer aims to maximise utility he will aim to reach Y. But XX' also gives the relative prices of x and y, i.e.

$$\text{slope } XX' = \frac{P_x}{P_y}.$$

Now the slope of XX' equals the slope of i_2 at Y, so that the consumer maximises his satisfaction where

$$\frac{MU_x}{MU_y} = \frac{P_x}{P_y}.$$

If, for convenience, we set $P_x/MU_x = 1$, i.e. establish this commodity as the 'numeraire', we obtain, by simple rearrangement,

$$P_y = MU_y.$$

In short, price reflects the worth to the individual of the commodity (state) y, and similarly for all other commodities.

Now, if an individual pays price P_y for commodity y he must be *willing to pay* that price, otherwise he will go without it. It is exactly this willingness to pay which defines a *benefit*, so that we obtain the important equivalence:

$$\text{benefit} = \text{willingness to pay} = \text{price,}$$

an equivalence which will require modification shortly.

1.7 THE AGGREGATION OF PREFERENCES: MAXIMISING 'SOCIAL UTILITY'

As far as the individual is concerned, the maximisation of utility can be analysed in terms of an ordinal utility indicator. For most economic problems, nothing is gained by attempting to measure the 'intensity' of a preference. Thus, demand theory rests upon ordinal utility only, and, in dispensing with the measurability of utility, demand theory is free of many of the problems which 'cardinalism' produces. However, if our interest is in *society's* preferences – and it is the basic assumption of cost–benefit analysis that policies are to be recommended on this ground – there is a difficulty of *aggregating* the recorded preferences of individuals. In arriving at some concept of social preference it does make a difference if individual preferences *qua* preferences are aggregated, or if the intensities of preferences (assuming they could be measured) are aggregated.

Chapter 3 demonstrates that difficulties arise in aggregating ordinal utilities, but the essential distinction between the two possibilities can be made clear with the aid of a simple example.

Suppose 'society' has to choose between two states, x and y, and that there are three persons, 1, 2 and 3. Then, where P_1 means 'preferred by 1', we might have

$$xP_1y$$
$$xP_2y$$
$$yP_3x$$

so that 1 and 2 'vote' for x, and 3 'votes' for y. On the assumption that each preference should count, and count equally, x is preferred to y by the majority – i.e. by society, where society is construed as a simple aggregation of the individuals that comprise it (thus the 'individualist' ethic is transposed to the social level: the 'state' or 'society' is not in any way regarded as a separate entity). To summarise this 'ordinal' approach, social welfare, SW, can be written

$$SW = SW\ [R_1(x), R_2(x), \ldots, R_n(x)]$$

i.e. social welfare depends on the rankings (R) by the individuals $(1, 2, \ldots, n)$ of the state x relative to other states.

Now suppose that some allowance is made for the *intensity* of preference of the individuals for x relative to y. It could be that 1 and 2 'barely prefer' x to y, but that 3 'very much prefers' y to x. Suppose some cardinal measure of the kind outlined in section 1.4 existed, common to 1, 2 and 3 such that these intensities could be recorded as

$$U_1(x)-U_1(y) = \quad 10 \text{ units}$$
$$U_2(x)-U_2(y) = \quad\ \ 5 \text{ units}$$
$$U_3(x)-U_3(y) = -50 \text{ units (i.e. 3 'disprefers' } x \text{ to } y)$$

so that, if the units are added, we get a net social *loss* of 35 units $(10+5-50)$. In other words, allowing for the intensity of preference, y is preferred to x by 'society'. This approach is equivalent to adding up the preferences of the individuals and weighting those preferences by the relative intensities of preference, so that

$$SW = SW\ [\alpha_1.R_1(x)+\alpha_2.R_2(x)+ \ldots \alpha_n.R_n(x)]$$

where $\alpha_1, \alpha_2, \ldots, \alpha_n$ are the respective weights.

In Chapter 3 it is shown why measurability in this sense contradicts one of the conditions of the 'Arrow Impossibility Theorem', although it provides an escape from the paradox produced by that theorem, and it will also be shown why the first approach to aggregation can give illogical outcomes once preferences are ordered by each individual over three or more states. For the moment it is necessary only to look at the underlying assumptions of the second approach.

The most important aspect of this cardinal approach is the assumption of *interpersonal comparisons of utility* (IPCU). IPCU requires that the utility of one individual be comparable with the utility of another person. The problem here is that the concept of utility relates to the concept of preference, as was shown in section 1.2, and it seems logically odd to speak of these preferences as being comparable. Thus, if 1 ranks x as being 'much better' than y, and 2 does likewise, are the two expressions of intensity of preference identical in terms of the scale on which utilities are recorded? If 1 has a scale, with a chosen unit of preference intensity and a zero point, there appears to be no reason to assume that these scales are the same for 1 and 2. 1 may *mean* by 'much better' something different from 2's 'much better' – there appears to be no way of finding out. The problem has already been encountered in the discussion of Armstrong utility in section 1.4.

Notice that two requirements have been stated as necessary for an IPCU: identical units of measurement, and identical zero points. The previous hypothetical example has shown that the existence of identical zeros does not matter very much. Thus, if 1 prefers x to y by 10 units and 2 prefers x to y by 5 units, and 1 and 2 mean the same thing by a 'unit', it does not matter if 1's preference relates to a move from 90 to 100 units and 2's from 60 to 65; the outcome for the decision problem is the same.

It is the apparent non-existence of a definitive unit of measurement that creates the difficulties. Luce and Raiffa ([13] pp. 33–4) make this clear:

> Suppose two people are isolated from each other and each is given a measuring stick marked off in certain and possibly different arbitrary units. With such limited communication it is clearly possible for the second man to construct a scale model of the object, but it will only be of the correct size if it happens that both measuring rods are marked in the same units. Clearly once the barriers on communication are dropped, the two men can determine with fair accuracy the relationship between their two units. The big difference between utility and length measurement is that we do not seem to have any 'outside thing' which can be measured by both persons to ascertain the relation between the two units.

The economist of the 'dominant' view tends to take the impossibility of IPCUs as proven. It would be misleading to suggest that this view is unassailable, but it is not directly relevant here to explore the criticisms in detail. Once again, philosophical arguments are involved concerning the existence of 'other minds' and communications between minds. The essential criticism is that there are reasons for supposing that scales of feeling are communicable as long as the scale for any one individual can be established. That is, if preferences are measurable for any one individual there is no problem of interpersonal comparison simply because there is no problem of 'other minds'. Here again, we can do no more than refer the inquiring reader to the works of Wisdom [14], Strawson [15] and Churchman [16] for a discussion of these problems.

An indicator of social benefit, then, can be obtained, in theory at least, in two major separate ways: by 'counting heads' and by aggregating the intensities of preference. The two may not yield the same result. Which approach underlies cost–benefit analysis? To establish this it is necessary to return to the benefit–utility–price equivalence established at the end of section 1.6.

It was established that if state x is preferred to state y by individual 1, this is the same as saying $U(x) > U(y)$ for 1. But these utilities will be reflected in prices, generally speaking, which in turn reflect willingness to pay (WTP). Suppose that, for three individuals 1, 2 and 3, it is possible to write

$$xP_1y \Rightarrow U_1(x) > U_1(y) \Rightarrow \text{WTP}_1(x) > \text{WTP}_1(y)$$
$$xP_2y \Rightarrow U_2(x) > U_2(y) \Rightarrow \text{WTP}_2(x) > \text{WTP}_2(y)$$
$$yI_3x \Rightarrow U_3(y) = U_3(x) \Rightarrow \text{WTP}_3(x) = \text{WTP}_3(y)$$

where the symbol '$\Rightarrow$' can be read as 'entails that'.

Adding up the willingness to pay would appear to give the same result as adding up preferences by 'counting heads'. In this case x is socially preferred to y on a count of heads. If 1 and 2 are willing to offer, say, £5 for x and, say, nothing for y, while 3 is willing to offer £5 for either, the relevant WTPs are WTP(x) = £15, and WTP(y) = £5.

However, prices do more than reflect simple preferences – they reflect to some extent relative intensities of preference. If 3 'dispreferred' x, and was willing to pay, say, £12 for y and nothing for x, a simple aggregation of WTPs would result in WTP(x) = £10 and WTP(y) = £12, so that the ranking would be reversed compared to a counting of heads. Essentially, it is this latter procedure which underlies cost–benefit analysis: partial allowance is made for intensities through willingness to pay and, as Chapter 2 shows, through requirements for compensation when there are losers. This principle should become more clear after the discussion of how benefits and costs are valued.

It is not the case, however, that willingness to pay fully reflects the intensity of preference. The reason is simple. The price that an individual is willing to pay for an outcome is partly dependent upon his income. He may desperately want something and be willing to spend a large part, perhaps the entire amount, of his income on it. A similar price might be offered by someone with a very much larger income, but the price offered in the latter case may not 'mean' as much to the individual concerned as the price offered in the first case. Essentially, the willingness-to-pay concept does not allow for differences in the *marginal utility of income*: the £1 of a poor man may yield more utility than the £1 of the rich man. Instead of the equation given in section 1.6, we require

$$MU_i = P_i . MU_Y$$

a formal proof of which is given in the appendix to this chapter. This condition states that the marginal utility of good i is equal, in equilibrium, to the price of good i multiplied by the individual's marginal utility of income. In the expression in section 1.6 marginal utility of the good was equated with price alone.

In this way an important proposition is derived. For projects or policies to be judged in terms of their contribution to social utility, the willingness-to-pay concept will not suffice unless either

(a) adjustments are made for the marginal utility of income, or
(b) arguments are advanced which justify ignoring the income utility factor.

It is fair to say that cost–benefit analysis generally proceeds on the basis of (b). The arguments that are advanced are considered in Chapter 2.

1.8 THE VALUATION OF BENEFITS

So far it has been established that the objective of cost–benefit analysis is to guide the decision-maker in the choice of capital projects and expenditures which will maximise the gains to social welfare. Social welfare has been related, albeit loosely for the moment, to some aggregation of individuals' preferences, and these in turn are represented by the individuals' willingness to pay for commodities. Market prices therefore play a central part in the valuation of benefits, although substantial modifications have to be made to these links to allow for market imperfections and for situations in which no market exists in the product of the project. The issue of indirect costs and their valuation is postponed to the next chapter.

Given, for the moment, that society's preferences for goods are relevant to the objective function, it is necessary to see how the appropriate valuation of a benefit is obtained.

Fig. 1.8.1 shows a familiar downward-sloping demand curve for some product. Suppose that market forces set the price of the good at P and the quantity sold at Q. Then, consumers pay out an

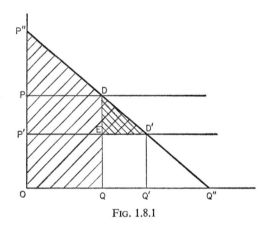

FIG. 1.8.1

amount PDQ – this is their *effective* payment for the good. It is not, however, a measure of their *willingness* to pay and hence of their true preference for the good. It is usual to approximate the willingness to pay by adding to the effective payment the consumer's surplus triangle $P''PD$. Essentially, the argument is that there are some consumers who *would have paid* more than P for the product: their preferences are recorded on the demand curve above the ruling price. (If there is only one consumer it is still the case that the first units of the commodity would have attracted a higher price.) The total willingness to pay is therefore given by the large lightly-shaded area in Fig. 1.8.1, so that

$$\text{Total WTP} = P.Q + S$$

i.e. the total willingness to pay for any good is equal to the purchase price multiplied by the amount purchased, plus the consumers' surplus (S).

Since the effect of an investment project is usually to alter the amount of the good already in existence, it is the *change* in WTP that is relevant. In other words, if quantity increases from Q to Q' in Fig. 1.8.1, benefits are computed as the willingness to pay for this increased output. From the diagram it can be seen that this change is equal to

$$OQ'D'P'' - OQDP'' = QQ'D'D$$

which in turn is equal to the change in quantity multiplied by the new price, plus the triangle $ED'D$. Writing ΔP for the change in price of A, and ΔQ for the change in quantity, the change in willingness to pay becomes

$$\Delta \text{WTP} = \Delta Q \cdot P' + \tfrac{1}{2}\Delta P \cdot \Delta Q$$

where the last expression is the area of the heavily-shaded triangle $ED'D$.[1]

This expression reduces to

$$\Delta \text{WTP} = \Delta Q\left(P' + \frac{P - P'}{2}\right)$$
$$= \Delta Q\left(\frac{P + P'}{2}\right).$$

The appropriate valuation of benefits therefore becomes the change in physical quantity multiplied by a simple average of the price previous to the investment and the price after the investment.

If the investment alters prices only *marginally*, or not at all, then, for valuation purposes, $P = P'$ and the rule reduces to

$$\Delta \text{WTP} = \Delta Q \cdot \left(\frac{2P}{2}\right) = \Delta Q \cdot P.$$

In other words, the ruling market price is an appropriate indication of the WTP per unit of output.

The use of market prices needs to be qualified in a number of circumstances, discussed in Chapter 4.

1.9 THE VALUATION OF COSTS, AND THE BENEFIT–COST FORMULA

Since economic resources are limited, it should be obvious that the undertaking of a public investment will divert resources from an

[1] Since the area of a triangle equals half base times altitude. This will hold true only if the segment of the demand curve DD' is linear.

alternative use – perhaps another public investment, or an investment in the private sector. There is an *opportunity cost* to carrying out the expenditure. The cost–benefit analyst must therefore be interested in the benefits to be derived from the expenditure in question *compared to* the benefits that would have been obtained if the money had been used elsewhere. Since the aim of CBA is to reflect the structure of society's preferences, it follows that the chosen *ranking function* should reflect the difference between the benefits obtained from a given project, say x, and the benefits that would have been obtained from the project which is forgone, say w. Essentially, then, we require a measure of the willingness to pay for the forgone project. Faced with several projects, x, y and z, the choice of any of which would mean going without w, the ranking function becomes

$$\text{WTP}(i) - \text{WTP}(w), \quad i = x, y, z.$$

If this difference is higher for, say, x than for y or z, then x is the most preferred project. $\text{WTP}(w)$ is properly regarded as the *cost* of project i.

The problem is to obtain a measure of the WTP for the forgone project, w, or the 'social opportunity cost'. If the resources used in x had been used in y they would have produced a certain physical output, say Q_d, which would sell at a price P_d. But, ignoring consumers' surplus and subject to the modifications to be discussed in Chapter 4, P_d must reflect the marginal social benefit of w. Hence, $P_d . Q_d$ is the willingness to pay for w. But, clearly, the resources displaced by x are represented by the money cost of x, and this money cost would appear in turn to be equal to $P_d . Q_d$. Subject to some qualifications to be made shortly, it follows that *the WTP for the forgone project is equal to the money cost of the chosen project*.[1]

To compute the *net* benefits to society of any project it is therefore necessary to estimate

$$\text{net } B = b . p - C$$

where b is the physical benefit, p the product price and C the costs of supplying the product. Since the amount supplied can be varied – the investment can vary in size, or *scale* – it is useful to write each of these variables as functions of size, so that the ranking function becomes

$$\text{net } B(x) = b(x) . p(x) - j(x) . w(x)$$

[1] The forgone project here is w. Clearly, if x is chosen it is also the case that y and z are forgone. The results are the same if the ranking function differences between WTP for x and y, y and z, z and w are computed.

where $b(x)$, for example, simply means the physical benefits which result from some chosen scale x; $j(x)$ is the amount of physical resources used in the project; and w is the market price of these resources. This in turn reduces to

$$\text{net } B(x) = B(x) - C(x).$$

As yet, time has not been introduced into the picture. The benefits and costs will be distributed over the 'life' of the project. To complete the formula for the ranking function it is necessary to write $B_t(x)$ for the benefits in year t, with a similar notation for costs. It will then be necessary to sum the benefits over the time periods, so that $\sum_{t=0}^{n} B_t$ simply means 'the sum of all the benefits in each of the years from 0 to n', where the nth year is the year in which the project ceases its 'life'. Again for completeness, we introduce the discount factor d_t, which allows for the fact that £1 of benefit (or costs) in later years is not to be regarded as being as large as £1 of benefit or cost now. The rationale of 'discounting' is discussed in Chapter 6. The discount factor will get larger as time increases (i.e. d_t will get smaller), so that d_t will vary with time. The final formula becomes

$$\text{net } B(x) = \sum_{t=0}^{n} B_t(x) \cdot d_t - \sum_{t=0}^{n} C_t(x) \cdot d_t$$
$$= \sum_{t=0}^{n} (B_t(x) - C_t(x)) \cdot d_t.$$

It will soon be seen in Chapter 4 that, under certain circumstances, market prices are inadequate representations of marginal social valuations in the case of benefits. The same problem arises with costs, since these are readily translated into the WTP for the forgone project. There are two general reasons for supposing that the price of the resources used in the chosen project will be an inadequate guide to the true opportunity cost of the project:

(1) Resource prices may rise because of the transfer of resources from one sector to the sector in which the project is to take place, i.e. from w to x or y or z in our case.
(2) The resources may come from sectors which have imperfectly competitive product markets or have imperfectly competitive resources markets.

In case (1) the resource cost of the chosen project could be measured at the resource prices *before* the change or *after* the change. But the actual loss of welfare from the project that would otherwise have been undertaken is not measured by either valuation. Fig. 1.9.1 demonstrates this point.

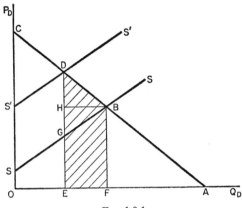

FIG. 1.9.1

The demand and supply curves are shown for the forgone project, *w*. The effect of the chosen investment is to raise factor prices so that the product supply curve is shifted from *SS* to *S'S'*. The total loss of WTP on the project *w* is therefore shown by the shaded area *EFBD*, and it is this area which is the proper valuation of the 'opportunity cost' of the chosen project. In practice, however, the use of market prices for resources will entail a valuation equal to the area *EFBG*, so that there is a 'bias' equal to the lost consumers' surplus *DHB* and the lost 'producers' surplus' *HBG* (see Dunn [17] and Stober *et al.* [18]).

Case (2) is shown in Fig. 1.9.2. The forgone output would have occurred in an imperfectly competitive context, so that the appropriate marginal revenue curve needs to be considered, as well as the demand curve. In Fig. 1.9.2 the diversion of resources from project *w* is assumed to raise resource prices so that the marginal cost curve shifts upward from MC to MC'. The change in the profit-maximising price is from *P* to *P'*. The loss in WTP is shown by the shaded area, whereas the usual valuation, based on market prices of resources, would compute only the area *Q'QCD*. There is therefore an understatement of the true WTP by the area *DCPP'*, which can be thought of as two areas: *BCD*, the effect of bidding up the resource prices, and *BCPP'*, the effect of withdrawing resources from an imperfectly competitive context.

A ranking function should measure the difference between the

WTP for the project in question and the WTP for the output for-gone. Only under simplified conditions will the money cost of the chosen project, based on revealed market prices of resources, repre-sent the forgone benefits. In practice there is likely to be at least one source of bias.

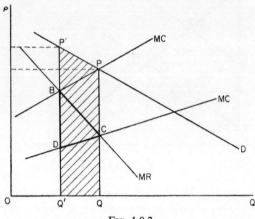

FIG. 1.9.2

1.10 SUMMARY

This chapter has concerned itself with the welfare foundations of cost–benefit. It was shown that CBA adopts as its criterion of social gain an improvement in social utility (welfare). It was therefore necessary to investigate in some more detail the meaning of the term 'utility'. A contrast was drawn between utility in its 'ordinal' and 'cardinal' senses. The possibility of cardinal measurement was discussed and it was argued that cost–benefit analysis reflects a welfare concept which is neither strictly ordinal nor cardinal. Will-ingness to pay reflected some part of preference intensity, but the essential distinction between criteria based on willingness to pay and criteria based on completely measurable utility lay in the con-cept of marginal utility of income. It was pointed out that 'con-ventional' cost–benefit analysis does not incorporate any allowance for the marginal utility of income. The idea of consumers' surplus was introduced and the relationship between market prices and willingness to pay was demonstrated. At the same time, attention was drawn to an asymmetry in the analysis of benefits and costs: the latter should strictly be measured in terms of society's willingness to pay for the forgone alternative.

APPENDIX

WELFARE MAXIMISATION AND COST–BENEFIT ANALYSIS: SOME SIMPLE MATHEMATICS

Suppose a society comprises n individuals ($i = 1, \ldots, n$), each with a utility function of the form

$$U_i = U_i(X_{i1}, X_{i2}, \ldots, X_{im}) \quad j = 1, \ldots, m \quad (1.1)$$

where X_{i1} is the amount of good 1 available to individual i. Since individual i will be supplying some goods (his labour, for example) and receiving others, some of the X_{ij} will be negative (inputs), and some positive (goods).

The income of individual i is Y_i and

$$Y_i = \sum_{j=1}^{m} P_{ij} \cdot X_{ij}$$

where P_j is the price of good j, so that

$$Y_i - \sum_{j=1}^{m} P_{ij} \cdot X_{ij} = 0. \quad (1.2)$$

The individual's utility is maximised when the following Lagrangean expression is maximised:

$$W = U_i(X_{i1}, \ldots, X_{im}) + \lambda_i(Y_i - \sum_{j=1}^{m} P_{ij} \cdot X_{ij}) \quad (1.3)$$

where λ_i is the Lagrangean multiplier. The relevant maximising condition is

$$\frac{\partial W}{\partial X_{ij}} = \frac{\partial U_i}{\partial X_{ij}} - \lambda_i \cdot P_j = 0$$

i.e.
$$\lambda_i = \frac{\partial U_i}{\partial X_{ij}} \Big/ P_j \quad (1.4)$$

where λ_i is the marginal utility of income to individual i, since $\partial W / \partial Y_i = \lambda_i$. Also from (1.4)

$$\frac{\partial U_i}{\partial X_{ij}} = P_j \lambda_i. \quad (1.5)$$

Any change in income to individual i will comprise changes in the goods and inputs X_j. It follows that an increase ΔX_1 in the amount of X_1 available to i will raise i's utility by

$$\frac{\partial U_i}{\partial X_{i1}} \cdot \Delta X_{i1}$$

and similarly for all goods comprising the change in income. Hence the change in income will change the utility of individual i by

$$\Delta U_i = \frac{\partial U_i}{\partial X_{i1}} \cdot \Delta X_{i1} + \ldots + \frac{\partial U_i}{\partial X_{im}} \cdot \Delta X_{im}. \tag{1.6}$$

Substituting (1.5) in (1.6) we have

$$\Delta U_i = \lambda_i P_1 \cdot \Delta X_{i1} + \ldots + \lambda_i \cdot P_m \cdot \Delta X_{im} \tag{1.7}$$

i.e. $$\Delta U_i = \lambda_i \cdot \sum_{j=1}^{m} P_j \cdot \Delta X_{ij} \tag{1.8}$$

which tells us that the utility from the increment of income is equal to the change in income multiplied by the marginal utility of income.

To find the change in *social* welfare arising from a change in national income, we assume that

$$\Delta SW = U_1 + U_2 + \ldots + U_n = \sum_{i=1}^{m} U_i \tag{1.9}$$

i.e. that the individual's utilities can be aggregated. Hence,

$$\Delta SW = \sum_{i=1}^{n} \sum_{j=1}^{m} \lambda_i \cdot P_j \cdot \Delta X_{ij}. \tag{1.10}$$

Now some of the X_{ij} are outputs and some inputs. Treating the former as *physical benefits* (b_j) and the latter as *physical costs* (c_j), we can expand (1.10) to

$$\Delta SW = \sum_{i=1}^{n} \cdot \left[\sum_{j=1}^{k} \cdot \lambda_i P_j \Delta b_{ij} - \sum_{j=l}^{m} \lambda_i P_j \cdot \Delta c_{ij} \right]. \tag{1.11}$$

If the marginal utility of income is assumed equal for all persons, so that $\lambda_1 = \lambda_2 = \ldots = \lambda_n = \lambda$, and if the change in national product is assumed to be distributed across the community, (1.11) can be simplified to

$$\Delta SW = \lambda \left[\sum_{j=1}^{k} P_j \cdot \Delta b_j - \sum_{j=l}^{m} P_j \cdot \Delta c_j \right]. \tag{1.12}$$

Since the *absolute* magnitude of SW is not relevant, the social welfare function being an aggregation of individual utility functions which are defined only up to a monotonic transformation, (1.12) can be written

$$\Delta SW = \sum_{=1}^{k} P_j \Delta b_j - \sum_{j=l}^{m} P_j \cdot \Delta c_j. \tag{1.13}$$

Let B_j, the money value of the benefit $j, = P_j \, \Delta b_j$, and let $C_j = P_j \, \Delta c_j$, so that

$$\Delta SW = \sum_{j=1}^{k} B_j - \sum_{j=l}^{m} C_j. \qquad (1.14)$$

2 Pareto Optimality, Compensation Tests and 'Equity'

2.1 PARETO SOCIAL WELFARE FUNCTIONS AND OPTIMALITY

Chapter 1 implied that CBA enabled the decision-maker to choose outcomes which are socially 'most preferred', no complete allowance being made for differing *intensities* of preference between individuals. It follows that there must be some overall state of the economy which is most preferred, and that the objective of CBA can be reformulated as that of guiding choices such that this most preferred state, or 'social optimum', is achieved. Clearly, this objective could only be fulfilled if

(a) CBA criteria were extended to *all* decision contexts;
(b) CBA criteria were rigidly applied – i.e. information was such that the rules were *capable* of universal and precise application;
(c) society rested content with a concept of an optimum based on revealed preferences.

In practice, conditions (a) and (b) are not met, nor are they ever likely to be. Condition (c) merely suggests that in practice the objective functions might need restatement in light of some 'chosen' aims – e.g. minimum levels of income, or education, or health: in place of 'social preferences' we would obtain 'planners' preferences', or a mixture of both.

Leaving aside the problems encountered in situations contained in (c), a clear definition of a social optimum is called for.

If preferences are aggregated it would seem impossible to take exception to a rule which declared policy x better than policy y if *everyone* prefers it. Such a rule is the Pareto 'unanimity' rule.[1]

The unanimity rule is clearly unexceptionable: the real problem is that it hardly, if ever, has relevance to actual decision problems. For the Pareto rule says that if everyone prefers x to y, x is a socially acceptable policy. Its scope is widened a little in that policy x is also

[1] Vilfredo Pareto was an Italian sociologist and economist at the end of the nineteenth and beginning of the twentieth century. His *Manual of Political Economy* was first published in Italian in 1906.

held to be socially preferred if a number of individuals are *indifferent* between x and y, and some individuals *prefer x to y*. If some people prefer x to y, and others prefer y to x, the Pareto rule offers no guidance: it does not permit the 'counting of votes' to see if the majority prefer one state rather than another. The reason for this is that the Paretian welfare theory denies the possibility of interpersonal comparisons of utility. Hence, if some gain and some lose in respect of a policy change, there is no way of discovering whether the extra utility of the gainers exceeds the extra utility of the losers.

With these simple illustrations it is possible to define relations between alternative states in terms of Pareto rankings.

(1) xP_sy (x is Pareto preferred to y) if *either xPy* for all individuals comprising society, *or xPy* for some individuals and *xIy* for the remainder.

(2) xI_sy (x is Pareto indifferent to y) if *xIy* for all individuals comprising society.

(3) xR_sy (x is either Pareto preferred or Pareto indifferent to y) if *xRy* for all individuals. Rules (1) and (2) are clearly sub-rules of rule (3).

(4) x and y are 'Pareto non-comparable' if for any one individual *xPy* and for any other individual *yPx*.

(5) Any state, say x, is said to be *Pareto optimal* if, given the tastes of consumers and the prevailing technology, there is no other state, say y, such that yP_sx. That is, Pareto optimality is defined as a state in which no one can be made better off without someone else being made worse off.

Clearly, these relations are highly restrictive in their application.[1]

[1] The Pareto criterion as economists interpret it *is* restrictive, but it would be wrong to suggest that Pareto himself confined his attention to limited orderings of the kind described here. Pareto used the term 'ophelimity' to describe what we have called 'utility' – i.e. preferences resulting from 'economic' causes. It was his argument that distributional problems involved interpersonal comparisons of ophelimity, and no decision could be reached in terms of economic analysis alone. However, he also argued that 'weights' could be assigned to gains and losses 'on grounds of ethics, social utility, or something else . . .'. In other words, resolving the distributional issue is essentially a political problem, and the term 'utility' was reserved by Pareto for this wider usage. Pareto dealt at some length with the issue of assigning 'utilities' in his *Sociology*. For an extremely interesting discussion of Pareto's sociological analysis and his use of the terms 'ophelimity' and 'utility', see V. J. Tarascio, 'Paretian Welfare Theory: Some Neglected Aspects', *Journal of Political Economy* (1969).

Pareto rankings can only be described for states which are Pareto comparable. Since policies frequently involve losses to some and gains to others, the states prior to, and resultant of, these policies cannot be Pareto-ranked. Hence Pareto ranking is a *partial* ranking as compared to the *complete* ordering obtained by the cardinal utility system and the 'majority preference' system outlined in sections 1.4 and 1.7.

However, the concept of Pareto optimality lies at the heart of cost-benefit analysis. For choosing policies which maximise the difference between benefits and costs is prima facie equivalent to

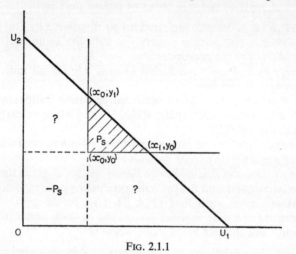

FIG. 2.1.1

moving the overall state of the economy towards a Pareto optimum. The essential problem is that CBA is specifically designed to deal with the fact that policies do involve losses for some people. In consequence the Pareto unanimity rule needs revision.

A simple diagram (Fig. 2.1.1) should help to underline the restrictiveness of the Pareto criterion.

Suppose the utility functions of individuals 1 and 2 are recorded on the two axes (no cardinal concept is implied). The line $U_2 U_1$ describes the maximum possible combinations of utilities which can be achieved by 1 and 2 given their tastes and the state of technology.[1] The set of points inside the triangle $O U_1 U_2$ are 'attainable' points. The set of points outside the triangle are non-attainable. Suppose the economy is at point (x_0, y_0). Then any move into

[1] $U_2 U_1$ is a 'utility possibility frontier', drawn here as a straight line, for convenience.

the triangle P_s (north-east) is a Pareto improvement. Any move into the rectangle $-P_s$ is a Pareto deterioration. Any move south-east or north-west of (x_0, y_0) involves Pareto non-comparability. *Any* point on the segment (x_0, y_1) to (x_1, y_0) is a Pareto optimum, points on the boundary being Pareto incomparable. Points *lying south-west* of a point on the boundary can be judged inferior. Note also that points on the boundary *cannot* be declared Pareto superior to points lying south-east or north-west in the shaded triangle.

2.2 COMPENSATION CRITERIA

The Paretian social welfare function outlined in the previous section tells us that a policy is 'acceptable' (i.e. is in accord with the basic individualist ethic) if at least one member of society prefers the new state and no one 'disprefers' it. But projects tend to involve gains to some and losses to others – i.e. there will usually be at least one person who 'disprefers' the policy. The Pareto rule needs refinement to allow for this obvious fact of life.

The most celebrated attempt to allow for non-unanimity while retaining the concept of Pareto optimality was the 'compensation principle' formulated in slightly different ways by Kaldor [1] and Hicks [2]. In simple terms, the Kaldor–Hicks principle declares a social state y 'socially preferable' to an existing social state x if those who gain from the move to y can compensate those who lose and still have some gains left over. In this way, the idea of 'Pareto optimality' appears to be preserved because the compensation paid to the losers is defined to be such that it leaves the losers *no worse off* than they were before, in state x. If the gainers can pay this compensation and still have something left over then there is a net social gain in that some people will prefer y, while the losers, having been fully compensated, must be indifferent between x and y. Such a situation is consistent with a Pareto improvement since we have xIy for the losers (once they are compensated) and yPx for the gainers (if they can 'over-compensate').

It is just this principle which underlies cost–benefit analysis. If the monetary value of benefits exceeds the monetary value of the costs, then the gainers (those who receive the benefits) can hypothetically compensate the losers (those who bear the costs) and still have some gains left over. The excess of gains over required compensation is equal to the 'net benefits' of the project.

Because the Kaldor–Hicks compensation principle is so fundamental, it needs to be explored a little more closely.

First, the Kaldor–Hicks principle does not require *actual* compensation to be paid. It is necessary only that the beneficiaries *can* compensate the losers. Fig. 2.2.1 repeats the essentials of Fig. 2.1.1. Assume the *status quo* is given by position x and it is proposed to move to y, a move which involves gains to 2 and losses to 1. Hence

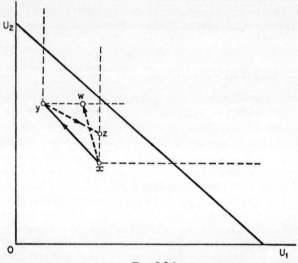

FIG. 2.2.1

y is Pareto incomparable with x. But suppose that, in moving to y, 2 *could* compensate 1 such that 1 is no worse off than he was at x, while 2 would be better off than he was at x. This is the situation at z, where 1 is no worse off and 2 is still better off. The *actual* move is from x to y, and the *hypothetical* move is from y to z. Thus, position z is not actually attained: it is only necessary that it could be reached from y. Since z can be reached from y, and z is Pareto superior to x, the Kaldor–Hicks principle argues that y is Pareto superior to x. Thus the Paretian rule appears to be preserved, and no interpersonal comparisons of utility have been made.

Now suppose the *status quo* is at y and a move to x is contemplated. This involves gains to 1 and losses to 2. It is quite possible that 1 could pay 2 to accept a move to x. If 1 can pay 2 enough to make him as well off as he was in y, a position such as w could be reached. At w, 1 is better off and 2 no worse off compared to situation y. By the same reasoning as before, if w can be reached from x and w is Pareto superior to y, it follows that x is Pareto superior to y.

There is clearly a paradox. A move from x to y is 'socially preferred' on the Kaldor–Hicks principle, but a move *back* from y to x is also socially preferred. The oddity of this 'reversal' was noted by Scitovsky [3].

Clearly, no problem arises if the move from x to y is accompanied by *actual* compensation. But the payment of compensation means that position z is actually reached, and z is Pareto comparable with x. If actual compensation is paid, (*a*) nothing is added to the Pareto ranking, and (*b*) state y is not reached anyway. On the other hand, if compensation is *not* actually paid, it is not the case that xIy for the losers, so that there is not an actual Pareto improvement.

If compensation *is* paid it is necessary that two conditions pertain. Firstly, the compensation must be paid out of the gains of the beneficiaries. Payment out of general government taxation, for example, would involve effects on the utilities of the general taxpayer. Clearly, if the only 'losers' from a project are the taxpayers themselves – e.g. through paying for the capital cost of the project – it would be absurd to raise taxes to compensate the taxpayer. Where the *same person* gains and loses – i.e. pays taxes in order to receive a benefit – the compensation problem does not really arise. Where the set of gainers is not the same as the set of losers, however, the transfer must be between the two groups. Secondly, the transfers should be in the form of lump sums so as to leave incentives to work unaffected.

It is useful to present the Scitovsky paradox in terms of prices and quantities. These can be the prices and quantities of marketed or non-marketed goods. In the latter case, the prices are 'imputed' or 'shadow' prices. Essentially, the Scitovsky paradox arises because the change in income distribution between states x and y alters the set of relative prices which rule in those states. Fig. 2.2.2 shows two goods x and y on the axes, and two price lines $y_1 x_1$ and $y_2 x_2$ showing the relative prices in situations 1 and 2. The relevant real income levels are also shown by the price lines, the line (P_2) showing year 1 quantities valued at year 2 prices, and the line (P_1) showing year 2 quantities valued at year 1 prices.

Consider a move from Q_1 to Q_2. Then the change in real income valued at year 1 prices is

$$P_1 Q_2 - P_1 Q_1$$

which is negative because $P_1 Q_1 > P_1 Q_2$. Hence Q_1 is preferred to Q_2. If the move is valued at year 2 prices, we get

$$P_2 Q_2 - P_2 Q_1$$

which is positive since $P_2Q_2 > P_2Q_1$. In other words, Q_2 is preferred to Q_1.

Essentially, then, the Scitovsky paradox occurs because the transition from one state to another can be shown to be 'better' (worse) when valued at the prices ruling in the initial state, but 'worse' (better) when valued at the prices ruling in the new state. Prices will alter because the distribution of income has altered.

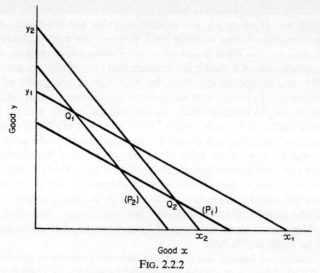

Fig. 2.2.2

A further problem arises. How is the compensation – actual or hypothetical – determined? Clearly, in order to judge a policy change it is necessary to find out what the compensation would need to be. The policy is most likely to involve some capital expenditure. It seems reasonable to suppose that the general taxpayer will require a sum equal to these capital costs in compensation. Chapter 1 argued that what the taxpayer loses is the benefit of the policy that *would have been* carried out if the chosen policy was not undertaken. That is, the compensation requirement would be the true *opportunity cost* of the chosen policy. The forgone project might be another 'lump' of public investment, in which case the opportunity cost is likely to be *less* than the money cost (otherwise the chosen policy would not have been undertaken first). But it is possible for the opportunity cost to exceed the capital cost if the precluded project is in another sector of the economy, say the private sector, and there is limited transference of funds between the two markets – i.e. 'better' projects are not necessarily undertaken first.

The benefit–cost maximand allows, in some measure, for the existence of welfare losses arising from projects. Invariably, public projects impose some costs on third parties – noise from motorways or aircraft, loss of amenity through unsightly electricity pylons, etc. This section has shown that, to some extent at least, CBA will still be consistent with the objective of Pareto optimality *and* can allow for losses of the kind described, once compensation criteria are considered admissible. As long as the benefits of a project exceed the costs, hypothetical compensation will preserve the requirement for a Pareto improvement, namely that some people prefer the final outcome while others (the losers) are at least indifferent to it, the latter's indifference being the result of their receipt of compensation.

The problem, as noted, is that the mechanism of compensation does not operate in practice, or rarely so at least. Some possible decision-rules to govern these situations are required.

2.3 PARETO IMPROVEMENTS, THE DISTRIBUTION OF INCOME AND 'EQUITY'

Even where the money value of benefits does outweigh the money value of losses, the compensation criterion provides an inadequate foundation for the link between the benefit–cost maximand and welfare maximisation as long as the compensation is not actually paid. The problem is that income will be redistributed if losers are not compensated. Three situations are possible.

(1) The beneficiaries bear all the costs, and the losers share in the net gains such that the existing distribution of income is maintained.
(2) The beneficiaries bear all the costs, but the net gains are retained by them.
(3) The beneficiaries do not compensate the losers.

Situation (1) requires that losers be compensated *and* share in the net social benefits. Not only is no one worse off, but everyone is better off, and the initial distribution of income is not changed. Situation (2) relates to a compensation context where losers are actually compensated – i.e. the move is a Pareto improvement. Situation (3) relates to the Kaldor–Hicks context and the move is an improvement only if that test is held to be justified.

Suppose now that there is some distribution of income which is held to be 'optimal'. Exactly what this might mean is discussed later. A dual criterion for a social improvement is now in order: gainers must be able to over-compensate losers (Kaldor–Hicks) *and* the re-distribution of income must be acceptable. Notice that the Scitovsky paradox could still be present even with this extension of the principle.

Clearly, if the *initial* distribution of income is optimal, situation (1) guarantees a social improvement because benefits exceed costs *and* the optimal distribution is preserved. But situations (2) and (3) involve a move *away* from optimal distribution because losers do not share in the net social gains. Indeed, in situation (3) the redistribution is more noticeable than in situation (2) because no compensation is actually paid. It follows that, if the existing distribution of income is optimal, situations (2) and (3) require that the redistribution effects be measured and that some criterion be established to enable a comparison of the 'distribution' effects with the 'efficiency' effects.

Now suppose the initial distribution is *not* optimal. There is even less that can be said in this case. Situation (1) involves no worsening of the distribution, but neither does it improve the distribution. Situations (2) and (3) on the other hand involve redistributions which could be either 'good' or 'bad', according to (*a*) who actually receives the benefits and who loses, and (*b*) what constitutes an improvement or worsening in the income distribution. Once again, clear-cut criteria for distributional changes are required before anything can be said about situations (2) and (3).

In fact situation (3), where losers are not compensated at all, is the relevant one. Nearly all projects involve gains for some and losses for others, and no real mechanism exists for the payment of compensation in the manner set out in section 2.2, i.e. lump-sum transfers between beneficiaries and losers. Given that a redistribution of income *does* result from undertaking projects, what alternatives face the decision-maker?

The first option, and the one which underlies most, though not all, cost–benefit analyses is to argue that the redistribution is not significant (Krutilla [4], Eckstein [5]). This is tantamount to ignoring the welfare effects of a redistribution because the magnitude of the change is small. To put it another way, the Gordian knot of the Scitovsky paradox is cut by saying that the effect of the redistribution on prices is not significant. If relative prices do not change, the Scitovsky problem does not arise; neither does any problem of judging the optimality or otherwise of the income distribution at the *status quo*. In general, proponents of this view would argue that, whatever view is taken of this distribution, the project which is to be the subject of a CBA will not alter that distribution in a significant fashion. In terms of welfare economics, this view accepts the Kaldor–Hicks compensation test, but preserves the dichotomy between 'efficiency' and 'distributional' effects by rejecting the relevance of the distributional problem to these situations.

Against this view several arguments must be posed. Firstly, even if the redistributional consequences of the investments so far subjected to cost–benefit analysis have been slight, this can be no guide for the future. CBA is being applied in ever-expanding fields and to larger and larger investments which have noticeable redistributional consequences (the Third London Airport study [6], for example – see Chapter 9). Secondly, even if the redistributional consequences for a single project are slight, the cumulative effects of many investments will be substantial. To ignore the consequences for a single project may be to compound an error over many investments. Thirdly, the change in real income is explicitly being valued in terms of ruling prices, which in turn will reflect the *existing* income distribution. That is, the very process of applying cost–benefit analysis, which requires some concept of social preference, implies acceptance of the existing distribution of income as being socially most preferred. Many proponents of the general view under discussion would agree with just this view. They put two arguments forward. Firstly, incomes reflect differences in marginal productivity. Hence individuals, being paid according to their marginal product, are paid according to their contributions to national product. This in turn implies some statement to the effect that they therefore *deserve* their existing incomes. Hence the existing distribution of income is 'socially approved'. Secondly, if society did not approve of the existing distribution of income it would change it through policies specifically aimed at altering the distribution. Indeed, it may be more efficient to use explicit redistribution policies rather than 'use' investment projects in this way.

The marginal productivity argument is not a strong one. It is by no means clear that people are paid according to their marginal product, and it would certainly be difficult to argue that they receive their marginal *social* product. Even if they do, the argument would be fallacious in implying that marginal productivity payments are *deserved*. No prescriptive or value statement can be derived from a descriptive statement about marginal productivity, even if the description was a true one. In addition, the idea that existing income distributions are socially approved implies a peculiarly 'static' view of the world. In practice, of course, efforts are made continually to change it. Neither is it the case that society can achieve the distribution of income it regards as optimal in a straightforward manner. Policies to change the distribution may involve side effects that are frequently unknown to the policy-maker and the final effect may be different from his intention. Also, explicitly redistributive policies might not be socially preferred. Arthur Maass cites a hypothetical example of supplying irrigation water to several groups, including low-income American Indians. As he argues, 'the community would probably be willing to give up some efficiency [of the irrigation project] to see the living standards of the Indians improved by their own labors rather than by the dole' (Maass [7]).

Accordingly, the first view is rejected and it is argued that distributional consequences should be integrated in some fashion into any criterion of social improvement.

The second line of support for ignoring redistributional consequences rests on the ground that their incorporation would involve apparently 'ascientific' considerations. In other words, whereas optimality is a well-defined concept in connection with the size of the real income change, it appears to require some value judgement when applied to distribution. What exactly is 'optimal' distribution? Any definition would involve some value statement, and these, so the argument goes, are best avoided.

This view is difficult to accept. It has already been argued that CBA involves one major explicit value judgement – that individual preferences should count. Why then ignore society's preferences about the distribution of income? Of course, if a policy involves an excess of benefits over costs and a worsening of the distribution of income (according to some social judgement which defines optimality), a further problem arises in assessing the importance of the distributional change relative to the 'efficiency' change. Thus, Little [8] quite explicitly rejects a move which involves an improvement in efficiency and a worsening of the distribution (his concept of optimality for distribution is usually interpreted as meaning equality of incomes). The problem, of course, would be to find out what kind of income distribution society approves.

A third option, then, is to make an explicit attempt to allow for the distributional consequences of a policy either by trying to observe social preferences concerning distribution, or by other means. There are several possibilities.

First, the cost–benefit analyst can indicate the consequences for distribution and allow the decision-maker to apply his own 'weights' to the gains and losses of the various sections of the community. In other words, given a social welfare function of the Paretian form, and observing that some of the elements of the function will be positive, some negative, a set of weights, $\alpha_1, \ldots, \alpha_n$ are applied to the gains and losses, so that the function becomes

$$SW = SW(\alpha_1 . R_1(x), \quad \alpha_2 . R_2(x), \ldots, \alpha_n . R_n(x))$$

which is the same as that in section 1.7, although the αs there were construed as 'intensity of preference' weights. The gains of individual 1 are weighted by some factor α_1. Individual 2 may lose and his losses are weighted by α_2. If the decision-maker considers individual 2 more 'deserving' than individual 1 he will weight 2's losses more heavily than 1's gains – i.e. $\alpha_2 > \alpha_1$. The most straightforward form of such a welfare function is an *additive* one – i.e. money values are placed on $R_1, \ldots, R_n$, say $U_1, \ldots, U_n$, and $\alpha_1, \ldots, \alpha_n$ are derived from the decision-maker's own judgements, so that

$$SW - \alpha_1 U_1 + \alpha_2 U_2 + \ldots \alpha_n U_n.$$

Indeed, if the simplifying assumption that $\alpha_1 = \alpha_2 = \ldots = \alpha_n$ is made, we revert to the original formulation of a cost–benefit maximand which simply requires the money values reflecting $R_1, \ldots, R_n$ to be estimated and then summed to obtain 'social welfare'. The assumption that $\alpha_1 = \alpha_2 = \ldots = \alpha_n$ means that an extra unit of real income to 1 is valued in exactly the same way as an extra unit of real income to 2. This is the concept of 'dollar democracy' – the constancy of the marginal utility of income across individuals – and it is important to recognise that such a social welfare function is indifferent to the distribution of money gains. It is precisely this function which is generally used in cost–benefit practice.

If the decision-maker is not indifferent to distribution he must assign some set of weights. However, leaving it to the decision-maker to derive these weights may not always be particularly helpful. The net (unweighted) benefits of a project can be presented as a number (assuming all the gains and losses can be evaluated). The information required for weighting, on the other hand, must be fairly complex. Integrating the two aspects – efficiency and distribution – will not necessarily be easy. Certainly, the decision-maker will have no obvious way of reducing the two outcomes to a single numerical value. His final judgement will therefore have to be qualitative and based upon some subjective adjustment of cost–benefit rankings (Dorfman [9]). To many economists this aspect of the decision problem is quite acceptable since the adoption of weights appears to be ascientific. However, there are dangers. The cost–benefit analyst may be abrogating responsibility by leaving the

C

problem to the decision-maker: at the very least he must present him with detailed information. He must also suggest tests of consistency between distributional judgements – a set of weights for one policy may not be the same as for other policies. He must also ensure that the weighting procedure has the desired effect: frequently the intentions of governments are not matched by the outcome, as several studies have shown (Bonnen [10]).

Can the cost–benefit analyst reduce the problem to more manageable proportions? A second approach would be to observe the weights implicit in past government decisions. These weights, if they could be observed, would presumably reflect the decision-maker's value judgements concerning the relevant 'deserts' of groups and individuals within the community. As such, derivation of these weights in numerical form would reflect 'planner's preferences'. This approach commands considerable support from several cost–benefit analysts. Weisbrod [11] has illustrated a method of deriving numerical coefficients for groups of individuals (i.e. the $\alpha_1, \ldots, \alpha_n$ would refer to groups, not individuals) by analysing past government decisions in respect of the distribution of benefits between the groups. Maass [7] has also remarked that 'there is a capacity in the legislative process to make the trade-off decisions that can then govern the design of project and programs' (p. 210). Others make less enthusiastic claims for such a procedure: 'The point is not to generate some particular reasonable community welfare function (let alone a "true" one); rather it is to discover and express the manager's preference in a communicable form. Hence, reference to the inherent plausibility of the underlying welfare function derivable from a manager's preferences can only provide a general check against absurdities' (McGuire and Garn [12] p. 884).

The last-quoted statement is perhaps the most apt comment on these procedures. They assume that intentions are in fact fulfilled so that the observation of *ex post* results will indicate *ex ante* intentions. As we have seen, information is rarely adequate for governments to assess the final distributional consequences of a policy. Unless governments consider distribution in great detail it is unlikely that the weights implicit in their decisions are anything other than accidental. More significantly, perhaps, the assumption that past government decisions reflect the *correct* weights would tend to render their explicit inclusion in cost–benefit studies redundant: i.e. the weights would be 'naturally' incorporated into public decisions.[1] A separate, pragmatic objection to any approach

[1] The point is made by R. Musgrave, 'Cost–Benefit Analysis and the Theory of Public Finance', *Journal of Economic Literature* (1969).

which explicitly incorporates distributional weights is that decision-makers tend to be obsessed with non-efficiency considerations anyway. The cost–benefit analyst, therefore, has a duty to counter-balance this bias by acting as 'efficiency partisan' – i.e. by stressing the efficiency aspects. Clearly, this objection will depend on the nature of the institutional context in which the decisions are made: there is increasing evidence that government departments are becoming more and more efficiency conscious, so that the pendulum may well be swinging the other way.

A variant on the 'past-decision' approach is the most frequently suggested (Krutilla and Eckstein [13]). This involves the use of marginal rates of taxation as weights. Since the marginal rate of taxation tends to rise as income rises, it would appear that society – represented by successive governments – assigns less weight to a £1 gain to a richer person than to a poorer person. If the marginal rate of tax rises with income, the marginal social valuation of income is falling. Thus, suppose we have an income range £500–£1000 (Y_1) with a marginal rate of 25p in the £, a rate of 50p for £1000–£2000 (Y_2) and a rate of 75p for the range £2000–£3000 (Y_3). The relevant weights would be in the ratio

$$\alpha_1 = 4 : \alpha_2 = 2 : \alpha_3 = 4/3.$$

In other words, the gains (or losses) of lower-income groups would be weighted more heavily than the gains of high-income groups.

This approach suffers some of the defects of the more general approach of using 'implicitly observed' weights. In particular, marginal rates often do not vary over very substantial income ranges. Does this imply constant marginal social valuations? If it does, the 'primitive' form of the cost–benefit social welfare function is justified for many contexts, since it would imply $\alpha_1 = \alpha_2 = \ldots = \alpha_n$. The fallacy lies in the supposition that marginal tax rates have very much to do with social valuations of income. For what is being observed is *some approximation* (no more than that) of past and present societies' views on 'equity'.

More seriously, the use of marginal *income*-tax rates implies that society makes no use of other taxes for 'equity' purposes. Yet many 'luxury' goods are taxed more heavily than non-luxury goods. If this principle was consistently applied, some attempt would have to be made to assess the marginal incidence of *all* taxes – a substantial task.

A third approach to the distribution problem is to impose an explicit value judgement on the social utility function. One simple approach is to scale down higher incomes and scale up lower incomes to 'equalise' their influence on the cost–benefit outcome. Foster [14] has suggested an approach whereby gains and losses are weighted by the ratio of the average national personal income to the individual's income, so that

$$\alpha_1 = \frac{y_a}{y_1}, \quad \alpha_2 = \frac{y_a}{y_2}, \quad \text{etc.,}$$

where y_a is the average personal income for the nation. The object here is not to say anything about marginal utilities of income, only to adjust valuations to allow for the fact that larger-income groups will have a larger 'vote' in assessing projects if benefits are assessed according to 'willingness to pay'. As such, Foster's approach involves an explicit value judgement about equity, a value judgement which the decision-maker can accept or reject. Similar approaches have been suggested in which y_a is the officially designated 'poverty line' income.

Finally, some attempt could be made to estimate weights by assessing the likely shape and elasticity of a marginal utility of income function. Such a procedure is inherently attractive since it is precisely this that is required for the 'complete' social welfare function referred to in section 1.7. However, it too encounters serious problems. Firstly, the choice of an elasticity will be arbitrary unless some of the many empirical observations which purport to measure income utilities are accepted, and secondly, the economist would appear to be indulging in explicit interpersonal comparisons of utility, having begun with a decision rule which avoided this theory problem.

It is worth noting, however, that there is a conceptual distinction between the marginal utility of income weighting approach and weighting for 'equity' considerations. If the social welfare function is defined in terms of 'cardinal' measures of utility, then it is still possible to speak of the equitable distribution of *utility*. That is, the concept of 'deservingness' does not entail that the weights reflect income utilities; the two approaches are quite distinct. If this is accepted, it is perfectly feasible for the social welfare function to appear as

$$SW = \alpha_1 . \beta_1 . U_1 + \alpha_2 . \beta_2 . U_2 + \ldots + \alpha_n . \beta_n . U_n$$

where the αs are the respective income-utility weights and the βs are the 'equity' weights.

Overall, there is no obvious solution to the distributional problem. The observation of 'planners' preferences' would appear to be the most promising source for weights, but it needs to be emphasised that it is planners' *intentions* which have to be measured.

Most seriously, however, this section has only discussed the pros and cons of various ways in which weights could be derived; it has not considered *whose* responsibility it is to suggest the weights, nor indeed whether the derivation of such weights is consistent with the general idea of reflecting individual preferences. It is to this question that Chapter 3 is devoted.

2.4 SUMMARY

This chapter has shown that 'conventional' cost–benefit analysis proceeds on the basis of equating social gains with Pareto-type improvements. Since all projects and policies tend to involve some sections of the population in welfare losses, the simple Pareto rule has to be modified by the Kaldor–Hicks hypothetical compensation principle. In the absence of actual compensation, however, it was seen that the principle generated a number of problems. These problems suggest that, in addition to the 'efficiency' objective, changes in distribution should also be incorporated into the objective function. Various methods of allowing for distributional consequences were discussed, ranging from 'weak' methods which indicate the likely consequences of assuming particular weights to be attached to preferences, to 'strong' methods which explicitly incorporate direct weighting systems. The latter approaches included the technical possibility of adopting a 'compound' weighting system in which income-utility weights were attached to preferences, and further weights were then attached to the income-utility weighted results. Essentially, the method demonstrated the distinction between weighting for income-utilities and weighting for 'equity' considerations. Each possible approach was seen to generate a number of problems, and counter-arguments against the inclusion of distributional effects into the objective function were noted. Overall, however, it was suggested that efficiency and distribution were not conceptually distinct aspects of the objective function.

3 Social Welfare Functions

COST–BENEFIT analysis, so it has been argued, is a means of identifying policies which society prefers. The difficulty lies in deciding what precisely is meant by 'society prefers'. In the context of CBA, saying 'society prefers x to y' constitutes in effect a recommendation that A be adopted. Hence no definition of social preference can be value-free. The discussion so far has, for example, been based on the value judgement that individual preferences should count. This implies that social preference is interpreted as an aggregate to be constructed from individual preferences. The question then is: in what way is it to be constructed?

One possible answer to this question, namely that social preference should be identified with Pareto optimality, was discussed in Chapter 2. Thus, the welfare foundations of 'conventional' CBA have been defined. But the present chapter is concerned with a logically prior question, viz. is a meaningful aggregation of individual preferences into social preference at all possible? This chapter is based largely on the work of Arrow [1] who first explored this question in a systematic way.[1]

The plan of this chapter is as follows. Arrow's concept of the social welfare function is discussed in section 3.1. Section 3.2 contains a statement of Arrow's Theorem on the Impossibility of a Social Welfare Function. Section 3.3 discusses various escape-routes from the Impossibility Theorem. Some implications for CBA are pointed out in the concluding section.

3.1 THE CONCEPT OF A SOCIAL WELFARE FUNCTION

The full significance of Arrow's analysis can be appreciated only by placing it in the context of earlier discussions of the social welfare function.

That the problem of social choice can be rationally discussed in terms of a postulated welfare function for society was first suggested by Bergson [3, 4]. Its implications for welfare economics were

[1] On some questions as to the correct interpretation of Arrow's results, we have found Sen [2] particularly helpful.

further explored by Samuelson. Indeed, the Bergson concept of a social welfare function is frequently referred to as the Bergson–Samuelson concept.

Bergson defined a social welfare function in very general terms. In essence, all that it involves is that social welfare be regarded as a real-valued function SW, 'the value of which is understood to depend on all the variables that might be considered as affecting welfare'.

In principle, SW is regarded as defined over all social alternatives. Given SW, the job of the economist is to choose policies which maximise SW subject to prevailing constraints, e.g. those imposed by technology. As long as the social welfare function is regarded simply as a way of organising one's thought about social choice, the extreme generality of this definition has its advantages. On the other hand, being able, even in principle, to draw conclusions requires that the concept be considerably narrowed down in scope. In his own discussion of the social welfare function, Bergson makes the concept more restricted in at least two respects.

First, he distinguishes between economic and non-economic variables. Both sets of variables affect welfare. However, he assumes that while the non-economic variables can affect economic variables, they are not affected by them. Bergson concedes that this assumption may not always hold. Political change, for example, may not only influence economic factors but may itself depend on such factors. However, Bergson argues that for relatively small changes in economic variables 'other elements in welfare' will not be significantly affected. To the extent that this is so, a partial analysis will in his view be possible.

This interpretation has now become an accepted part of the received doctrine of welfare economics,[1] and has dominated most cost–benefit analysis to date. However, uncritical acceptance of it could well lead to the neglect of non-economic factors even when the 'marginal' argument does not hold. Thus, if a highway project could damage the beauty of the countryside, there is no valid reason for neglecting this unfavourable effect on social welfare when

[1] Cf. Graaff ([6] pp. 5–6): 'So we shall instead regard a person's choices, or general welfare, as determined by a large number of variables, some of which have traditionally interested economists and some of which have not. Those which have we shall call *economic variables*. Welfare economics then proceeds on the assumption that the non-economic ones all remain unchanged. They can be thought of as exogenous – that is, as influencing the economic variables without being influenced by them.'

deciding whether or not the project should be undertaken. Such considerations are discussed in Chapter 5.

The second modification consists in regarding social welfare as a function, in the first instance, of *individual* utilities, the latter themselves being functions of the relevant variables.

Thus, if society consists of n individuals, U_i denotes the utility index of the ith individual ($i = 1, 2, \ldots, n$) and SW is the Bergson social welfare function, we now have

$$SW = SW(U_1, \ldots, U_n)$$

which is the formulation introduced in Chapter 1.

This interpretation of the social welfare function has been described as the 'individualist type of Bergson social welfare function'. It can be regarded as an expression of the principle that individual preferences count.

Subsequent discussions of the social welfare function have almost exclusively been about welfare functions of the individualist type.

Bergson's modified definition of the social welfare function still leaves a basic question unanswered. Given that SW is a function of the individual utility indices, how is the shape of the function to be determined? Since it is the shape of the SW function that will determine the relative weights to be given to the utility indices of different individuals in arriving at an aggregate index of social welfare, the importance of the question is self-evident, and has already been noted in Chapter 2.

According to Bergson, the shape of the function is 'determined by the specific decisions on ends that are introduced into the analysis'. But this does not tell us who provides these decisions on ends.

One answer to the question is provided by Little [7], who regards decisions on ends as given by an individual ethical observer. Little argues that decisions on ends involve value judgements, that a value judgement is necessarily a judgement by some individual person and hence that the social welfare function postulated by welfare economics must be interpreted as such a value judgement.

Thus, according to Little, rather than write, with Bergson, $SW = SW(U_1, \ldots, U_n)$, we can write simply $SW_i = SW_i(U_1, \ldots, U_n)$, ($i = 1, \ldots, n$), to indicate that this indicates the judgement of the ith individual.

According to Little, 'We can deduce the whole effective corpus of welfare economics from, say $W_{10}(U_1, \ldots, U_n)$ – remembering only to put "in the opinion of individual No. 10" after "welfare" whenever we use the term' ([7] p. 424).

Clearly on this view the social welfare function SW is not to be regarded in any sense as an ordering by society as a whole, but rather as the opinion of a particular individual.[1]

This is one possible answer. However, there are others. The decisions on ends represented by the Bergson social welfare function may just as well be 'the dictates of an oligarchy or the whims of a dictator or the values of a class or even be given simply by tradition' (Sen [2] p. 34). The Bergson concept of the social welfare function is general enough to accommodate any of these.

Arrow's contribution to the theory of social choice consists essentially in attempting to get another answer to the question: how should the Bergson social welfare function be determined? The social welfare function, according to Arrow, is to be regarded as a social decision process. Specifically, it is a method, a 'collective choice rule' for deriving a social ordering from individual preferences. What Arrow is concerned to show is that a collective choice rule satisfying conditions that are generally thought to be reasonable will not, in general, exist. Clearly, if this is true it is of some importance. For Chapter 2 showed that CBA reflected what can now be called a Bergson social welfare function of the individualist type. But if such a function cannot be determined from individual preferences, then cost–benefit is, in some sense, without a logical foundation.

Formally, Arrow's definition of a social welfare function is as follows. Suppose a society consists of n individuals. Each individual i is assumed to have a weak preference (i.e. 'preference or indifference') ordering R_i of available alternatives which determines his choices between them.

Arrow then defines a social welfare function to be a process or rule which for each such set of individual orderings $R_1, \ldots, R_n$ of alternatives (one ordering for each individual) states a corresponding social ordering of alternatives R.

The logic of Arrow's approach may be stated as follows. The concept of a social welfare function was introduced into theoretical welfare economics as a device for expanding the range of welfare economics beyond the Pareto optimality criterion which is an extremely restrictive one. The social welfare function if it exists allows the ordering of any two social states, Pareto optimal or otherwise. It thus aims to overcome the problem noted in section

[1] Cf. 'Thus the so-called "social welfare function" postulated by welfare economists should in my view be regarded as a social ordering *only* in the sense that it orders states of society' (ibid.). Note that Little does not distinguish between an 'ordering' and a 'function'. On this point, see below, p. 75.

2.1 that points on the frontier in Fig. 2.1.1 could not be Pareto-compared. However, if the social welfare function is interpreted simply as an individual's value judgement ('the opinion of individual No. 10', in Little's phrase), the question of *which* individual is to judge becomes decisive. Since individuals often vary widely in their value judgements, the difficulties of deriving a rationale for social decisions in this way are obvious. Hence the appeal of the alternative approach favoured by Arrow which explores the possibility of constructing a social ordering from individual preferences subject to satisfying a number of conditions which, it is thought, are likely to command wide assent.

While Arrow's definition of a social welfare function is closely related to that of Bergson, there are some differences. Neglecting them has sometimes led to confusion. The following points are particularly relevant in this respect.

Arrow defines a social welfare function as a collective choice rule for deriving a social ordering from individual orderings. On the other hand, a Bergson social welfare function (of the individualist type) is a more general concept where the social ordering may be derived from individual orderings in any other way as well, for example by a specified ethical judgement. The meaning of an ethical judgement and that of a collective choice rule are not in general the same.

There are two riders to this. Firstly, as Bergson has pointed out, Arrow's interpretation of the social welfare function may itself be regarded in a certain sense as a special case of the 'ethical judgement' approach. Thus, if the social welfare function is regarded as an ethical judgement, this implies that it is not just a statement of personal likes or dislikes but that it expresses the concern, central to welfare economics, for counselling individual citizens as to wise choice. On the other hand, Arrow's version of the social welfare function is designed to counsel, not citizens generally, but the public official who may be regarded as standing for society as a whole in this respect, and whose 'one aim in life is to implement the values of other citizens as given by some rule of collective decision-making' (Bergson [8] p. 242).

Secondly, Arrow's version of the social welfare function raises the following logical difficulty. The collective choice rule to be used may itself be a matter on which individuals have an ordering, some such rules being preferred to others. The majority decision rule, for example, may be valued as such, independently of the alternatives which it favours.

One way of getting round this difficulty is to assume that the job of the social welfare function (the collective choice rule) is indeed to aggregate in an appropriate way individual preferences as expressed by the R_is. However, once the choice rule derives a particular social ordering, individuals are committed to it, irrespective of what was stated earlier by their individual orderings.

At the other extreme, we can assume that individuals are committed to their particular R_is to the extent that they would reject any choice rule that does not lead to the adoption of these.

In practice, individual attitudes to collective choice rules may well be somewhere between these extremes (cf. Sen [2] p. 65).

The difficulty in question is one which is inherent in any social decision process based on individual preferences. However, this does not, as some have suggested (e.g. Little [7]), invalidate Arrow's concept of a social welfare function. The point rather, as Sen correctly observes, is to distinguish between a person's preferences as such and what he thinks he could accept as a basis of public policy given the preferences of others and his own values on collective choice rules ([2] p. 66). Indeed, it is in the context of this distinction that the question of imposing some 'conditions of reasonableness', which a social welfare function must satisfy, assumes importance.

We shall conclude this section by pointing out a difference in terminology between Arrow and Bergson.

In the Bergson–Samuelson discussion of social welfare functions, 'function' tends to be used in its strict sense. On the other hand Arrow's concept of a social welfare function is really based on the concept of a social *ordering* rather than that of a *function*.

While economists often tend to use the two words interchangeably, strictly speaking they have different meanings. Thus, there are some orderings (rankings) of alternatives, e.g. the lexicographic ordering, which are incapable of being depicted by any real-valued function (numerical representation) (see above, p. 25). However, as was pointed out in Chapter 1 (p. 24 above), we generally make certain assumptions which ensure equivalence between the existence of an ordering or ranking and that of a function (numerical representation) such that it is order-preserving, i.e. such that

$$u(x) > u(y) \Rightarrow xPy$$

$$u(x) = u(y) \Rightarrow xIy$$

$$U(x) < U(y) \Rightarrow yPx.$$

Indeed, only if we do make the assumptions referred to above, does the possibility of a conflict between the Bergson–Samuelson and the Arrow definitions vanish.

However, this is not what Arrow himself suggests. He argues rather that, for the purpose at hand, there is no need to make such assumptions. Arrow's point really is that if, both for the individual and for society, all we are interested in are ordinal properties of a welfare index, the construction of a *function* to represent social welfare adds little to the analysis.

Indeed, for the purpose of enabling us to choose between alternative policies, it is not really necessary that such a real-valued function should exist. A complete social *ordering* is sufficient.

Unfortunately, Arrow continues to use the older terminology, though the sense is different.

3.2 ARROW'S 'IMPOSSIBILITY THEOREM'

The main result that Arrow derives from his approach to the concept of a social welfare function is a negative one. It states that under certain conditions that appear to be generally accepted as reasonable no social welfare function can exist.

This result is often referred to in the literature as Arrow's theorem or, more precisely, as the Impossibility Theorem. To see exactly what the theorem asserts, it is necessary to spell out both the conditions under which it holds and the logic underlying them.

We shall start by going back to Arrow's formulation of the problem. Society consists of n individuals. Let R_i denote the (weak preference) ordering of alternatives by the ith individual and let R be the social (weak preference) ordering. Similarly, P_i and I_i denote strict preference and indifference for the ith individual while P_s and I_s denote the social preference and indifference respectively.

Now each individual is assumed to be rational in the sense that his ordering of alternatives satisfies the properties of connectedness and transitivity (see section 1.2 above).

The first requirement that Arrow imposes on the social welfare function can now be stated. It is that *social* choice should have the same rational structure as *individual* choice – i.e. the social ordering R, which is to determine social choice, must be connected and transitive.

This requirement is sometimes regarded as part of the definition of a social ordering rather than as a separate condition which it should satisfy. For ease of exposition we shall refer to it as condition 0.

The next condition, referred to below as condition 1 or the 'Free Triple' Condition, is concerned with ensuring that the social welfare function is wide enough in scope. By sufficiently restricting the domain of the social welfare function (viz. the range of admissible sets of individual orderings to which it is meant to apply), one can in principle ensure that a social welfare function exists. However, such a social welfare function would be of little interest to anybody. In discussing the question whether a social welfare function exists, it is important to exclude such trivial cases from consideration. This is done by stipulating the Free Triple Condition.

Condition 1 (the Free Triple Condition)
Given any three alternatives, no matter what the individual orderings of these alternatives are, the social welfare function must give rise to a (connected and transitive) social ordering. In effect, this means that the aggregation rule represented by the social welfare function must apply to all logically possible sets of individual orderings and not just to a selected few.

The purpose of the next condition (condition 2) is to ensure that the social ordering and individual orderings should move in the same direction, i.e. that the social ordering responds positively, or at least not negatively, to any change in individual orderings.

The condition can be stated as follows.

Condition 2 (Non-negative Association)
If one alternative social state rises or remains still in the ordering of every individual without any other change in those orderings, we shall expect it to rise, or at least not to fall, in the social ordering.

This condition is referred to as the condition of Non-negative Association between individual orderings and the social ordering. It is in essence an expression of the basic value judgement that individual preferences should count.

A more formal statement of the condition of Non-negative Association is as follows.

Let $R_1, R_2, \ldots, R_n$ be a set of individual (weak preference) orderings and $P_1, \ldots, P_n$ the corresponding strict preference relations.

Let R_s be the social ordering corresponding to this set of individual orderings and P_s the corresponding social preference relation.

Let $R'_1, \ldots, R'_n$ be another set of individual orderings and $P'_1, \ldots, P'_n$ similarly be the corresponding strict preference relations. Let R'_s represent the social ordering and P'_s the social preference relation corresponding to this new set of individual orderings.

Suppose that for each i, the two individual ordering relations, the 'old' and the 'new', are connected in the following ways:

(a) for x' and y' distinct from a given alternative x, $x'R'_iy$ if and only if $x'R_iy'$;

(b) for all y' if xR_iy' then xR'_iy';

(c) for all y' if xP_iy' then xP'_iy'.

Then if xP_sy, we must have xP'_sy.

This can be interpreted as follows. Suppose as between two sets of individual orderings we want that a particular alternative x be *not* lower on each individual's ordering while all other comparisons remain unchanged. This means that:

(1) If x is not involved in a pairwise choice, the two sets of orderings give identical results (for each individual). This is stated by (a).

If x *is* involved in a comparison, the assumption is that (for each individual):

(2) x is preferred on the new ordering to an alternative to which it was formerly preferred.

(3) x is *preferred or indifferent* on the new ordering to an alternative to which it was formerly indifferent.

In view of (3), (2) can also be replaced by (2′): x is preferred or indifferent on the new ordering to any alternative to which it was formally preferred or indifferent.

(2′) corresponds to the proposition (b) above, while (3) is equivalent to (c).

Together (a), (b) and (c) state that no individual ranks x lower on the new ordering than he previously did and that apart from this no other change in any ordering occurs.

We then require that if society formerly ranked x above y, it should still do so, which is equivalent to our statement above that if xP_sy we must have xP'_sy. This explains the formal statement of condition 2.

The next requirement that Arrow imposes on the social welfare function is (like condition 0) concerned with the rationality of social choice. It is known as 'the independence of irrelevant alternatives' and can be stated as follows.

Condition 3 (*Independence of Irrelevant Alternatives*)
The social ordering of a set of alternatives should depend only on the orderings by individuals over this set and not on the existence or ordering of alternatives outside this set.

Formally, the condition implies the following. Let $R_1, \ldots, R_n$ and $R_1', \ldots, R_n'$ be two sets of individual orderings and let $\bar{x}$, $\bar{x}'$ represent the socially *most* preferred alternatives corresponding to these two sets of individual orderings respectively. Also for any two alternatives x, y in the admissible set, and all i, let

$$xR_i y \text{ if and only if } xR_i' y.$$

Then $\qquad\qquad \bar{x} = \bar{x}'.$

Thus, the social ranking among states in any set depends only on the individual rankings of states *over the elements of that set*. Hence, if one alternative is *deleted* from the set, the choice as between the rest is not affected thereby. At the same time, the social ordering depends only on individual *orderings* and not, for example, on their intensities of preference.

The two remaining conditions are similar to condition 1 in that they express some aspect of the basic value judgement that individual preferences are to count. They are as follows.

Condition 4 (*'Non-imposition'*)
The social welfare function must not be 'imposed'. A social welfare function is said to be imposed if a pair of distinct alternatives x, y exist such that $xR_s y$ for every set of individual orderings $R_1, \ldots, R_n$, i.e. if there is some pair of alternatives x and y such that society can never express a preference for y over x, irrespective of individual preferences (for example even if all individuals prefer y to x). An imposed social welfare function would thus make some preference orderings taboo. Condition 4 rules this out. Finally, there is:

Condition 5 (*'Non-dictatorship'*)
The social welfare function must not be dictatorial, i.e. social orderings should not be determined solely by the preferences of a particular individual member of society.

Formally, there should be no individual h such that for all states x, y and all sets of individual orderings other than that of h

$$xP_h y \text{ implies } xP_s y.$$

In other words, there should be no individual such that whenever he strictly prefers x to y, society strictly prefers x to y, no matter what other individuals' preferences are.

To recapitulate, conditions 0 and 3 are meant to ensure that the social ordering to which the social welfare function leads is rational. Condition 1 defines the scope of the social welfare function: it ensures that the range of individual orderings to which a social welfare function is applicable is as wide as possible.

Conditions 2, 4 and 5 are different aspects of the value judgement that individual preferences should count.

Arrow proved that no social welfare function which simultaneously satisfies the conditions stipulated above can exist. This result is known as the Impossibility Theorem.[1]

In effect, Arrow's theorem states that there exists no method for determining the social ranking of alternative social states which is both based on individual preferences and satisfies some intuitively plausible criteria of 'reasonableness' for social choice. The links between collective rationality and individual preferences are thus severed. Hence, Arrow's work has damaging consequences for the theory of welfare economics which has traditionally been regarded as providing precisely such a link. And if this link does not exist for welfare economics, it does not exist for cost–benefit analysis, which is based upon welfare economics.

3.3 Escapes from the Arrow 'Barrier'

Attempts to rescue welfare economics from the consequences of Arrow's theorem can be divided into two broad categories, viz. those that reject his methodology as such and those that question some of his specific conditions. These 'escapes' will be considered in turn.

It has been suggested that Arrow's concept of a social welfare function differs fundamentally from that used in the theory of welfare economics and hence that his Impossibility Theorem is irrelevant.

In particular, two such differences have been emphasised by Little [7]. In the first place, in traditional welfare economics, the social welfare function has been regarded as forming a welfare

---

[1] Some alternative versions of the Impossibility Theorem, based on slightly different sets of 'reasonableness' conditions, are discussed in Sen [2], esp. chap. 3.

judgement. Arrow's social welfare function on the other hand is essentially a social decision process.

Secondly, the traditional theory regards individual tastes as given; on the other hand, Arrow's concern is largely with ensuring the consistency of the social ordering in response to variations in individual preference orderings (under his conditions). Little argues that no sense can in fact be attached to the notion of given individuals with changing tastes and hence that Arrow's formulation of the problem of social choice is inappropriate.

As regards the first criticism, Arrow's social welfare function is indeed to be regarded essentially as a social decision process, and specifically as a method of deriving a social ordering from individual preferences. Arrow's Impossibility Theorem is intended to demonstrate that a 'reasonable' method of going from individual preferences to a social ordering, i.e. one which satisfies the requirements indicated by Arrow's conditions, does not exist. However, even when a social welfare function in this sense does not exist, it is perfectly possible that a social welfare function in some other sense may exist.

However, to recognise this does not appear to constitute sufficient grounds for rejecting Arrow's theorem as irrelevant.

To insist on any one interpretation of the social welfare function as the only relevant concept, even as the only relevant concept for welfare economics, seems unduly arbitrary. The appropriate interpretation surely depends on the problem under investigation. In the context of cost–benefit analysis, it is the rationality of the social decision process that would appear to be the appropriate point of departure.

Indeed, cost–benefit analysis is itself best regarded as a tool for social decision-making. From this point of view it is Arrow's approach to the social welfare function which appears to be the relevant one.[1]

As regards the second point of contention, relating to the admissibility of allowing individual tastes to vary, the validity of this criticism clearly depends on the interpretation given to the social welfare function. If the latter is interpreted as a welfare judgement *tout court*, individual tastes may be taken as given – as they are in Little's formulation. On the other hand, if the social welfare

---

[1] Cf. Arrow ([1] p. 106): '[In the second place], the location of welfare judgements in any individual, while logically possible, does not appear to be very interesting. "Social Welfare" is related to social policy in any sensible interpretation; the welfare judgements formed by any single individual are unconnected with action and hence sterile.'

function is regarded essentially as a rule of correspondence between individual orderings and a social ordering, it is natural to take into consideration not merely the relationship of the social ordering to a given set of individual orderings but also what the social ordering would have been if the individual orderings had been different. The nature of such variation is clearly an essential part of the meaning of a correspondence rule.

Thus, the validity of the second criticism mentioned depends upon that of the first, which has already been examined.

Even if one accepts Arrow's general approach to the problem of social choice, the significance that one attaches to the Impossibility Theorem will necessarily depend on the extent to which one regards Arrow's criteria of reasonableness for a social welfare function as binding. A number of writers have argued in favour of rejecting one or more of Arrow's criteria, in which case the Impossibility Theorem ceases to be of interest. To this type of criticism we now turn.

Consider first the 'rationality' conditions (conditions 0 and 3) which Arrow imposes on the social welfare function. Most people will accept the requirement that social choice between alternatives should be determined in a rational (i.e. logical and consistent) manner.[1] The suggestion is that Arrow's conditions might not be a necessary part of rationality in this sense and hence could be relaxed appropriately.

The first suggested modification concerns condition 0 and consists in dropping the requirement that the social ordering must be transitive:[2] i.e. the requirement that given any three social states x, y, z, if $xR_s y$ and $yR_s z$ then $xR_s z$.

However, dropping the transitivity condition has drastic implications not all of which appear to have been appreciated by those suggesting such an approach. For instance, it means that the social ordering ceases to be independent of the order in which we take up the alternatives given for pairwise comparison.

To see this, consider the well-known paradox of voting. Society consists of three individuals 1, 2 and 3, and there are three alter-

---

[1] Most, but not all. Cf. Yeats:

> Tho' logic-choppers rule the town
> And every man and maid and boy
> Marks a distant object down
> An aimless joy is a pure joy!
> *(Collected Poems)*

[2] For variants of such proposals, see Kemp [9].

natives x, y and z. Individual 1 strictly prefers x to y and y to z. Individual 2 strictly prefers y to z and z to x. Individual 3 strictly prefers z to x and x to y. Assume that the social ordering is chosen on the majority voting principle. We then have the result that in the social ordering x is preferred to y and y to z, but z to x, violating the transitivity requirement. This has been regarded as a basic failure of majority voting as a basis of social choice.

Relaxing transitivity means that this particular criticism is no longer regarded as binding. However, this does not tell us what the social choice should be. If, forgetting about transitivity, we simply try to apply the majority decision rule as such, we come up against the difficulty mentioned above, viz. the dependence of the outcome on the sequence in which alternatives are taken up for choice. If the first choice is between x and y and the winner is then put to the vote against z, the social choice will be z. If, on the other hand, we start with y and z, the winner then being faced with x, the outcome is x.

Social choice would thus depend on the sequence in which alternatives are compared rather than on the alternatives themselves. This is clearly unsatisfactory. The proposed 'solution' thus amounts to throwing out the baby (rational social choice) along with the bath-water (the transitivity condition)!

A more serious case can be made out for rejecting Arrow's condition 3, viz. the Independence of Irrelevant Alternatives. The issue turns on the choice as between ordinal and cardinal measures of utility.

For what the condition in question asserts is that as long as individual orderings of a set of achievable alternatives remain unaltered, so does their social ordering. This means *inter alia* that only individual *orderings* matter; preference intensities do not. To take a simple example, suppose the only difference as between two sets of individual orderings is the following. In case I, individual 1 *just* prefers x to y while individual 2 *just* prefers y to x. In case II, individual 1 *just* prefers x to y, as before, but individual 2 *desperately* prefers y to x. According to condition 3, the social ordering in case II must necessarily be the same as in case I. Is this reasonable?[1]

In seeking an answer to this question, the discussion of cardinal versus ordinal measures of utility in Chapter 1 provides a convenient point of departure. Two proposed approaches for cardinalising individual utility – the perception-threshold approach

---

[1] Coleman [10] suggested that actual collective decisions *do* tend to reflect preference intensities. Hildreth [11] indicated early on in the debate the cardinalist 'escape'.

and the von Neumann–Morgenstern approach – were discussed in that context.

For the present purpose, there are two separate questions to be considered. Firstly, does cardinalisation provide a meaningful cardinal utility index for each individual? Secondly, if it does, will this enable the construction of a social welfare function?

As far as the individual utility index is concerned, the point was made in Chapter 1 that while cardinalism required an additional assumption (viz. that *degrees* of preference are measurable), in most contexts it did not add anything new to the results. This indeed was the principal argument in favour of the ordinal approach. The argument does not apply to the present case where the introduction of preference intensities does appear to make a difference.

Moreover, the discussion of specific methods of cardinalisation suggested that while each method has its problems they are not necessarily insuperable. Indeed, the trend of the discussion went against the view that there were any decisive theoretical objections against regarding individual utility as measurable up to a linear transformation (i.e. measurable except for scale and origin).

Unfortunately, the answer to the second question must be much less optimistic. For even if such a utility index for each individual can be constructed, this does not in itself enable us to make an aggregation of individual utility indices into a utility index for society as a whole. In order that aggregation be possible, we require further that the indices for different individuals should be comparable. The precise meaning of comparability in this context was indicated earlier (see above, pp. 42–3). Essentially, it involves that the scaling unit for utility should be the same for each individual.

Suppose, for example, that we are using a preference-threshold approach to construct a cardinal utility index for each individual and that we assume further that all individuals have the same utility unit. From the point of view of constructing a social ordering from individual preferences this implies the value judgement that a movement from one discrimination level to the next higher one is to be regarded as equally significant, irrespective of which individual moves up.

Such a value judgement may well be regarded as unreasonable, for example, since all persons may not be equally 'sensitive'.[1] This

---

[1] The point is well stated by Sen [2] who argues that '. . . there are individuals who tend to be extremists and find things either "magnificent" or "horrible" while others finely differentiate between such things as "excellent", "good", "mediocre", "poor" and "awful". It seems manifestly unfair to make the ethical assumption that the welfare sig-

involves the familiar difficulties of making detailed interpersonal comparisons of utility which it was the purpose of Arrow's social welfare function approach to avoid.

Similarly, even if von Neumann–Morgenstern utility indices can be derived for all individuals, one cannot regard them as comparable to each other; hence one cannot aggregate them into a social welfare function without introducing fairly specialised value judgements.[1] Essentially, this is because the von Neumann–Morgenstern indices are only unique up to a linear transformation. There is no 'natural' origin and, which is more important, no 'natural' scaling unit.

There is yet another way of escaping from the impasse created by the Impossibility Theorem, which is to impose some restrictions on the individual orderings to be considered. Arrow was looking for a social welfare function that would yield a social ordering starting from every logically possible set of individual orderings. This is perhaps too demanding. At a given time and in a stable society, the orderings of alternatives by individuals are likely to reflect a shared culture and hence to show certain similarities among themselves.[2] Much of the recent literature on the existence of a social welfare function has been concerned with formulating such similarities more precisely, i.e. with imposing the appropriate restrictions on the admissible set of individual orderings, and with stating the conditions under which they enable us to derive a social ordering with acceptable properties.

The point of departure for this discussion is provided by the 'single-peakedness' condition (Black [14]; see also Arrow [1] chap. 7). A set of individual orderings is said to be single-peaked if there is some 'basic arrangement' of the alternatives such that in passing from one alternative to the next in this arrangement each individual monotonically rises to the peak of his preferences and/or monotonically drops off. For this 'basic' arrangement of alternatives, the

---

nificance of moving the first individual from what he regards as "horrible" to what he finds as "magnificent" is no more than moving the second individual from what he finds "poor" to what strikes him as "mediocre" ' (p. 94).

[1] See above, p. 42. For a deeper analysis of the relationships between attitudes to risk, moral judgements and the social welfare function, see Harsanyi [12] and Pattanaik [13].

[2] This need not necessarily reflect the prevalence of a 'democratic culture'. It may just as well result from pervasive political and social pressures on the individual to conform to the views of 'the establishment'.

map showing the direction of preference of each individual over all the alternatives will then appear, geometrically, to be single-peaked.[1]

For example, consider the following set of orderings by three individuals 1, 2, 3 of three alternatives x, y, z. Individual 1 strictly prefers x to y and y to z. Individual 2 strictly prefers y to z and z to x. Individual 3 strictly prefers z to y and y to x. These orderings are represented graphically in Fig. 3.3.1.

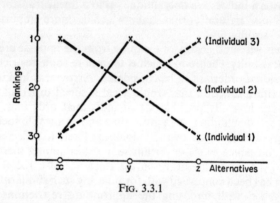

FIG. 3.3.1

Fig. 3.3.1 is constructed as follows. The alternatives x, y, z are arranged in that order on the horizontal axis. For each individual the orders of preference among alternatives (the rankings 1, 2, 3) are arranged on the vertical axis, where 1 indicates that the alternative is most preferred, 2 that it comes next in the preference order and 3 that it comes last.

The 'single-peaked' or 'unimodal' pattern of preferences of each individual with respect to the 'basic arrangement' of alternatives x, y, z is clear from the graph.

While such a geometrical interpretation helps us to visualise the nature of individual orderings implied by single-peakedness, it is not strictly necessary for the definition of the single-peakedness condition.

An equivalent 'algebraic' definition of single-peakedness, with three alternatives denoted by x, y, z respectively, is as follows.

Let x, y, z (in that order) be a basic arrangement of the alternatives. Then the single-peakedness condition implies that any individual who does not strictly prefer y to x must strictly prefer y to

[1] Note that this need not hold for all arrangements of alternatives but for at least one, viz. the basic arrangement.

z, while any individual who does not strictly prefer y to z must strictly prefer y to x.

In effect, this means that every individual is agreed in not regarding y as the worst alternative.

Similarly, if the basic arrangement is y, z, x, single-peakedness is equivalent to z not being regarded by any individual as the worst alternative. If the basic arrangement is z, x, y, the condition is equivalent to x not being regarded by anyone as the worst alternative. It is in this sense that the single-peakedness condition can be regarded as a form of similarity among individual orderings.

For the condition to hold, all individuals must agree that a specified alternative is not worst in the triple.

It can easily be checked that the set of individual orderings cited above (viz. individual 1 strictly prefers x to y and y to z; individual 2 strictly prefers y to z and z to x; while individual 3 strictly prefers z to y and y to x) satisfies the formal definition of single-peakedness. On the other hand, consider the set of individual orderings cited on p. 82 above as an example of the paradox of voting, where individual 1 strictly prefers x to y and y to z; individual 2 strictly prefers y to z and z to x; and individual 3 strictly prefers z to x and x to y. Clearly, this set of individual orderings is not single-peaked with respect to the 'basic arrangement' x, y, z since individual 3 does not strictly prefer y to z yet strictly prefers x to y. Similarly, it can be shown that it is not single-peaked with respect to any other possible basic arrangement. Hence it is not single-peaked.

This would seem to suggest that the single-peakedness condition and the transitivity of the majority decision-rule are related. Such is indeed the case. It has been proved that if the individual orderings are single-peaked and the number of individuals is odd, the majority decision-rule will be transitive (Arrow [1] chap. 8).[1]

In assessing the interpretative significance of this proposition, the following considerations are particularly relevant.

---

[1] A more general type of restriction on individual orderings which will ensure that the majority decision-rule is transitive has been developed by Sen. This is called the 'value-restriction' condition and requires 'that all agree that some alternative is not best or all agree that some alternative is not worst or all agree that some alternative is not medium in anyone's ranking of the triple' ([2] p. 168).

Since all agreeing that some alternative is not worst is equivalent to single-peakedness, the condition of value restriction includes single-peakedness as a special case.

Sen has proved that if value restriction holds for every triple and the number of voters is odd, majority rule will be transitive.

Firstly, the requirement that the number of individuals be odd is both restrictive and intellectually unsatisfactory. However, while majority decisions can indeed be intransitive if the number of individuals is even, even when the single-peakedness condition is satisfied, this is so only if there is a special kind of balance between conflicting orderings. It can be shown that the probability of such a precise balance diminishes as the number of individuals increases. Hence for large groups this condition can be relaxed.

Secondly, the single-peakedness requirement violates the free triple condition. The special relationship between individual orderings imposed by single-peakedness will always rule out *some* individual orderings. Hence single-peakedness implies the absence of a free triple among admissible alternatives. Intuitively this is not particularly surprising, for the purpose of the free triple condition was to make the range of situations to which the social welfare function can apply as wide as possible. The rationale of postulating similarities between individual orderings, of which the single-peakedness condition is a particular example, is on the contrary to make this range narrower. In effect the single-peakedness condition is to be interpreted as replacing Arrow's condition 1, the Free Triple Condition, for a social welfare function, the other conditions remaining unchanged.

Thirdly, and most important, it is not at all clear that actual preference patterns in a modern society are likely to be single-peaked.

One way of interpreting the single-peakedness condition is to regard it as a certain kind of consensus as to how the various alternatives are to be labelled in terms of some chosen dimension. This labelling corresponds to what has been previously called 'the basic arrangement' of alternatives. For example, all individuals might agree that a preference for one particular alternative implies a higher degree of 'liberalness' than a preference for another. If every possible pair of alternatives can be so compared, an agreed arrangement of alternatives in a descending order of liberalness can be constructed.

Suppose, for example, that the following ranking of the alternatives concerned: (1) integrated schools, (2) medicare, (3) conservation, (4) the space programme and (5) an anti-ballistic missiles system, is regarded by all as a descending order of liberalness, (1) representing the most and (5) the least liberal alternative. If each person in any pairwise choice of alternatives prefers the one which is relatively closer to his own position on the scale of 'liberalness', the orderings of individuals will be single-peaked. However, since individual values tend to be multi-dimensional, the particular dimension (such as 'liberalness') may not be sufficient to provide a relevant basis for choice. This will be more so the greater the complexity of choice being considered. Further, even if there were only one relevant dimension, agreement on how alternatives are labelled in terms of it may not be forthcoming. Single-peakedness is more difficult to achieve than it looks.

To sum up, although much ingenuity has been spent in thinking up ways of escaping from the implications of the Impossibility Theorem, no escape route that does not depend either on interpersonal comparisons of utility or on the clustering of individual preferences in a special way seems yet to be available.

3.4 THE IMPOSSIBILITY THEOREM AND COMPENSATION CRITERIA

Arrow showed that the Kaldor–Hicks principle of compensation as originally formulated was inconsistent with condition 3 – the Independence of Irrelevant Alternatives.[1] Moreover, Scitovsky had already demonstrated the possibility that both xP_sy and yP_sx could be fulfilled by the Kaldor–Hicks test. Significantly, Arrow further demonstrated that the Scitovsky 'double criterion' contradicted the collective rationality conditions. The double criterion could be interpreted as an acceptance of the compensation test if 'reversibility' was impossible, and a declaration that states be declared indifferent if xP_sy and yP_sx. Arrow constructed an example ([1] pp. 44–5) to show that, given states x, y, z, then

$\qquad$ (a) yP_sx
$\qquad$ (b) by redistribution of goods in x, xP_sy
so that $\quad$ (c) xI_sy, by the Scitovsky double criterion.
Similarly, (d) zP_sy
$\qquad$ (e) by redistribution of goods in y, yP_sz
so that $\quad$ (f) zI_sy.

By (c) and (f), it follows from transitivity that

$\qquad$ (g) xI_sz.

But Arrow's example shows

$\qquad$ (h) zP_sx, which contradicts (g).

[1] Arrow ([1] p. 40). He does in fact restate the Kaldor–Hicks test to make it consistent with condition 3.

Effectively, then, Arrow showed that the 'new' welfare economics did not meet the criteria of reasonableness. In turn, to the extent that CBA rests upon the compensation criteria for its own foundations, CBA contradicts the Arrow conditions.

3.5 THE IMPOSSIBILITY THEOREM AND COST–BENEFIT ANALYSIS

From the point of view of CBA the main lesson of this discussion seems to be the following. CBA has been generally interpreted as a method of aggregating individual preferences so as to provide a basis for social choice. The Impossibility Theorem claims to show that no such aggregation is possible without introducing ethical judgements of a more specialised kind than requiring simply that individual preferences should count. The explicit introduction of ethical judgements into CBA thus appears inevitable. This immediately raises the following problem.

Given that the social welfare function necessarily involves ethical judgements, in what way should the economist who sets out to use cost–benefit analysis for the formulation of policy approach his task?

One possible approach would be to use a social welfare function which incorporates his own ethical judgements. The ethical judgements of the economist are indeed often particularly relevant for CBA because, *inter alia*, he may be expected to have special knowledge about the economic structure within which such judgements are to be made effective. Nevertheless, there are other members of the community whose claims to special knowledge may also be deemed equally legitimate. Moreover, in decisions with far-reaching social consequences, claims based on specialist knowledge are themselves likely to be regarded with suspicion, at least under political democracy. Hence basic ethical judgements which may underlie the economist's approach to policy decisions will only be serious claimants for social use if they happen to be widely shared in the community at large, or if economists happen to be a particularly powerful social group. Neither seems to be generally the case.

A more serious contender for use in determining the social welfare function would be the ethical judgements of political authorities. Adopting these has sometimes been justified by recourse to some variant of 'the organic theory' in which representatives of the state are regarded as the unique choosers of social ends. However, such theories seem to be based on mysticism and do not lend themselves well to rational argument.

Alternatively, such a procedure could be interpreted as being logically implied by an individualist but *two-stage* decision process, viz. (i) the choice of representatives by majority voting and (ii) the choice of objectives by those elected. The ethical judgements of the government are thus regarded as a proxy for those of the community as a whole. While this position is increasingly fashionable (see Buchanan and Tullock [15]), its intellectual basis is open to doubt.

In the first place, the majority voting principle is intransitive, except when the spectrum of opinions is sufficiently 'similar'.

Secondly, the relationship of voting to individual preference is more complex than the simple 'two-stage' model implies, essentially because the result of my vote depends on how others vote. One such complication is the possibility of 'strategic', i.e. insincere, voting (cf. Majumdar [16]).

In practice the ethical judgements of political authorities are often neither given in advance nor sufficiently specific to be operational. This suggests yet another approach to the use of ethical judgements, that the economist follows through his exercise in CBA on the basis of some specified ethical judgement without necessarily committing himself to this particular judgement. What he would then be doing would be to work out the implications of the specified ethical judgement for CBA – i.e. to derive the decisions which would follow *if* one accepted it. Someone who happened to accept such an ethical judgement could then recommend these decisions on the basis of the work done by the economist.[1] This possibility was also discussed in Chapter 2.

Yet another possible approach, which may indeed be described as a logical outcome of the one just described, would be to regard the choice of a social welfare function as a first step towards setting up a meaningful dialogue between professional economists and the community as a whole. On this view, the models discussed by the economist are useful to the extent that they stimulate decision-makers throughout the economy to examine the decisions facing them in the light of the basic preference orderings set for the economy as a whole. In turn, their reactions should have a feedback

---

[1] This procedure is given a qualified approach by Little: 'The economist can, of course, investigate what follows from any set of value premises he likes to choose. If the value premises are made explicit and are not hidden, the result will be informative and interesting – and cannot be misleading. So long as there are some people who would be prepared to accept the stated premises, the result cannot be entirely useless' ([17] p. 83).

effect on the original specification of social welfare. An interactive process may thus ensue which, hopefully, could converge towards some kind of a consensus. The social welfare function is on this approach regarded in effect as a social learning process rather than as being fixed *ab initio*.

If one takes this kind of approach, one may further argue that in an area where the problems involved are fundamental, complex and generally unfamiliar, to take the choice of a particular welfare function as one's point of departure may well be inappropriate. Rather, the economist should see his task as that of spelling out the consequences of adopting *different* welfare functions – in particular of working out the alternative time-paths of consumption implied by these different welfare functions – and thus enabling essentially political decisions to be made on a more rational basis than would otherwise be possible.

To conclude, we mention some of the implications for CBA of our discussion in this chapter.

Firstly, our discussion provides little support for the view that 'efficiency criteria' (see Chapter 2 above) necessarily provide the best possible basis for CBA. The neglect of the distributional effects of projects is justified by the argument that (i) such effects will 'cancel out' or that (ii) the desired distribution will be achieved by other means.

However, (i) is essentially an appeal to the theory of probability. Hence, it can only be analysed properly on the basis of a well-defined probabilistic theory of social welfare functions. Such a theory is still lacking.

As regards (ii), it implies among other things that the policy instruments are themselves welfare-neutral. The theory of the social welfare function, which is concerned with the social ordering of 'alternatives' or 'social states' in a general sense, does not make any such assumption.

Secondly, the question of the proper scope of CBA has often been raised.

According to one view, the difficulties involved in reaching an agreed ranking of social objectives limit the applicability of CBA to a strictly limited range, viz. to the relative appraisal of projects with *one* common objective. CBA is thus regarded essentially as applying only to 'choice of techniques' problems within a relatively homogeneous 'programme'.

As against this, there is a more 'positive' view which argues that CBA should not merely acknowledge the multiplicity of objectives but also attempt to estimate the trade-offs between them. This would require (i) econometric estimation of structural relationships in the economy as a whole, and (ii) quantitative analysis of the consequences of different sets of weights being given to the objectives.

However, neither view seems to be entirely accurate. Thus, for example, limiting CBA to projects within a broadly homogeneous programme does not eliminate all the difficulties, since the time-profile of benefits accruing from different projects will tend to differ, thus necessitating interpersonal comparisons (see Chapter 6 below).

Similarly, as regards the second view of CBA, while knowledge of the consequences of policies with different sets of weights given to the objectives is important, someone has still to decide which set of weights is to be adopted. This necessarily involves value judgements – hence the need for a social welfare function.

What emerges from our discussion is that *how* CBA is to be applied for decision-making is a far more important question than the kind of decisions it is to be applied to.

If we remember that value judgements are inescapable in reaching policy decisions and that such value judgements can themselves be rationally argued about, CBA can be an extremely useful tool of decision-making. For by making such judgements explicit and, as far as possible, spelling them out in precise quantitative terms, it makes clear thinking about policy matters possible. However, it can never be a substitute for thought.

3.6 SUMMARY

Chapters 1 and 2 developed the concept of a social welfare function in which individual preferences were added together. Weights could then be attached to the individual utilities, producing what this chapter showed to be a Bergson–Samuelson type of social welfare function. But the problem with such a function is that it offers no guidance as to how the weights are to be derived, and by whom. This problem was partly discussed in Chapter 2, which was mainly concerned with alternative ways of deriving weights. This chapter concentrated on a more fundamental problem, namely, whether it is logically possible to derive a Bergson–Samuelson type of social welfare function from a set of individual preferences. This was the question to which Arrow addressed himself in his work on the Impossibility Theorem. Without actually proving the theorem, the chapter investigated the foundations of Arrow's theorem and argued that the only possible escapes – via cardinalisation to avoid Arrow's condition 3, or via the imposition of restrictions on the 'domain' of individuals' preferences – each foundered upon serious obstacles. In the first case, interpersonal comparisons of utility intervened, and in the second the restrictive conditions, centred mainly upon 'single-peakedness', appeared unduly unrealistic. In consequence, the Arrow problem remains.

As far as cost–benefit analysis is concerned, the continued existence of the Arrow problem means that the process of aggregating preferences cannot be achieved without violating at least one of Arrow's criteria of 'reasonableness'. But these in turn centre largely upon the idea of consumers' sovereignty, which Chapter 1 argued was the supposed underlying philosophy of CBA. Therefore, cost–benefit proceeds in a fashion which is at odds with its own apparent philosophy. To this end, the question of value judgements was raised again and the question of 'who decides?', which was hinted at in Chapter 2, was discussed in terms of a suggested 'interactive' procedure whereby economists pose alternative social welfare functions and show the consequences of using them.

Part Two

Accounting Prices

4 Accounting Prices

CHAPTER 2 suggested that, as a first approximation, market prices of final outputs indicated the 'proper' valuation of benefits, and market prices of resources the 'proper' valuation of costs. The maximand of benefits minus costs, valued in this way, was seen to satisfy the requirement for a ranking function which ordered alternative projects in terms of their social preferredness. The extent to which these prices do comprise a proper valuation must now be investigated.

4.1 THE MEANING OF ACCOUNTING PRICES

Given that resources are limited, the use in one project will entail an opportunity cost – the benefit they would have yielded in an alternative use. Whatever the objective function, then, there will be a cost involved in meeting that objective by the use of resources in one project rather than in another. The ratio of the two WTPs for these alternative uses is given the term 'shadow' or 'accounting' price. These terms will be used interchangeably. These shadow prices can be thought of as the marginal rate of substitution between the 'outputs' in question, the amount of one output which we have to sacrifice in order to obtain another output. An extra unit of health may mean one unit less of education; one extra unit of water for irrigation is one unit less for direct consumption. There is always a 'trade-off' between the two uses, and it is the shadow price of the output which reflects this true cost.

The adjective 'shadow' is a useful one, since shadow prices are not necessarily observed. Health and education are 'outputs' but they are not always sold on the market. There is no observable price, but there is a 'shadow' price, since each must have an opportunity cost in terms of some forgone alternative. Even where outputs are sold on the market, there need be little correspondence between observed (market) prices and shadow prices, for reasons shortly to be discussed.[1]

[1] Shadow or accounting prices will be used in this general sense. The reader should note that many authors reserve the term 'shadow' price for outputs which are not sold in a direct market.

D

The terminology of shadow prices derives from mathematical programming. For an extensive treatment of programming and the meaning of shadow prices in programming problems, the reader is referred to Samuelson, Dorfman and Solow [1].

Now the precise values which shadow prices take on will depend upon what is maximised, i.e. on what the objective function is. If the transfer of resources from use *A* to use *B* involves a sacrifice of some outcome *X*, this element of opportunity cost will not be reflected in the shadow price if *X* is not an argument (i.e. one of the factors involved) in the chosen objective function. If *X is* introduced into the objective function, the shadow price is altered. This argument should be sufficient to emphasise the very important point that shadow prices reflect the chosen objective function.

For the moment we continue to work with a Pareto-type objective function with the existing income distribution being regarded as optimal. Hence, our concern is with 'efficiency benefits' and 'efficiency costs' in the Pareto sense. At the risk of labouring the point, it is most important that this be understood. CBA has traditionally confined itself to the Pareto criterion (modified with the compensation test argument), but this criterion reflects *one* set of value judgements about individual preferences. It carries no more moral compulsion about it than any other SWF.

Given that there is a set of shadow prices implicit in Pareto optimality, what are they? The next section provides a fairly elementary proof that, *under certain conditions*, the shadow prices implicit in Pareto optimality are identical with the market prices.

4.2 ACCOUNTING PRICES AND PARETO OPTIMALITY

Pareto optimality exists when no individual within the economy can be made better off without someone being made worse off. This condition was redefined in Chapter 2 to allow for some people being worse off. The requirement then became that an optimum exists if gainers could *only just* compensate losers. If they could over-compensate, then scope existed for the adoption of policies to yield a Pareto improvement; if they could only under-compensate, the policies in question should not be undertaken.

Three overall requirements are necessary for Pareto optimality to exist.

(1) *The Resources-to-Outputs Condition.* Resources should be allocated between outputs such that no reallocation would increase the national product.

(2) *The Goods-to-Consumers Condition.* Goods should be allocated between consumers such that no reallocation would increase total utility.

    Note: This condition does *not* involve us in deciding the optimal distribution of income. It merely refers to the exchange of goods between consumers; it does not tell us whether individual 1 should have more of all goods than individual 2.

(3) *The Optimal Output Set Condition.* This rule indicates the best set of outputs – i.e. whether there should be $10x+5y$ or $7x+7y$, or whatever.

With the aid of elementary algebra the shadow prices implicit in these rules can be derived. It is assumed that only the recorded national product matters, that there is *non-satiation* (i.e. consumers prefer more of everything), and, as has been assumed to date, the analysis remains 'static'. Only two goods, x and y, are considered.

Rule 1.
$$\frac{\mathrm{MP}_L(x)}{\mathrm{MP}_K(x)} = \frac{\mathrm{MP}_L(y)}{\mathrm{MP}_K(y)}$$

where L is the labour input, K is the capital input and $\mathrm{MP}_L(x)$ reads 'the marginal product of labour in producing x'.

    Proof. Let some amount dL be taken from y and given to x. The net effect on combined outputs is

$$-dL \cdot \mathrm{MP}_L(y)+dL \cdot \mathrm{MP}_L(x). \qquad (4.1)$$

Now move dK from x to y such that the output of y is held constant – i.e. the capital movement compensates for the labour movement. Then

$$\left|dK \cdot \mathrm{MP}_K(y)\right| = \left|dL \cdot \mathrm{MP}_L(y)\right| \qquad (4.2)$$

so that

$$\frac{dL \cdot \mathrm{MP}_L(y)}{dK \cdot \mathrm{MP}_K(y)} = 1 \qquad (4.2\textsc{a})$$

and there is a net loss of output of

$$-dK \cdot \mathrm{MP}_K(x)+dK \cdot \mathrm{MP}_K(y). \qquad (4.3)$$

Now suppose the optimality condition does not hold, such that

$$\frac{\mathrm{MP}_L\,(x)}{\mathrm{MP}_K\,(x)} > \frac{\mathrm{MP}_L\,(y)}{\mathrm{MP}_K\,(y)}. \qquad (4.4)$$

Multiplying (4.4) by dL/dK gives

$$\frac{dL \cdot \text{MP}_L(x)}{dK \cdot \text{MP}_K(x)} > \frac{dL \cdot \text{MP}_L(y)}{dK \cdot \text{MP}_K(y)} \tag{4.5}$$

which, by (4.2A), reduces to

$$\frac{dL}{dK} \cdot \frac{\text{MP}_L(x)}{\text{MP}_K(x)} > 1$$

i.e. $\qquad\qquad dL \cdot \text{MP}_L(x) > dK \cdot \text{MP}_K(x)$. (4.6)

Now the result of the moves in (4.1) and (4.3) is, overall,

$$-dL \cdot \text{MP}_L(y) + dL \cdot \text{MP}_L(x) - dK \cdot \text{MP}_K(x) + dK \cdot \text{MP}_K(y)$$
$$= +dL \cdot \text{MP}_L(x) - dK \cdot \text{MP}_K(x) \quad (4.7)$$

(since the first and last terms are equal, by (4.2A)).

But (4.7) must be greater than zero because, by assumption, (4.6) shows the first term to be greater than the latter. Hence, if the optimality condition does *not* hold, it is possible to increase the total output by reallocation of resources. The ratio of the marginal products expressed in this way is called the *marginal rate of technical substitution* ($\text{MRTS}_{K,L}$), so that the condition can be expressed as

$$\text{MRTS}_{K,L}(x) = \text{MRTS}_{K,L}(y).$$

Rule 2. $\qquad\qquad \dfrac{\text{MU}_x(1)}{\text{MU}_y(1)} = \dfrac{\text{MU}_x(2)}{\text{MU}_y(2)}$

where 1 and 2 are consumers, and $\text{MU}_y(1)$ reads 'the marginal utility of y to 1'.

Proof. The proof is essentially the same as that given for rule 1, with MU substituted for MP. Move dx from 2 and give it to 1, and move dy from 1 to 2 such that $U(2)$ is the same. Calculate the net effect and see if the reallocation raises total utility if the optimality condition does not hold. It will.

Rule 2 can be written as

$$\text{MRS}_{x,y}(1) = \text{MRS}_{x,y}(2)$$

i.e. the 'marginal rates of substitution' between the two goods must be the same for all consumers.

Rule 3. $\qquad \text{MRS}_{x,y}(1) = \text{MRS}_{x,y}(2) = \text{MRT}_{x,y}$

where MRT (not to be confused with MRTS) refers to the 'marginal rate of transformation' between x and y, i.e. the rate at which x needs to be given up in order to obtain an increment of y. This rate of transformation can therefore be written dx/dy.

Now dx is the change in output of x and this must be equal to

$$dx = -[dL . \text{MP}_L(x) + dK . \text{MP}_K(x)].$$

Similarly

$$dy = -[dL . \text{MP}_L(y) + dK . \text{MP}_K(y)].$$

With some manipulation, we obtain

$$\frac{dx}{dy} = \frac{-\text{MP}_L(x)}{\text{MP}_L(y)} = \frac{-\text{MP}_K(x)}{\text{MP}_K(y)}$$

so that rule 3 can be rewritten

$$\text{MRS}_{x,y}(1) = \text{MRS}_{x,y}(2) = \frac{\text{MP}_L(x)}{\text{MP}_L(y)} = \frac{\text{MP}_K(x)}{\text{MP}_K(y)}. \quad (4.8)$$

A simple example should demonstrate that rule 3 is a sufficient condition for an optimum. Suppose the equation does *not* hold. A reduction of one unit of x will yield an increase of 3 units of y. Suppose the $1x$ is taken from just one of the consumers. To compensate him so that his total utility is not changed he requires only $1y$ since his MRS is equal to 1. But this leaves $2y$ spare since the surrender of $1x$ enabled $3y$ to be obtained. Hence, the $2y$ can be distributed between the consumers so as to raise the total utility.

Rule 3 states the requirement for an 'overall' Pareto optimum, and with this rule stated it is possible to derive the shadow prices. For any firm, the following relation will hold:

$$\text{MC}_x = \frac{W_x}{\text{MP}_L(x)} = \frac{R_x}{\text{MP}_K(x)} \quad (4.9)$$

where MC_x is the marginal cost of producing x, W_x is the wage in industry x, and R_x the rate of interest pertaining to industry x. In the short run, capital can be assumed fixed so that MC is determined by labour's marginal product and wage. In the long run, both capital and labour will vary, so that equation (4.9) will hold. Rearranging (4.9) gives

$$\text{MP}_L(x) = \frac{W_x}{\text{MC}_x}. \quad (4.9\text{A})$$

In Chapter 1 it was shown that, if the consumer is in equilibrium,

$$\frac{\text{MU}_y(1)}{\text{MU}_x(1)} = \frac{P_y(1)}{P_x(1)}. \quad (4.10)$$

Substituting (4.9A) and (4.10) in (4.8) gives

$$\frac{P_y(1)}{P_x(1)} = \frac{P_y(2)}{P_x(2)} = \frac{W_x . \text{MC}_y}{W_y . \text{MC}_x} \quad (4.11)$$

where P_y and P_x are in fact the 'shadow prices' of y and x respectively.

If price discrimination is not practised, the prices to 1 and 2 of the same goods must be the same, and wage rates will be the same, so that

$$\frac{P_y}{P_x} = \frac{MC_y}{MC_x}. \tag{4.12}$$

Optimality therefore requires that product prices be proportional to their marginal costs. The 'strict' version of this rule requires prices to be *equal* to marginal costs, a requirement which emerges once factor supplies are allowed to vary.[1]

Consider leisure time. This is both a consumption good and an input. For each consumer there are substitution possibilities between leisure and the goods which would otherwise be obtained by working. It follows that for a situation to be optimal, this MRS must be equal to the MRT between leisure (as an input) and the good, say x. We require

$$MRS_{D, x} = MRT_{D, x} \tag{4.13}$$

where D is leisure. Now the marginal rate of transformation of leisure into good x must be the output which would be produced if the leisure time was used as work, and this will be equal to

$$\frac{dx}{dD} = MP_L(x). \tag{4.14}$$

Also, the MRS between leisure and good x will be equal to the ratio of prices. The price of leisure is simply the wage rate forgone, W_x. The optimality requirement of (4.13) becomes

$$\frac{W_x}{P_x} = MP_L(x) = \frac{W_x}{MC_x} \tag{4.15}$$

using the relationship between marginal cost and marginal product given in (4.9).

Equation (4.15) clearly requires $P_x = MC_x$. It follows that, once factor supplies are allowed to vary (in this case, labour), a strict equality of price and marginal cost is required.[2]

If the proper shadow price of final goods is equal to their marginal cost, it is simple to derive the shadow price of inputs. From equation (4.9) we know that

[1] The apparent sufficiency of the proportionality requirement was emphasised by Kahn [2].

[2] There are other reasons for requiring equality rather than proportionality (see McKenzie [3]). For a dissenting view which attempts to preserve the proportionality argument, see Dobb [4].

$$\text{MC}_x = \frac{W_x}{\text{MP}_L(x)}$$

so that, since $P_x = \text{MC}_x$, we obtain,

$$W_x = P_x \cdot \text{MP}_L(x) = \text{VMP}_L(x).$$

The shadow price of labour is therefore equal to the price of the product multiplied by the marginal product of labour, which is termed the 'value of the marginal product'. A similar condition will hold for other inputs.

It has taken a little while, but the shadow prices relevant for Pareto optimality have been derived in a formal way. The immediate corollary is that these shadow prices are the relevant ones for purposes of valuing costs and benefits in cost–benefit analysis, in theory at least.

Will market prices be the same as the requisite shadow prices? Only under certain conditions, namely those of perfect competition. For in perfect competition, firms maximise profits where price equals marginal cost. Perfect competition, however, is a state of the economy which is rarely if ever approximated. It follows that market prices will tend to diverge from equivalence with marginal costs, depending on the degree of imperfection. These circumstances are dealt with in section 4.4.

4.3 Marginal Cost and Willingness to Pay

In the absence of any qualifying factors, to be discussed in section 4.4, the marginal cost of any final output reflects the appropriate shadow price. In a perfectly competitive economy market prices equal marginal costs, so that market prices are themselves adequate shadow prices.

It may be useful to relate marginal cost pricing to the idea of maximising the difference between benefits and costs as measured by willingness to pay.

Fig. 4.3.1 shows a demand curve for a product together with the relevant marginal and average cost curves. Price will be *BE* if marginal cost pricing is adopted, and total willingness to pay will be *ABEO*. The *net* willingness to pay (benefits minus costs) will be *ABJ = ABEO−OEBJ*, where *OEBJ*, the area under the marginal cost up to the selected output *OE*, is the total cost of providing the output *OE*.

Now, by setting price equal to marginal cost, the shadow price implicit in the Pareto optimality conditions, the net willingness to pay should be maximised. That is, any other pricing policy should

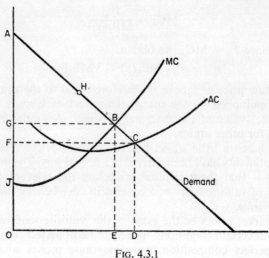

Fig. 4.3.1

not result in a 'total surplus' greater than *ABO*. If price was set
equal to average cost, for example, the total willingness to pay
would be *ACDO*, but the net willingness to pay would be *ACF*, an
area which, by inspection, is seen to be smaller than *ABO*. If the
reader can imagine a marginal revenue curve to the left of the
demand curve, the profit-maximising price would be, say, *H*. Output would be less than *OE*, and so would the total surplus. In other
words, *marginal cost pricing will maximise the net willingness to
pay*.

For the reader familiar with the elementary integral calculus the
proof is straightforward. Maximise

$$\int_0^{q_1} p(q) . dq - c(q_1)$$

which, when differentiated, gives

$$p(q) = \frac{dc}{dq}$$

where q is the quantity of the output, p is price and c is cost. The
expression dc/dq is simply marginal cost, so that the relevant
pricing rule is shown to maximise the net willingness to pay.

4.4 QUALIFICATIONS ON USING MARKET PRICES

The use of market prices for valuation purposes will be improper if

(a) market prices are not equal to marginal costs;
(b) marginal cost does not reflect the true social cost of resources.

In a perfectly competitive world there is no reason to suppose that marginal costs will reflect true social costs because of the phenomena of 'external effects', discussed in detail in Chapter 5. In an imperfectly competitive world, price will tend to be above marginal cost, *and* external effects will exist, so that both conditions will pertain. The sources of these divergences are:

(i) *Imperfect competition.* In the product market under imperfectly competitive conditions the profit-maximising firm will equate marginal revenue, not price, with marginal cost, so that price will be above marginal cost. The extent of this divergence will depend upon the 'degree of monopoly'. If there are many firms the demand curve may be very elastic, so that the final market price will not be too far above marginal cost. Some cost–benefit practitioners have relied upon this argument for a justification of the use of market prices. Technically, however, market prices will overstate the proper shadow price to be applied to outputs, and an adjustment should be made.

The same considerations will apply to the market for resources, the shadow prices of which should reflect the *value* of the marginal product. Under imperfect competition, however, producers will buy resources to the point where factor prices equal the *marginal revenue product* which will be less than the value of the marginal product.

(ii) *Imperfect competition in the factor market.* Where the producer buys resources in an imperfect market, the price of the resource is likely to rise the more it is purchased. Since all units of the same resource will have to be paid the same (the last man cannot be paid more than other men doing the same work), the 'intra-marginal' units, the ones employed before the marginal unit, will receive payments in excess of their true opportunity cost. They are in fact receiving elements of 'economic rent', and, technically, this rental element should be deducted The bias implicit in the use of market prices was discussed at the end of Chapter 2.

(iii) *Unemployment of resources.* If a public project employs a resource which would otherwise have been unemployed, the true cost to society of employment is (virtually) zero. In times of recession, then, the shadow cost of labour would be nearer to zero than it is to the wage actually paid. Where the costs are distributed over a period of time it would be necessary to know whether the level of unemployment is likely to continue at its existing rate. If there is reason to suppose that it will, the appropriate valuation will remain at zero. If, as is perhaps more likely, the recession is not expected to last, future labour would need to be valued at the likely ruling wage rate.

(iv) *Non-marginal changes in price.* This problem has already been discussed in Chapter 2, where some average of the new and old price was suggested as the best approximation of the willingness to pay. There are several drawbacks to this rule, however. Firstly, the demand curve may not be susceptible to linear approximation. In this case the shape of the demand curve over the relevant range should be calculated and the resulting area should be estimated by more complex rules. The error involved in linear approximation may not, however, be significant and it may be that the search for precision is more than offset by costs of actually estimating the change. Secondly, it may be extremely difficult to estimate the new price. In this case, the cost–benefit analyst must resort to some guess, or simply use existing and known market prices. Thirdly, the outputs may not be final outputs – e.g. fertilisers or irrigation water. The demand for these goods is of course a demand derived from the demand for the final product – agricultural output. The relevant valuation is the value of the final output *minus* the value of any inputs other than the intermediate products in question. In short, WTP is measured by the 'value added' by the intermediate products which are to be valued. Fourthly, the measurement of consumers' surplus by the area under the demand curve for the final product will not indicate the change in willingness to pay if the income effects of a change in price are at all significant. What this amounts to is that the assumption of the constant marginal utility of income underlies the use of consumers' surplus as an indicator of WTP. Basically, the consumer is in equilibrium if the ratio of the marginal utility to price is equal for each good consumed by him. Constant marginal utility of income implies that a change in the price in one good will not affect the ratios for any other good he consumes; i.e. the only adjustment to price is in the amount purchased of the affected good. It is only of this assumption, made by Marshall, that the consumers' surplus 'triangle' is operationally useful. Now it is unlikely that this requirement will hold in practice, so that the valuation procedure is not a correct one. A full discussion of the relationship between consumers' surplus and WTP is to be found in Hicks ([5] pp. 38–41). Although consumers' surplus is widely used as a measure of utility change, the constancy of the marginal utility of income tends to receive acknowledgement only in footnotes, an indication perhaps of the difficulties of actually taking it into account when carrying out practical studies. In a number of situations there is no problem, since the outputs in question are intermediate products. In these cases the area under the demand curve does not require adjustment (Marglin [6]).

Lastly, where *relative* prices change over time, allowance should be made for the fact in the cost–benefit analysis. Predicting changes in the absolute price level is not without its hazards, but the absolute price level is irrelevant to cost–benefit analysis, which is carried out in terms of constant prices, the base year for benefits being the year in which the output commences, and the base year of costs being the year in which they are first incurred (see Chapter 6). Predicting changes in relative prices is likely to be extremely difficult. Indeed, one writer has remarked that 'the cost-per-unit of high-quality information about substitution ratios five years from now is usually like the per-unit cost of Holy Grails: it is very high' (McKean [7] p. 42). On the other hand, some indication of the likely bias from using unchanging ratios is required in projects where outputs are likely to be far more highly valued in real terms in later years, as with recreational facilities for example.

(v) *Increasing returns.*[1] The existence of increasing returns will mean that marginal cost will be *below* average cost. For the purposes of valuing benefits, the actual use of prices which reflect marginal cost will therefore involve the public enterprise in a loss. But the losses have to be financed and the methods of financing will themselves have welfare effects. In addition, increasing returns industries have a tendency to monopoly so that the problems arising under (i) will be relevant.

(vi) *Taxation.* Market prices will, in practice, contain elements of indirect taxation, or, alternatively, may be below the true cost in so far as the product is subsidised. Where a product is highly taxed, the use of unadjusted market prices will exaggerate the maximum benefits, while the benefits of a subsidised product would be undervalued. To correct for these biases, all outputs should be valued net of indirect taxes and subsidies, i.e. at 'factor cost'.

[1] In terms of the marginal conditions of section 4.3, increasing returns will mean that a particular range of the production possibility frontier will be concave to the origin instead of convex. As such, the equation of MRT with combined MRSs is not sufficient to guarantee an optimum. In such conditions, the use of pricing for the decentralisation of decision-making is not generally possible.

Whereas private investment decisions should rightly estimate the rate of return on investments (i.e. the private benefits) *after* tax, the return to a public investment should be estimated before tax since the before-tax returns are the proper indicator of benefits (Prest and Turvey [8] p. 603).

(vii) *Multiplier effects*. Allied to the point concerning unemployment is the fact that investments will yield multiplier effects if resources are not fully employed. On a global scale, it would appear that the benefits to the project are considerably greater than those indicated by the revenue of the project. This issue is discussed in more detail in Chapter 5.

(viii) *External effects*. An external effect may exist if the consumption activities of one consumer affect the utility level of other consumers (a consumer–consumer externality), and if the production activities of one producer affect the profitability of another product (a producer–producer externality). Similarly, externalities can exist if producers' activities affect consumers' utility levels, and consumers' activities affect producers' profits. But before these interdependences are deserving of the label 'external effect' *it must be the case that they are not priced in a market*.

That is, if effluent from an upstream producer affects the cost and hence the profits of a downstream producer, an externality does not exist if the upstream producer fully compensates the loser. If the compensation is paid, the upstream producer's costs will rise, and those of the downstream producer will be reduced to their 'natural' level. A nuisance can therefore exist without it being an externality – an uncompensated or unappropriated cost or benefit. External effects are discussed in more detail in Chapter 5.

(ix) *Public goods*. These are goods which, when supplied to one person, are supplied to others because of 'joint supply' and the impossibility of excluding others by pricing policies. If benefits are yielded, those who receive the benefits as a by-product of the supply to a particular section of the population will, if they act rationally, understate their true valuation of the benefit, knowing that they will obtain the product free as long as it is supplied to at least one person. Clearly, the market price will not be a valid indicator of the social benefit in this case. Public goods necessarily exhibit the characteristics of external effects and are discussed more fully in Chapter 5.

Clearly, from the preceding list it can be seen that market prices will rarely coincide with the shadow prices which are theoretically necessary to value benefits and costs. This complexity raises the whole issue of whether it is really worth trying to obtain shadow prices at all. The pros and cons of this argument are discussed at the end of the chapter. There remain, however, two further important problems in the pricing of benefits.

4.5 The 'Second Best' Problem

The shadow pricing argument suggests that benefits should be valued at prices which reflect marginal costs. The preceding section suggested some modifications to this rule, modifications which can best be summarised by saying that a correct pricing rule values benefits at their marginal *social* cost – i.e. taking account of market imperfections and external effects. Once again, it is worth remembering that this rule will be relevant for policies which are designed to move an economy in the direction of a Pareto social optimum.

However, even if benefits are valued at their marginal social cost, a problem arises. Cost–benefit analysis is specifically designed to deal with public-sector investment. But for an overall Paretian optimum it will be necessary for prices to be equal to marginal social cost in *all* sectors. It seems highly unlikely that prices will reflect marginal social costs in the private sector where the aim of the firm is to maximise some private objective function, which is usually assumed to be profits, but which could equally well be sales revenue, or managerial prestige. If marginal social cost pricing is adopted in the public sector but not in the private sector, will the economy be nearer a Pareto optimum than if neither sector used the appropriate shadow prices? It is tempting to think that if some people are pursuing the 'right' policy and others are not, this must be better than a situation in which no one pursues the right policy.[1]

However, it has been suggested that marginal social cost pricing in this context will not guarantee a move in the right direction. Indeed, it may move the economy away from a social optimum in Pareto terms. That is, given that a 'first best', where all prices reflect marginal social costs, is not obtainable, it is not possible to

[1] This would appear to be the philosophy underlying the requirements which now exists for United Kingdom nationalised industries, namely that they set their prices to reflect long-run marginal cost. The exceptions are the decreasing-cost industries, which would make a loss if they set prices equal to marginal cost, and industries in which there is a state of excess demand or excess capacity. In addition, prices need not reflect marginal private costs if there are significant social benefits or social costs to be taken into account.

state what pricing rule in the public sector will, in the presence of the constraints set by pricing policies in the private sector, take the economy as far as possible towards a Pareto optimum. This is the essential import of the celebrated paper by Lipsey and Lancaster [9].

If the second-best theorem is correct, the implications for shadow pricing are drastic. For it means that there is no obvious justification for using marginal social cost as the appropriate shadow price, *and* that a set of shadow prices must either be determined all together, or not at all. Cost–benefit analysts are well aware of the problems imposed by the second-best theorem, but, as one writer has re-marked, 'these arguments are deferred to in footnotes and then ignored. Unfortunately for the analyst who has to advise govern-ments, the decision-makers, or at least their staff economists, have heard these arguments and their requests for clarification cannot be as easily avoided' (Margolis [10] pp. 72–3). Economists are divided on the appropriate course of action to take. Some use the theorem to support their own doubts about shadow prices in general (McKean [7]), others argue effectively for the abandonment of the optimality objective since no rigorous welfare pricing rules can be found (Wiseman [12]), while the 'optimists' continue to argue for some form of marginal cost rule in the absence of any better rule; after all, some shadow price has to be adopted – it is impossible not to price (Turvey [13]). Still others have sought to derive rules for the attainment of a second best, but the rules are immensely complex and could scarcely be described as operational for a decision-maker (Rees [14]).

Some welfare theorists have criticised the Lipsey–Lancaster theorem, declaring that the existence of certain conditions makes the theorem largely inapplicable (Davis and Whinston [11]).[1] If these criticisms are correct there may be little to worry about. These arguments, which have special relevance for developing countries, can be summarised as follows.

The second-best theorem really contrasts the different results

[1] The presentation is somewhat complex. Essentially, however, the Lipsey–Lancaster theorem is argued not to hold if utility and trans-formation functions are 'separable'. If a utility function is of the form $U = U(x_1, x_2, \ldots, x_n)$, it is additively separable if $U = U_1(x_1) + U_2(x_2) + \ldots + U_n(x_n)$. If utility and transformation functions exhibit this form, it is tantamount to saying that the interdependence between the relevant variables in the economy is very weak, indeed sufficiently so for changes in one not to affect significantly the values of other variables. A criticism of Davis and Whinston can be found in M. McManus, 'Private and Social Costs in the Theory of Second Best', *Review of Economic Studies* (July 1967).

which arise with a 'partial' as opposed to a 'general equilibrium' approach to appraisal. Thus, it may be argued that since everything depends on everything else, adjustment in any one price will necessitate adjustments in all others. If this is so, we cannot hope to estimate a particular accounting price without at the same time estimating all other prices in the system, which might mean in effect that we cannot estimate any accounting price at all.

Several rejoinders can be made to this line of argument. In the first place, everything does *not* depend on everything else in any significant degree. There is evidence to suggest that interdependence between activities is not so marked as the second-best theorem would seem to imply. The basic idea is that there are 'key' sectors or activities which play a crucial role in the economy.[1] There is then a case for paying special attention to a number of particular activities or sectors, and hence by implication to a few specific accounting prices, in the planning calculations. The special importance of the accounting price of foreign exchange is a case in point. Since a great many commodities can, at the margin, be traded, estimating the accounting price of foreign exchange eliminates the need for calculating the accounting prices of many such goods, or at least provides benchmarks against which alternative estimates of accounting prices can be checked.

From this point of view, the most important type of commodities for which separate calculation of accounting prices is necessary are non-traded goods and in particular non-traded intermediate goods such as electricity and transport.

Secondly, while partial results are necessarily approximate, it is important to remember that the 'correct' degree of approximation of any results depends on the purpose for which the results are desired. Hence the question of the accuracy of accounting prices must be seen in its proper context, namely the decentralisation of investment appraisals and of investment decisions. In most developing countries, for example, a great deal of decentralisation is generally regarded as desirable, or at least as unavoidable, so that projects must, in general, be assessed separately. There is then a problem of ensuring that the separate assessments – and decisions based on them – are consistent with one another.

In particular, we must ensure that it is feasible to carry out all the projects recommended within the limitations imposed by scarce

[1] Cf. A. T. Peacock and P. Dosser, 'Input–Output Analysis in an Underdeveloped Country: A Case Study', *Review of Economic Studies* (Oct 1957). The independence of sectors is summed up by saying that the input–output matrices tend to be 'triangular'.

economic resources and by imperfect social and administrative
arrangements. It is here that accounting prices of a few basic items,
even if these provide only rough estimates of the orders of magnitude involved, could be of great help in planning. The tendency to
decide on many costly projects – to be abandoned subsequently
when scarcities appear or constraints begin to bite – has been a
familiar aspect of planning in developing countries in recent years.
To the extent that the use of accounting prices helps to build the
most important scarcities and constraints into the planning calculations from the start, it should go some way in helping to curb this
practice.

4.6 ACCOUNTING PRICES IN THE ABSENCE OF MARKETS: 'INTANGIBLES'

Perhaps the greatest cause of the controversy over the use of cost–
benefit analysis is the attempts made by analysts to put values on
social effects in which there is no market, or in which there is reason
to suppose that existing markets do not value an effect completely.
There is, for example, no market in changes in the delinquency rate,
and yet urban renewal programmes will affect this rate, one way or
another. There is no market in defence – we do not buy it in the
same way that we buy other goods. There are no markets for many
types of disamenity such as noise and air pollution, although frequently these 'external effects' will affect property prices so that
there is at least some indication of the direction of change. It is unlikely, however, that these markets reflect the total externality costs.
There is a market in human life in the sense of insurance against the
risk of death, but it is a strange market since the beneficiary is, by
definition, not the person who pays the premiums! Alternatively, we
could think of human life being valued through death or accident
prevention schemes such as road barriers, lighting, speed limits and
so on. And yet the resulting *implicit* values would surprise most of
us. Perhaps the legal system could provide indicators through
damages awarded to persons involved in accidents or to their
dependants. That a human life should be valued at all in this way
will strike many as a morally reprehensible procedure, and yet these
values exist, whether we agree with them or not. In building a
motorway it is possible that the accident rate will increase. If life
has infinite value no motorways will be built. Hence the decision-
makers are already valuing lives at some 'shadow price' which is
at least less than the net measured benefits of building an accident-
generating motorway.

Labels for these types of benefits and costs are manifold, but they are frequently referred to as 'intangibles'. The term 'incommensurables' has also been used of human life and disamenity, but terminology of this kind prejudges an issue over which debate still rages. Logically, there can be no such thing as an 'incommensurable' good. By definition of the concept of a shadow price (see section 4.1), every outcome has a social opportunity cost, and hence a shadow price.

Why are there no markets for these outcomes? It may be that it is considered impracticable to charge for the benefits. Toll roads are one way of pricing for the use of road space, but the toll collection costs and general administrative costs may be prohibitive. Sometimes the prime beneficiaries are not the users of the project in question. Thus the Victoria underground railway in London was largely justified in terms of the benefits to *road* users in view of the reduced congestion on London's roads (Foster and Beesley [15]). It may be that the government has a distinct *policy* of not charging, for reasons of 'social need' or 'distributional equity'. This is the case with some irrigation schemes, and with the major part of the health and education services in the United Kingdom. Frequently, property rights simply do not exist and hence there is no market, as with fishing grounds outside territorial limits, or the seabed. Sometimes international legal agreement will invent property rights, as with seabed space in the North Sea for oil rigs. Sometimes it is too expensive to create the property rights (Demsetz [16]). Whatever the reason, it must be recognised that non-marketed benefits frequently play a substantial part in public investment decisions. The cost–benefit analyst must therefore come to terms with them, finding ways (*a*) to measure physical benefits and costs where no measure exists already, and (*b*) finding ways to estimate shadow prices once the physical measure of benefits and costs has been found.

Technically, once a physical unit exists it must also be possible to find a shadow price, the willingness to pay of society for those units. There is no necessity for purchasers to be aware of the units of measurement. We may have a good idea of what we are willing to pay to prevent aircraft noise, or, more correctly, what we require in compensation, even though we are unable to explain the mathematical properties of a decibel scale, or the meaning of a Noise and Number Index. Once the product has the attributes of a public good, however, the search for a shadow price may be doomed to failure, and the problem is that public investments frequently do exhibit just these characteristics. Thus, including services 'with pronounced external economies', Brownlee has estimated that, in 1960, public goods accounted for some 80 per cent of United States Government expenditure [17].

If the analyst decides that he can go no further than the measurement of physical outcomes, and that shadow prices cannot be ascribed, he can still prescribe 'best available' efficiency rules in terms of 'maximising physical benefits subject to a cost constraint' or 'minimising costs for a desired level of physical benefits'. Once he does this he undertakes 'cost-effectiveness' analysis which we distinguish here from cost–benefit analysis because of the absence of measures of willingness to pay (shadow prices).

Actually ascribing shadow prices can be immensely complex, so much so that the charge of 'arbitrariness' is difficult to counter. Several strategies are possible.

Firstly, consumer questionnaires can be used. Suitably phrased, it may be possible to find out what consumers would be willing to pay for x if x was sold on the market, or what consumers would require to put up with x if x is a nuisance. An example of this approach is given in a later chapter relating to the Third London Airport study. Suffice it to say here that questionnaires can be notoriously unreliable.

Secondly, there may be markets for similar goods outside the public sector. The obvious examples in advanced economies are education and health. Private education is obtainable and private health schemes exist. Are school fees and patient charges adequate surrogate prices? Allowance would have to be made for differences in quality (noticeable in both the education and health fields in the United Kingdom, for example) and in the likely effect on price if all education and health were marketed. In addition, it is marginal social cost that is relevant, and this may be difficult to measure, especially if the unit of output is unclear.

Thirdly, and least satisfactory, the cost of providing a service could be used to indicate its social value. Yet this assumes away any 'social profit' from the service, no allowance being made for willingness to pay exceeding average cost of provision.[1]

Fourthly, and as mentioned earlier, there are shadow prices implicit in government decisions. Benefits and costs are valued implicitly. The problems of adopting these implicit prices are the same

---

[1] This approach could be termed the 'national accounting' approach since public services are valued in this way in the national accounts. The national accounts do not, of course, purport to measure the social benefit of outputs, though many commentators treat them as if they do.

as those presented against the use of implicit distributional weights. Governments may not consciously take these 'intangible' effects into account, or, if they do, their valuation procedures need not bear any resemblance to the objective function adopted for the whole analysis.

Fifthly, the analyst may decide that the effort is not worth it: the degree of arbitrariness may be too high, or there may be no evident way of discovering values. If this is so, one procedure is essential. In the final analysis the non-valued benefits and costs must at least be listed as 'contingencies'. Thus, benefits may exceed costs by £10 million, and there may be a probable loss of 100 lives over the time period in question. At the very least, the decision-maker's problem is reduced to asking if those 100 lives are 'worth' the £10 million net benefit. Once the contingencies exceed more than one, however, the decision-maker will have difficulty in deciding the appropriate 'trade-off'. Net benefits may be £10 million, probable lives lost 100, and there may be some improvement in amenity. The decision-maker is forced to weight the gains and losses by his own preferences. The real danger to avoid is ignoring gains and losses simply because they cannot be valued. 'To base important policy decisions on only the dollar amounts that *can* be computed, just because they *are* the only dollar amounts, would be most dangerous; the underestimation of the most truly distinctive benefits of the program might be crucial' (Rothenberg [18]).

In terms of theory, all gains and losses have values. If a new airport saves time and brings trade, but inflicts noise and air pollution on the community, there is a trade-off. To say that the intangibles *cannot* be valued is possibly to say something true in the sense that it may be difficult, or even impossible, to estimate the trade-off. Some commentators imply a 'cannot' in the sense of *logical* impossibility, but this would be incorrect. At the other end of the spectrum, there will be the argument that some outcomes have infinite value. The destruction of a community, the irreversible loss of wildlife or plants, would seem to appear in this category. Yet if the community recognised them to have infinite value, there would be no change. Whatever the ethics of change, it does not put infinite prices on benefits and costs. But to say this much is not to be particularly helpful. The problem of benefit estimation remains, as the case studies at the end of the book show.

4.7 THE USEFULNESS OF ACCOUNTING PRICES

The derivation of relevant accounting prices is obviously an extremely difficult task. In consequence, many economists feel that the results do not justify the effort, given the degree of arbitrariness that must be involved. McKean [7] has emphasised the costs involved in obtaining shadow prices. Admitting that 'one often prefers imputed prices to no prices at all', he concludes, 'in what specific instances to impute prices, how far to go in refining those imputed prices, and whether to adjust market prices where they exist depends upon one's judgement about the cost and worth of the information' ([7] p. 57). The role of personal judgement is the real source of the criticisms of imputed price estimates, since it would appear to lend a large element of 'subjectivity' to a discipline which purports to be objective.

However, even if market prices exist, using them for the purposes of CBA might be no less subjective. Hence, the necessity of imputing prices in most cases cannot be avoided. In essence, the question of 'subjectivity' in CBA is related to the role of value judgements in policy decisions, which was discussed earlier in Chapter 3.

4.8 SUMMARY

The concept of an 'accounting' or 'shadow' price has been introduced. Given that the objective function in 'conventional' cost–benefit analysis is of the Pareto–Hicks–Kaldor type, the chapter derived the shadow prices implicit in the concept of Pareto optimality. At a first approximation, these prices were seen to be related to marginal cost for goods and services, and to the value of the marginal product for inputs. But the imperfections in the economic system which upset these equalities were noted, producing the conclusion that, *in theory*, market prices should not be used to value benefits and costs. Rather, some process of adjustment to secure the correct shadow price should take place. It was noted, however, that serious obstacles face anyone searching for 'true' shadow prices. Apart from the absence of markets in many cases – so that not even a first approximation to a shadow price can be made without establishing experiments in 'surrogate' markets – the 'second best' problem suggested that the use of a particular set of shadow prices in the public sector would not guarantee a move towards optimality if the relevant shadow prices were not in operation in all other sectors. It was suggested, however, that in some economies at least, the interdependence between sectors which underlies the 'second best' problem might not be very marked.

In conclusion, the doubts of economists about the *worth* of measuring shadow prices were recorded. The issue remains one of controversy.

5 External Effects and Public Goods

I T should be evident by now that CBA differs from a 'commercial' appraisal of a project or policy in that it attempts to embrace *all* costs and benefits, whether they accrue to the investing agency or not. A basic difference between commercial and social returns consists of the 'external' effects of the investment; hence the importance of these effects for CBA.[1]

So far we have provided no rigorous definitions of external effects or public goods, although both figured in section 4.4 as obstacles to the use of market prices.

5.1 DEFINING EXTERNALITIES

An external effect will be said to exist whenever

(*a*) economic activity in the form of production or consumption affects the production or utility levels of other producers or consumers;[2] and

(*b*) the effect is unpriced or uncompensated.

Condition (*a*) is the *interdependence* condition, and (*b*) is the *non-price* condition. Both conditions must obtain for an externality

---

[1] A number of terms have secured common usage. The reader should therefore be aware that external effects are frequently referred to as externalities, indirect effects, secondary benefits and costs, spillovers, repercussion effects and even 'linkages'. On some occasions, however, these terms are constrained to mean something more specific than the definition here. This is particularly true of 'secondary benefits' (see below, pp. 121–2).

External benefits and costs are external *to* some institution or set of persons. Usually, they are defined as being external to the investing agency, i.e. as being unreflected in its calculation of private benefit and cost. But they might equally well be external to any defined set of individuals.

[2] Strictly, it need not be just production and consumption. Externalities can arise because of government decisions, economic and non-economic.

to exist.[1] If interdependence exists, but the effect *is* priced, then the externality is said to be 'internalised'.

External effects may be either external benefits (economies) or external costs (diseconomies). In the former case, condition (*b*) can be restated as saying that there is *non-appropriation* of benefits. In the latter case, the costs are *uncompensated.* If the economy is divided into two sectors – producers and consumers – there are four types of interdependence for benefits and costs respectively. These are:

(i) *Producer–producer* externalities. In this case, the output of one particular firm depends directly or indirectly on the output of another firm or firms and the effect is unpriced. The externality may be 'input-generated' or 'output-generated'. Input-generated effects occur because of the use of particular inputs in the 'donor' firm. Output-generated effects arise directly from the output of the donor firm, independently of the nature of the production process. Usually, the distinction relates to situations in which a certain raw material is used (e.g. coal in coal-fired power stations, mercury in paper production) compared to situations where the final product itself has some waste component.[2]

(ii) *Producer–consumer externalities.* Whereas the interdependence condition for class (i) externalities requires the production or cost function of one producer to be partially dependent upon the output of another producer, producer–consumer interaction requires the consumer's utility function to be partly dependent upon the output of the 'donor' producer. For an externality to exist, of course, it must be the case that no trade, exchange or compensation occurs between the two. This category of externality is perhaps the most noticeable, and would include aircraft and motorway noise, air and water pollution, and many amenity losses.

(iii) *Consumer–producer externalities.* It is less easy to find examples of this type of interdependence, and they are probably correctly regarded as being unimportant.

[1] A number of writers regard the interdependence condition alone as sufficient for an externality to occur. See Buchanan and Stubblebine [1].

[2] Which in turn roughly corresponds to 'energy residuals' and 'materials residuals' – terms which now have an increasing use in the important and growing literature on environmental economics. 'Materials residuals' could also include materials as inputs, however. See A. V. Kneese, R. U. Ayres and R. C. D'Arge, *Economics and the Environment* (Baltimore, 1970). T. Scitovsky unjustly regarded the production–production type of externality as unimportant. See T. Scitovsky, 'Two Concepts of External Economies', *Journal of Political Economy* (Apr 1954), reprinted in Arrow and Scitovsky [1].

(iv) *Consumer–consumer* externalities. This type of externality has been extensively treated in the literature (Duesenberry [2], Kemp [3], Davis and Whinston [4], Dolbear [5] are useful references). A distinction is usually made between 'envy' and 'non-envy' externalities. In the former case, the welfare loss arises because the consumer is envious of another consumer's income or his possession of a certain good or set of goods. In the latter case, the envy effect is absent and the interdependence is similar to that in the producer–producer case. There is some disagreement as to whether envy is a 'proper' externality in that, although it clearly exists, some writers feel that, on ethical grounds, it should not be allowed to influence the rules for allocating resources (Mishan [6]).

Of the four categories it seems fair to say that the first two are the most noticeable and that, consequently, they are likely to figure significantly in cost–benefit analyses.

5.2 PECUNIARY AND TECHNOLOGICAL EXTERNALITIES

The externality relationships described in the previous sections can be either 'technological' or 'pecuniary'. The distinction between the two is conceptually clear: in practice, however, it may not be so obvious. Essentially, a *technological* externality occurs when the production function of the affected producer, or the utility function of the affected consumer, is altered. In the producer case, less (more) output is obtained for a given level of input because of the external diseconomy (economy). In the consumer case, less (more) utility is obtained from a given level of real income because of the diseconomy (economy). In short, technological externalities exist when the technical possibilities of transforming inputs into outputs are changed because of the actions of the externality-creating agent, and, it should be remembered, when this change in transformation possibilities goes unpriced.

A *pecuniary* externality relates to a change in the output or utility of a third party due to changes in the level of demand. Invariably, these effects will accrue to supply or processing industries (which corresponds to an earlier distinction between 'induced' and 'stemming' effects). An increased output of sugar beet, for example, will be reflected in a higher demand and hence higher profits for suppliers of agricultural machinery, seed suppliers and beet processors. Thus, pecuniary effects show up in changed prices and profits, but do not alter the technological possibilities of production.

It is usually argued that only technological externalities are relevant to a cost–benefit appraisal. In the sugar-beet example the valuation of increased beet output will already reflect the gains to suppliers and processors. To add pecuniary and technological effects would be to double-count. The fundamentally technological externalities reflect *real* gains or losses; pecuniary effects reflect only transfers from one section of the community to another, via changes in relative prices.[1] They are essentially transfers in the economic rents received by factors in less than perfectly elastic supply.

In so far as the pecuniary effects are mere transfers from one group to another, they clearly do not constitute an element of benefit or cost. But other non-technological external effects have been argued to constitute proper benefits or costs. These are comprised of output effects which result because of an increased (or decreased) scale of activity on the part of the third party, and which are not offset by losses (or gains) elsewhere. The condition for such non-technological output effects to occur is essentially that of under-full employment. In a full-employment context the output increase or decrease would be offset elsewhere in the economy. Prima facie, then, output generation effects in underemployment economies would seem to constitute 'proper' benefits (Hirschman [7]).

Against this argument it has been suggested that the inclusion of such output effects presupposes the continuation of under-full employment conditions, and that the forecasting of such changes is extremely difficult.[2]

[1] Pecuniary effects would, however, be very relevant if the social welfare function used in cost–benefit contained explicit distributional weights. In this case the incidence of the transfers would matter. It is shown below that externalities arise because of the failure of economies to extend the notion of a property right to what were once regarded as 'free' goods and resources. It has been suggested that, historically, in some circumstances, rights in existing prices have been established and that pecuniary externalities, in so far as they infringe upon those rights, are also relevant to social policy. 'If property rights are accepted, then Pareto-relevant externalities are defined, and it is logically consistent that they must be removed whether technological or pecuniary.' A. A. Schmid, 'Nonmarket Values and Efficiency of Public Investments in Water Resources', *American Economic Review, Papers and Proceedings* (1963).

[2] It is not always clear what the objections to the inclusion of 'secondary' output effects are. But they appear to be (*a*) that the increased demand for the 'secondary' product is at the expense of a demand expansion elsewhere in the economy, (*b*) that such demand expansions should be distinguished conceptually from the allocatory effects of a project and (*c*) that it is both unsafe and difficult to predict with any

5.3 THE SOURCE OF EXTERNAL EFFECTS

Externalities arise because of the failure to define and enforce property rights in certain areas of economic activity. Thus, the absence of property rights to watercourses and air space leads to the use of these resources as 'free goods', with the donor party feeling that he has a 'right' (since he has not been prohibited) to dispose of effluent into the water or the air, but with the recipient party feeling offended that *his* 'rights' to enjoy clean air and clean water have also been impaired. In other cases, rights are well defined, but enforcement of the law has fallen into abuse and the donor party comes to think of a resource as 'common property'. This is particularly true of rivers in the United Kingdom.

Clearly, externality problems can be 'resolved' by a complete definition and enforcement of property rights. But cost–benefit analysis tends to operate with the existing structure of property rights, which has led some writers to suggest that there is a fundamental asymmetry in the valuation procedure The asymmetry arises in that the need to obtain shadow prices is most urgent in cases of non-marketable outcomes, and these in turn are frequently the outcomes to which no property rights are ascribed. Other outcomes may have market prices attached to them. The non-market and market values are then added to obtain the overall net benefit figure. But suppose now that property rights were introduced in the

---

reasonable degree of accuracy the secondary employment effects, since it is not possible to say whether the unemployment in the secondary industries would have continued. Propositions (*a*) and (*b*) are expressed by P. D. Henderson, 'Some Unsettled Issues in Cost–Benefit Analysis', in P. Streeten (ed.), *Unfashionable Economics* (London, 1970). Proposition (*c*) is advanced in R. McKean, *Efficiency in Government through Systems Analysis* (New York, 1968). Thus, Henderson remarks that '. . . there are good grounds for adopting in project analysis a convention that any given increase in final demand, however induced and wherever it may take effect, should be regarded as precluding an equivalent increase elsewhere in the system. The justification for this procedure lies in the need to separate so far as possible questions of allocation from those relating to the determination of the total level of final demand' (p. 238). Henderson refers to I. M. D. Little and J. Mirrlees, *Manual of Industrial Project Analysis*, vol. II (O.E.C.D., Paris, 1970), but a reading of Little and Mirrlees suggests that their preference for ignoring these secondary benefits rests upon proposition (*c*). It is difficult to attach very much significance to propositions (*a*) and (*b*) since, *ex hypothesi*, they are inapplicable. Proposition (*c*) provides a forceful but pragmatic argument against the inclusion of secondary output benefits.

non-market outcomes. Would the resulting market values be the same as the imputed shadow prices obtained when no property rights existed? That they should be equal is one of the requirements for what some writers have called 'ideal' cost–benefit analysis.[1] In short, cost–benefit valuations should, on this argument, be independent of existing legal structures and institutions.

It is possible to see the asymmetry at work by contrasting the willingness-to-pay principle with the compensation principle. The first applies in situations where the property right does not yet exist, the latter where the right exists and is to be taken away. If a poor man has a right to a certain benefit, he might require a compensation sum of, say, £100 to compensate him for forgoing that benefit. But if he does not possess the right in the first place, his willingness to pay, being constrained by his income, to achieve the benefit might well be zero. The way in which property rights are distributed affects the valuations.

The argument has some force in so far as the existing distribution of property rights is historically determined and is therefore in some sense 'arbitrary'. Since the valuations in cost–benefit may reflect these property rights, these valuations are themselves, in this sense, 'arbitrary'. It is entirely analogous with the distribution of income argument of Chapter 2. We noted there that cost–benefit results tend to reflect the existing distribution of income. The debate concerning the admissibility or otherwise of distributional weights is equally applicable to the problem of property rights.

5.4 EXTERNALITIES, ALTERNATIVE TECHNOLOGIES AND CBA

Externalities arise because the 'donor' party engages in economic activity which either uses externality-generating inputs, or which involves the production of externality-generating outputs. Where production processes are constrained in number, the inputs giving rise to the externality might be a necessary condition of production at any level. Frequently, however, the donor party will have the choice of alternative activity: a firm, for example, may well have the chance of choosing a 'clean' technology as opposed to one which generates pollutants. This is true of 'recycling' procedures which aim at the reuse of inputs, such as water, within the production

[1] For Example, see E. J. Mishan, 'What is Wrong with Roskill', *Journal of Transport Economics and Policy* (Sept 1970), and the same author's *The Costs of Economic Growth* [8] chaps 5 and 6.

124   *Accounting Prices*

process. Most cost–benefit analyses tend to assume that the existing
technology is the least-cost one, and costs and benefits are valued
accordingly. It may well be, however, that the choice of an alternative technology is itself socially desirable in terms of producing
net social benefits. This section shows the relevance of cost–benefit
to this issue.

Fig. 5.4.1 shows the donor's *marginal* net gain function (G_D) in a
context of external costs. The function L_R is the *marginal* net loss
function of the recipient of the external cost, and, for convenience,

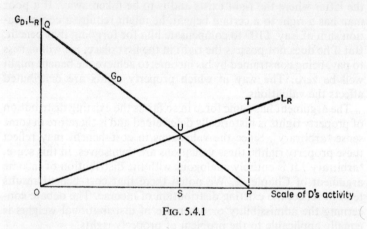

FIG. 5.4.1

each function is assumed to take on the simple properties shown in
the diagram. The vertical axis measures gains and losses; the horizontal axis measures the scale of D's activity. If D is a maximiser of
his own self-interest, he will operate at point P where his marginal
net gains are zero. At this point, R suffers total losses equal to the
area under the L_R function. Inspection of the diagram shows that P
is not a 'social' optimum in the sense of maximising the added gains
and losses of D and R. For net social gains at P are OQP minus
$OTP = OUQ - UTP$. But moving to a scale of activity S, net social
gains are OUQ, which is clearly an improvement. If activity is
reduced below S, social gains would be less than OUQ. Hence point
S is a point of socially optimal activity by D.

If a cost–benefit analysis was carried out to discover whether D's
activity is desirable, in the Pareto sense, it can be seen from the
diagram that D's operations at point P would be sanctioned. Social
benefits (OQP) are clearly greater than social costs (OTP). As long
as no compensation is *actually* paid by D to R, D can over-
compensate R in the sense that he can pay all the social costs and

still be left with net benefits. But if we use cost–benefit to assess the socially optimal *scale* of *D*'s activity, it will show that *D* should operate at point *S*. At *S*, *net* social benefits are maximised, as we showed in the previous paragraph. The example serves to illustrate the important distinction between the use of cost–benefit to assess a project or policy of *given scale* ($\bar{x}$) and its use in assessing the *optimal scale* (x^*). That is, writing the net benefit function as

$$B(x) - K(x) = \text{net } B(x)$$

the function may be used to assess whether

$$B(\bar{x}) - C(\bar{x}) > 0$$

or to find x^* where x^* is the value which maximises the net benefit function. Obviously, x^* is achieved where $\text{MB}(x) = \text{MC}(x)$, i.e. where the marginal benefits equal the marginal costs. This is formally equivalent to the scale *S* in Fig. 5.4.1. The 'given scale' approach is familiar in situations where the investment is indivisible, or where some concept of 'social need' has pre-empted the possibility of considering different scales of activity. The latter approach corresponds to the more traditional 'marginalist' analysis.

Depending on the way in which the project problem is formulated, then, cost–benefit will sanction *D*'s activity at *P*, *provided no compensation is paid to R*. If compensation is actually paid, *P* would operate at the socially optimal point *S* of his own 'volition'. At all points to the left of *S*, *D* can compensate *R* for each marginal unit of loss. To the right of *S*, however, he cannot do so, since his marginal benefits are less than the marginal costs he imposes on *R*.[1] Hence the existence of procedures which entail the payment of compensation will tend to bring about the optimal scale of *D*'s activity.

Notice that the optimal scale does not eliminate the externality.

[1] There is a considerable literature on the relative merits of such 'government-assisted' compensation remedies and their 'bargaining' counterpart. With the bargaining solution *R* would be willing to 'compensate' (though 'bribe' seems more apposite) *D* to move back from *P* towards *S*, since *R* suffers costs in excess of *D*'s gains. Whether compensation or bribes are adopted, the allocatory solution is the same. The resulting distribution of income is different, however, and the compensation alternative requires a legal framework which the bribe solution does not. As noted earlier, however, the idea of the bribe solution might strike many as ethically unacceptable. In addition, and most seriously, bargaining solutions are hardly ever likely to arise in real-life contexts of serious externalities such as air and water pollution. A very brief analysis of the main issues is to be found in Turvey [9].

What does disappear is what has been called the 'Pareto-relevant' externality – i.e. the area $SUTP$.[1] It follows that legislation to eliminate externalities may not yield the socially optimal results which would be recommended by cost–benefit analysis. Indeed, elimination could mean the end of the activity which generates the externality if alternative productive processes are not available. This is the reason sometimes advanced for the continuance of serious pollution activities.

In many cases, however, it is possible for an alternative productive process to be employed. 'Clean' technology may replace the existing technology. In general, clean technologies tend to be more expensive than existing technologies, so that their introduction would tend to raise D's costs and therefore shift his marginal gain curve in Fig. 5.4.1 to the left. On the other hand, it will reduce R's externally received costs. The situation is shown in Fig. 5.4.2 below.

In the upper part of the diagram, the loss function is shifted downwards on a pivot. The gain function is shifted leftwards, owing to the higher costs of the clean technology. For diagrammatic convenience, the new social optimum with the clean technology is assumed to coincide, in terms of D's activity, with the old social optimum. The lower part of the diagram traces out the net marginal social benefit functions relating to the old and new technologies.

The social benefits of the clean technology are best judged in comparison to the previous private optimum, with D operating at point P. In terms of the areas marked on the lower part of Fig. 5.4.2, the net benefits of D's activity were

$$(1)+(2)-[(3)+(4)+(5)].$$

Now, if D is allowed to maximise his own utility (profit) function while bearing the costs of the new technology, he will operate at P' and net social benefits will be

$$(1)-(3).$$

Hence the gains from introducing the new technology will be this second expression minus the first one, i.e.

$$-(2)+(4)+(5).$$

[1] A Pareto-relevant externality exists if modification of existing behaviour can take place in such a way as to make one party better off without the other party being worse off (see Buchanan and Stubblebine [1]). For reasons stated at the end of this chapter it should not be assumed, however, that policies designed to eliminate externalities altogether are undesirable. They may be so in the limited sense of Pareto optimality, but not in a wider context (see below, pp. 128–9).

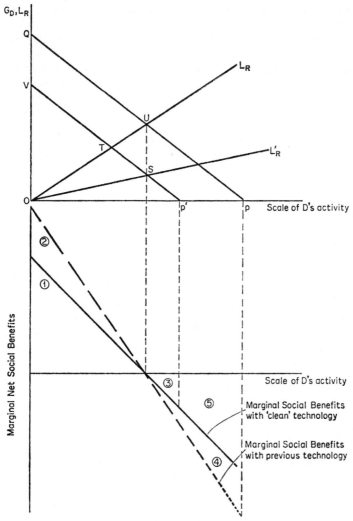

FIG. 5.4.2

Notice that the introduction of the new technology may therefore
yield fewer net social benefits than in the *status quo* situation. Notice
too that the chances of the new technology being considered socially
desirable are improved if D is also required to operate at the optimal
point S. In this case, the benefits of the change are

$$-(2)+(3)+(4)+(5)$$

which is an obvious improvement over the previous change in net benefits.

The evaluation of clean technologies is an increasingly important application of cost–benefit analysis. Water and air pollution abatement schemes frequently involve the introduction of cleansing and filtering apparatus, storage reservoirs to augment river flows during dry seasons, and so on. The same is true of noise-suppression devices for motor-cars and aircraft. The previous analysis shows, in terms of a very elementary model, that such changes are capable of evaluation but that further adjustments to the output of the donor party may be necessary even after the introduction of the new technology.

5.5 EXTERNALITIES AND FUTURE GENERATIONS

In the analysis of section 5.4 it was implicitly assumed that the gain and loss function of D and R were known. Further, the relevance of cost–benefit was described in terms of an assumed Pareto-type objective function. In practice, there are two major difficulties with this approach.

First, benefit and cost functions for all affected parties cannot always be specified. Chapter 4 illustrated some of the difficulties of deriving shadow prices for non-marketed outcomes. But, frequently, some externalities are largely unforeseen: for example, 'ecological externalities', which have as yet to receive proper attention from economists. Given that humans and other animal species exist in a context of complex interaction with their environment, changes in that environment will have repercussions on living species, including the existing generations and, more significantly, future generations. But the precise nature of the ecological links between humans and their environment is not known. Indeed, it seems fair to say that aspects of the links only become known when ecological 'mistakes' occur, such as the overuse of herbicides and pesticides. It follows that many projects will generate externalities the nature of which is not known. They may be rapid in their emergence, as with the detrimental effects of a mammoth irrigation dam, or they may bring about the change only slowly, as with the effects of DDT on wildlife and human health.

It would seem preferable to treat these externalities in the context of uncertainty. Since the consequences cannot, in the current state of knowledge, be easily foreseen, some assessment must at least be made of the possible effects.

By and large, little effort has been made to consider the ecological effects of major investments. Two reasons might be advanced as a justification. Firstly, the ecological effects of an individual investment might be considered marginal, while it is accepted that the effects of investment in the aggregate might be substantial. And secondly, the effects are usually of the slowly accruing kind. Since individuals (and politicians) tend to be notoriously myopic, they ignore consequences which are likely to affect them only in the distant future. Perhaps more significantly, many ecological changes will affect only future generations. This raises the second problem mentioned – that of adopting a Pareto-type objective function.

Almost by definition, the Pareto criterion precludes consideration of future generations. Since they do not yet exist (at least, not as preference-expressing agents) their preferences cannot be known. Judgements must therefore be made on one of two bases. Either the current generation *alone* must count, *or* the decision-maker must judge *on behalf* of future generations, guessing as to their likely preferences. Cost–benefit analysis tends either to limit society to present generations, or it implicitly assumes that future generations will have a want structure very much like the existing one. As such, the two approaches tend to produce the same answers. However, ecological externalities frequently take on the attribute of 'irreversibility'; that is, they produce effects which cannot be altered. In these cases, the most familiar of which are the elimination of wildlife species, the future generation is being denied the option of expressing a preference which diverges from that of the current generation, assuming that the current generation is aware of the consequence. There is no possibility of 'disinvesting' in such a way as to restore the *status quo*.[1]

In order that CBA may yield rules relating to the optimal use of exhaustible resources, an extension of the population reference implied by Pareto, or any other welfare criterion, to include future generations would be called for.

[1] We might of course have similar 'regrets' about the passing of the dinosaur, but the difference in the examples lies in the fact that the dinosaur disappeared at a time when other species were emerging. The current problem is that there is a distinct and real danger that we shall have fewer and fewer species, uncompensated for by the appearance of others. And, if some writers are correct, one species in danger of self-elimination is *Homo sapiens*. See, for example, P. and A. Ehrlich, *Population, Resources, Environment* (San Francisco, 1970).

E

5.6 COLLECTIVE GOODS

The necessary requirements that have to exist before a good can be called a 'collective' good have generated a considerable amount of confusing terminology in the literature (see Head [10], Buchanan [11], Musgrave [12], Samuelson [13], Mishan [14]). The competing claims of those who would use separate definitions are not discussed here. We propose the following classification of characteristics:

    (*a*) non-excludability;

    (*b*) non-rivalry in consumption.

Condition (*a*) states that if a good is provided to one person it is provided to others simply because the others cannot be excluded from the benefit (or cost if it is a 'public bad'). Condition (*b*) states that if the good is consumed by one person it does not prevent the good being consumed by another person; that is, consumption of the good by one individual is not at the expense of consumption of the good by another individual.

For a good to be a collective good, it will be argued that *both* conditions must apply. Various other combinations of the two characteristics and their opposites will define other goods. Thus, a good which is 'rival' in consumption and 'excludable' is generally a 'private' good, the normal type of good which is discussed in the economic literature.[1]

However, many goods can be provided jointly, including railway and bus seats. Yet these goods are not collective goods as defined here: they are goods in joint user supply, but they are not collective goods. The difference lies in condition (*b*) above. It is possible to devise discriminatory pricing systems to exclude some potential purchasers from enjoying the benefits of a railway seat. It is not possible to exclude other persons from enjoying the benefits of a defence system once it is introduced, or, at the very least, it is far less easy to devise a system of exclusion.[2] Thus collective goods are

---

[1] Very explicit accounts of the characteristics of public goods are given in Head [10] and Peston [18]. Head uses the term 'joint supply' for what is termed here 'non-rivalness'. The 'rivalry' terminology derives in turn mainly from Musgrave [12]. Joint supply is a somewhat misleading term in that, historically, it refers to joint production supply – e.g. wool and mutton. The joint supply concept used by Head is really joint *user* supply.

[2] The problem lies in defining what is meant by the *possibility* of exclusion. Scrambling devices could be used to discriminate between receivers of broadcasting signals, but the cost would be prohibitive. To this extent, the definition of collectivity is one of degree. On the relevance of exclusion costs, see Millward [15].

in joint supply in the sense that they are not only available to more than one user, but that all users share the goods equally.

The converse of a collective good is a collective 'bad' – air pollution, for example. Collective bads affect many users but the element of non-exclusivity is less pronounced. It is possible to devise a system whereby those who are willing to pay for air filters and smog masks can reduce the nuisance to themselves.

The two corollaries of the definition of a collective good are:

(a) That the consumption of the good by individual *A* does not reduce the consumption of the good by individual *B*. This characteristic differentiates collective and private goods, and is often referred to as 'non-rivalry' in consumption.
(b) What amounts to the same thing, that the marginal cost of supplying the collective good to an extra person is zero.

The effect of the existence of collective goods on the overall Pareto optimality conditions of Chapter 2 is to alter them as follows. If there are two goods, a private one *P*, and a collective one *C*, then optimality requires

$$MRT_{P,C} = MRS^1_{P,C} + MRS^2_{P,C}$$

i.e. the marginal rate of transformation between the two goods should be equal to the *sum* of the marginal rates of substitution of each consumer (1 and 2).[1]

Diagrammatically, this condition requires that the aggregate demand curve for a collective good be obtained by *vertically sum-*

[1] This is the condition derived in P. Samuelson, 'The Pure Theory of Public Expenditure', *Review of Economics and Statistics* (Nov 1954). In his article on externalities, Professor Buchanan has argued that externalities are analysable in terms of joint supply since they are essentially by-products of either the production or the consumption process. Buchanan therefore uses joint supply to mean both production jointness *and* user jointness (see Buchanan [11]). But Samuelson has restated the different optimality conditions required for goods in production jointness and goods in user jointness. The former require

$$MRT_{P,J} = MRS^1_{P,A+B} = MRS^2_{P,A+B}$$

where *J* is the joint product (say, sheep) and *A* and *B* are divisions of the joint product (e.g. wool and mutton). This condition is not the same as that presented for collective goods – i.e. goods in user jointness (see Samuelson [13]).

ming the individual demand curves, rather than *horizontally summing* them in the normal private goods case. The contrast is shown in Fig. 5.6.1 below.

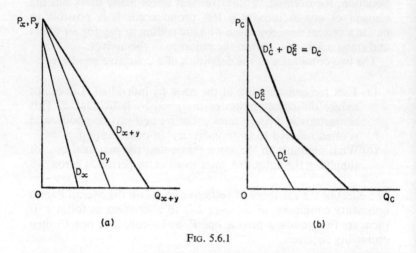

(a)   (b)

FIG. 5.6.1

In (a) the demand curves are added horizontally to obtain D_{x+y}, but in (b) the individual demand curves are summed vertically to obtain D_C since C is consumed in equal amounts by each person.

Given the existence of user-jointness and non-excludability, a problem arises in that consumers will have an incentive to understate their true preferences for a public good. For if the good is supplied to one individual it must necessarily be supplied to other individuals, so that any one individual can understate the benefits to him of securing the good. An observation of 'willingness to pay' therefore understates the true willingness to pay; the social benefits of public goods are therefore difficult to assess by direct reference to revealed preferences expressed in terms of monetary bids. Some other system of preference revelation is required and it must be one which overcomes the 'free rider' problem noted above. A simple voting procedure, for example, will tend to have this effect since each voter will know that the price paid for the good will be shared equally between voters (via tax payments, say).[1] However, simple

[1] Note that such taxes involve a distributional problem in that persons not willing to pay anything nonetheless have the good made available to them, and others will be willing to pay more than their tax burden for their 'share' of the good.

voting procedures do not meet the requirements of Pareto improvements, since the minority loses and is therefore worse off. Nothing in the voting system can guarantee that the majority can overcompensate the minority.

Clearly, the existence of collective goods poses a serious problem for cost–benefit analysis. The 'output' of many public projects frequently comprises goods which have a substantial degree of 'publicness'. Flood control, education programmes, health improvements, environment protection and depollution policies all share this characteristic. The fact that it is difficult (or, as many would argue, impossible) to discover the true preferences of individuals does not of course mean that no decision procedure based on individual wants is possible for collective goods. Political mechanisms provide potential means for the expression of 'non-market' preferences in these cases.

Suppose that the inhabitants of a particular area are asked to express a vote about the desirability of building a sewage plant, the benefits of which would accrue in the form of a cleaner local river which, in its clean state, can be used for recreational purposes. The cost is known, and it is calculated that local taxes would have to increase by 10 per cent per household to meet this cost. If the referendum limits replies to 'yes' and 'no', and if only the one price (i.e. the tax increase) is quoted, then a 100 per cent affirmative response would indicate a willingness to pay in excess of the cost. Indeed, in this situation, it can be said that WTP is *at least* as great as the cost of the project, since some residents are likely to have a WTP in excess of the tax increase – they have a consumer's surplus at that price. But it is not possible to determine whether a response that is less than 100 per cent affirmative implies an excess of WTP over costs. Thus, if 70 per cent answer 'yes', and each experiences no consumer's surplus at that price, then WTP is less than cost. But there is no direct way of finding out whether those in favour do have consumer's surplus at that price. The only acceptable procedure would be to vary the price by including in the referendum various increases in taxes, and asking each respondent to indicate at what point on the scale of tax changes his preference changes from negative to positive. In this way, the referendum simulates a market for the collective good.

Now, whether the 'free rider' problem arises depends on whether the local residents know that the project is to be financed by a tax affecting everyone in an equal fashion, or whether the tax will be proportional to their expressed willingness to pay. In the former case there is, technically, no free rider problem. But, by taxing each

resident equally, the price charged will not equal – except by unlikely accident – the benefit received by each resident. Individuals
will therefore be in disequilibrium in the sense that the price (i.e. the
increment in local tax) will not equal the marginal benefit gained.
There can then be no clear guide as to how much depollution should
be supplied. Of course, the individual disequilibria may lead to
adjustment mechanisms – some people may move from the area,
while others may engage in political activity to secure some altera-
tion in the supply of the collective good.

In the latter case, where taxes are related to willingness to pay,
each individual knows that he personally cannot influence the final
outcome of the referendum. It may be to his advantage, therefore,
to understate a true preference for the project in the expectation
that the preferences of others will secure the project. Since exclusion
from the benefits of the project is not possible, the 'free rider' individual secures the benefit at a cost to himself which is less than
that he is really willing to bear. As a further variant, the referendum
could imply that the project will be supplied free of charge if the
residents want it. As long as the project itself entails no external
costs (e.g. the sewage plant may itself be unattractive), a zero price
will attract a 100 per cent affirmative response. As Bohm [16] points
out, these alternative referenda – one with an incentive to understate preferences because of the free rider problem, the other with
an incentive to overstate because the benefits are thought to be free
(most usually because the project is financed from central government funds) – would at least set lower and upper bounds to the
WTP magnitude. Indeed, Bohm suggests that the means of finance
should be declared to be unknown, so that individuals are in a state
of uncertainty as to which form of bias they should exhibit in order
to serve their own interests. Given that the individual is now uncertain as to which strategy to pursue, it may well be that he will opt
for the 'safe' solution and declare his true preferences.

Whether such procedures are likely to avoid bias is largely a
matter of empirical testing. Bohm [17] has already produced a
simple pilot experiment which tends to confirm his thesis. In short,
it may well be that the 'free rider' problem is not so serious after all.
It is significant that it has become part of the established 'lore' of
welfare and cost–benefit problems without anyone once having
tested whether the misrepresentation of preferences actually does
occur.

An added problem arises when the collective good yields benefits
not just to the local population, but to residents outside the local
area. It is important to define the population that receives the

benefits of the collective good (or the disbenefits if the output is a collective 'bad'). For purposes of cost–benefit analysis, then, it is important to consider the population affected, and not just the population that is likely to finance the good.

5.7 SUMMARY

This chapter has been concerned with two types of 'market imperfection' which preclude the use of market prices as guides to shadow prices. The existence of external effects provides much of the justification for cost–benefit analysis, and the divergence between private and social costs necessitates either an adjustment to market prices to allow for externalities, or a separate assessment of the external benefits and costs. The latter is the procedure adopted in cost–benefit analysis. Public goods, which are clearly closely allied to goods exhibiting external effects, generate a serious problem of valuation since their market prices, if they have them, cannot be construed as proper indicators of willingness to pay. The non-revelation of true preferences exists because of the 'user-jointness' exhibited by public goods. It seems fair to say that no clear-cut procedure exists to guide the cost–benefit analyst in the evaluation of public goods (or bads).

6 The Social Rate of Discount

INVESTMENT in capital projects involves the sacrifice of present benefits in favour of future benefits. In this chapter we shall limit the definition of benefits to consumption goods, but, unless otherwise stated, the arguments can be restated in terms of general benefits. The sacrifice of present consumption would not be worth while unless the gains in future consumption are greater. Essentially, then, an investment is worth while if the future gains in consumption are regarded as being in excess of the current sacrifice of consumption, viewed from the point of view of the chosen social welfare function. It is important to define the meaning of 'future gains in consumption' carefully. These gains will be distributed over the lifetime of the project. One simple procedure would be to add up all the consumption benefits regardless of when they occur. But such a procedure would ignore the existence of 'social time preference' – a preference which society supposedly exhibits for present benefits over future benefits.

If *individuals* prefer £1 of consumption benefits now to £1 of consumption benefits in the future, the principle of consumers' sovereignty, which we noted was fundamental to most cost–benefit procedures, requires that the present ('year 1') benefit be weighted more heavily than the future benefit in calculating the *social* value of a project. Let the relevant weight, yet to be derived, on year 1 consumption benefit be 'w', and let consumption benefit in years 1 and 2 be C_1 and C_2. Then the worth from the standpoint of *present* society of the two consumption flows is

$$C_0 = w \cdot C_1 + C_2$$

where C_0 is the weighted sum of consumption benefits.

Essentially, if C_2 is regarded as 'numeraire', then w is the weight by which C_1 must be multiplied in order that C_1 and C_2 can be added together to give a measure of social benefit. If the present benefit is to count more heavily than the future benefit, then w must be greater than unity. In fact what we have is the 'accounting price' of present benefits as compared with future benefits: w can be construed as the price which reflects society's 'trade-off' between the present and the future.

The equation above could equally well have been written

$$\frac{C_0}{w} = \text{PV}(C) = C_1 + \frac{C_2}{w}$$

where PV(C) now reads the 'present value' of consumption benefits – i.e. the value to society from its present standpoint. The weight w is now divided into C_2 so that $1/w$ becomes a 'discount factor'. In general it will be found that $w > 1$, so that $1/w < 1$. The problems of deciding upon the appropriate value of w is the subject of this chapter.

6.1 SOCIAL TIME PREFERENCE

The reasons for supposing that the rate of time preference is positive and greater than unity could be:

(a) Society simply does prefer the present to the future – there is 'pure myopia'.

(b) Future generations are likely to have higher levels of consumption. If the principle of diminishing marginal utility of consumption operates, then the utility gains to future generations from a gain in consumption will be less than the utility gains to the present generation from the same gain. Hence, the future gain should be 'discounted'.

Reason (a) simply declares that individuals *do* prefer the present to the future. Reason (b) may take two forms. *Either* it gives a *reason* for individuals having a preference for the present, *or* it is a normative statement to the effect that decision-makers *should* discount future benefits because they will accrue to richer generations. If individuals are consciously aware of future generations' likely improved consumption levels, then the diminishing marginal utility argument might explain their preference for present benefits. The two reasons would effectively collapse into one. Since the underlying value premise of cost–benefit analysis is that there should be appeal to individuals' preferences, it follows that the discount factor can be derived from the expression of these preferences.

But the diminishing marginal utility argument is sometimes advanced as a separate normative judgement. This presumes that individuals are unaware of the utility argument concerning future generations. (They may nonetheless discount the future for reasons of 'impatience'. Whether such reasons are to be counted 'rational' or not is a moot point.) It may nonetheless be argued that those responsible for social decision-making should discount future benefits in light of the consumption-utility argument. In this respect the argument is a normative one and does not make reference to individuals' preferences.

Of course, with either approach the preferences of future generations are not recorded. The 'democrat' could argue that he is unable to take account of future generations' preference because he does not know them, and, further, democracy implies that *recorded* preferences only be taken into account. Thus, Marglin [1] remarks, 'Whatever else democratic theory may or may not imply, I consider it axiomatic that a democratic government reflects only the preferences of the individuals who are presently members of the body politic' (p. 97). Others might reply that this generation has a special collective responsibility for future generations and that individuals do not exhibit rationality in their time preference. To take account of irrational preferences may therefore be to jeopardise the welfare of future generations. It is this argument which is most commonly used against attempts to incorporate argument (*a*) into any derivation of a social time preference rate (STPR) (Pigou [2], Dobb [3], Sen [4]).

In addition, even if individuals are 'rational' in their expression of time preference, they may not be rational in the collective sense, as we note below.

Will market rates reflect social time preference? Certainly, the existence of positive interest rates suggests that people do discount future expenditures compared to present ones. If no allowance is made for risk, the relevant market rate would be the one which reflects individuals' willingness to make risk-free loans, i.e. the government borrowing rate. The use of this rate for social discounting has considerable attractions. Firstly, it is easily observed (though some decision has to be reached about whether it is the long or short rate which is used). Secondly, it appears to meet the requirement generally made in private investment decisions – that the rate of return should exceed the cost of capital to the firm. Since the cost of capital to the government is its borrowing rate, the analogy is met.

However, there is little reason to suppose that market rates actually do reflect time preference rates. Firstly, individuals may not express all their preferences concerning the future in the market place. Secondly, individuals behave in a 'schizophrenic' fashion (Marglin's term [1]). Their preferences expressed as individuals may not be the same as their preferences expressed when they see themselves as part of a community. Thus it is probable that society as a whole would have a *lower* rate of discount in its collective attitude than the observed market rates which reflect the individual's myopia.

The argument so far seems to suggest that, if one is a 'democrat', discounting is justified whatever the source of the present society's preferences for the present over the future. The 'authoritarian' argument (the epithet is Marglin's and tends slightly to prejudge the issue: the term 'utilitarian' is far more appropriate) gives this generation responsibility for future generations and therefore rejects any irrationality in time preference. The obvious fear of the utilitarians is that acceptance of irrational time preference will entail a higher discount rate (a high rate of time preference) and hence less investment, which in turn means less capital stock to be passed on to future generations. Clearly the issue of which argument to accept depends upon which set of value judgements is the most appealing.

What preferences are regarded as being 'irrational' by the utilitarians? The first source of myopia would seem eminently rational. Given the choice between £1 of consumption now and £1 later, the consumption goods being equivalent and tastes unchanging, there are two elements of risk involved in accepting the future bundle of goods. The goods themselves may not materialise and the recipient, being mortal, may not be able to receive the goods because he himself is dead. The first type of uncertainty has sometimes been used to substantiate some sort of risk premium being attached to any rate of discount (see Chapter 8). The latter type of uncertainty, the risk of death, would seem, in theory, to be a legitimate source for deriving some sort of pure time preference date. Eckstein [5] has calculated 'rational individual time preference' rates based upon this type of uncertainty. His results show rates of 0·4 per cent for the United States and 2·15 per cent for India for the 40–44 age group (approximately the median group in his table), with a range of 0·04 per cent (5–9 age group) to 7·45 per cent (80–84) for the United States, and 1·50 per cent to 10·55 per cent for India for the same age range. The rates for the United States are, as Eckstein remarks, 'amazingly low', and should be treated with some caution. In particular the results are outdated by the fall in the Indian death rate in recent years.

The utilitarian would still wish to reject the admissibility of risk-of-death time preference as far as the calculation of a social discount rate is concerned. His reasoning would be to the effect that *social* time preference relates to society, and not to an aggregate of present-day individuals. Although individuals are mortal, society is not (nuclear holocausts excepted, presumably). Thus, consumers' sovereignty is rejected in this respect also.

In an age when future generations face a high probability of inheriting substantial capital equipment, the utilitarian argument would seem slightly dated. But in another respect it is doubly relevant. For future generations most certainly do not seem likely to inherit natural resources on anything like the scale at present being exploited. In other words, some natural resources, such as arable and afforested land, will be seriously depleted. Over-utilisation of such resources can, and does, result in 'irreversible externalities' which, if the preferences of the future could be known, may be to the detriment of future generations, as we have seen in Chapter 5. There is then an argument for less present consumption of natural resources, and more investment in conservation. It may well be that dual criteria are needed, one for capital investments which do not yield significant externalities, and one for investments in conservation (national parks, coastline preservation, etc.). In short, the discount rate on conservation projects should be low, whatever the preferences of society. This argument, which has considerable importance in both advanced and underdeveloped economies, has been advanced by Baumol [6] and Tullock [7].

We turn now to argument (b), the DMUC argument. *If* it could be argued that the diminishing marginal utility of consumption is an observable fact, and *if* consumption per head is observed to rise over time, then the DMUC argument would also involve two value judgements, namely, that present preferences should count, and future preferences should count also. Since, by observation, future preferences for a given £1's worth of consumption are less than present preferences, a discount rate based on this DMUC is justified. The DMUC argument therefore belongs properly to the utilitarians, those who believe that present generations have some responsibility for future generations.

Of course, it is perfectly possible to be both a utilitarian and a democrat in respect of discount rates, i.e. to accept both arguments. The social rate of discount which results will then reflect both pure time preference and DMUC. If labels are required, we can summarise the argument as follows:

(i) democrat: $\text{STPR} = l + d$;
(ii) utilitarian: $\text{STPR} = r$;
(iii) 'democrat—utilitarian': $\text{STPR} = l + d + r$;

where l is the pure myopia rate of discount,[1] d the risk-of-death rate of discount and r the DMUC rate of discount. Notice that estima-

[1] That is, myopia in the sense that DMUC is not consciously determining individuals' intertemporal preferences.

tion of *l* would be excessively difficult. Finally, if current generations are not *aware* that future generations will be richer – i.e. if they do not consciously prefer the present because of this – the DMUC argument reduces to a purely normative proposition about inter-generational equity. One suspects that, in practice, people are aware of their offspring's expectations of increased levels of consumption.

6.2 THE DERIVATION OF SOCIAL TIME PREFERENCE RATE FROM DIMINISHING MARGINAL UTILITY OF CONSUMPTION

We consider now the derivation of a discount rate on the basis of the hypothesis of diminishing marginal utility of consumption.[1]

Assume that each individual has a utility function relating his utility to his consumption, the function being of the form shown in Fig. 6.2.1 below. The corresponding *marginal* utility function is shown in Fig. 6.2.2.

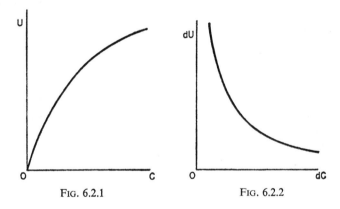

FIG. 6.2.1   FIG. 6.2.2

Fig. 6.2.2 depicts marginal utility (dU) against marginal changes in consumption (dC), and the curve is assumed to have a particular shape: it has a *constant* elasticity. This means that a percentage rise

---

[1] Clearly, there is a problem of testing for the diminishing marginal utility of consumption. Frisch [8] has argued for a diminishing rate on the basis of cross-section data – i.e. different income groups at some point in time – but others (e.g. Pearce [9]) doubt whether Frisch was measuring the marginal *utility* of consumption. Apart from problems of estimation, the issue is not significantly different for time-series data – i.e. observing changes in marginal utilities over time.

in consumption will lead to an equal percentage fall in marginal utility. There is nothing sacred about this particular shape of the marginal utility function, but it is convenient for purposes of computation.

The curve in Fig. 6.2.2 has the equation

$$\frac{dU}{dC} = aC^{-e} \tag{6.1}$$

where a is constant and $-e$ is the elasticity of the function.[1] This equation relates, for the moment, to consumption per head. Now equation (6.1) will hold for each time period, so that, writing dU/dC as $U'(C)$, we have for the time periods t and $t+1$

$$U'(C_t) = a \cdot C_t^{-e} \tag{6.2}$$

and $$U'(C_{t+1}) = a \cdot C_{t+1}^{-e}. \tag{6.3}$$

Now suppose $C_t < C_{t+1}$. The assumption of DMUC entails that

$$U'(C_{t+1}) < U'(C_t).$$

The ratio of the two marginal utilities therefore exceeds unity:

$$\frac{U'(C_t)}{U'(C_{t+1})} > 1.$$

Let this ratio equal $1+r$. Then

$$(1+r) \cdot U'(C_{t+1}) = U'(C_t). \tag{6.4}$$

What interpretation is to be attached to equation (6.4)? It tells us that the marginal utility of consumption in period $t+1$ needs to be multiplied by some factor greater than unity for it to be regarded as 'socially equal' to the extra utility derived from incremental consumption in period t.

Equation (6.4) can be rewritten as

$$U'(C_{t+1}) = U'(C_t) \cdot \frac{1}{1+r} \tag{6.5}$$

[1] By definition

$$-e = \frac{d^2U}{dC^2} \bigg/ \frac{dU}{dC} \div \frac{dC}{C},$$

so that

$$d \cdot \log \frac{dU}{dC} = -e \cdot d \cdot \log C$$

and, by integration,

$$\frac{dU}{dC} = a \cdot C^{-e}.$$

so that $(1+r)$ can be thought of as the weight to be attached to earlier consumption compared to later consumption, and the ratio $1/1+r$ can be thought of as the 'discount factor' which has to be applied to future consumption to give it a present value. In short, $1/1+r$ is the discount factor derived from the DMUC argument, and r is the actual rate of discount.

Equation (6.4) or (6.5) can be rewritten as

$$r = \frac{U'(C_t)}{U'(C_{t+1})} - 1. \tag{6.6}$$

Substituting equations (6.2) and (6.3) in equation (6.6) gives

$$r = \frac{a \cdot C_t^{-e}}{a \cdot C_{t+1}^{-e}} - 1$$

$$= \left(\frac{C_{t+1}}{C_t}\right)^e - 1. \tag{6.7}$$

Now let the rate of growth of consumption per head be b, such that

$$b = \frac{C_{t+1} - C_t}{C_t}. \tag{6.8}$$

Then

$$1 + b = 1 + \frac{C_{t+1} - C_t}{C_t}$$

i.e.

$$1 + b = \frac{C_{t+1}}{C_t}. \tag{6.9}$$

Equation (6.7) can therefore be written

$$r = (1+b)^e - 1 \tag{6.10}$$

which is the required expression for a social discount rate, r, based on the DMUC hypothesis. Two variables, the rate of growth of consumption per head, and the elasticity of the marginal utility function, are required for purposes of estimation.

The calculation of r has been in terms of consumption *per head*, since, with Meade [10], we argue that it is proper to take account not only of the total consumption available, but the number of persons who can share that consumption. The population variable can be made explicit. Where n is the rate of growth of population, and k the rate of growth of total consumption, then

$$b = \frac{k-n}{1+n}. \tag{6.11}$$

Substituting (6.11) in (6.10) gives

$$r = \left(1 + \frac{k-n}{1+n}\right)^e - 1$$

which reduces to

$$r = \left(\frac{1+k}{1+n}\right)^e - 1. \tag{6.12}$$

Equations (6.10) and (6.12) give the equivalent expressions for a utilitarian rate of discount. Addition of 'pure' time preference expands equation (6.12) to an expression for the 'natural rate of interest':

$$r^* = \frac{(1+k)^e(1+d+l)}{(1+n)^e} - 1$$

using the previous symbols.[1] Using equation (6.12), the rate of discount for the United Kingdom would appear to be of the order of about 4·5 per cent. This result is obtained by looking at rates of growth of total population, and of consumption in real terms, and by using an elasticity of -2.

One apparent oddity of the DMUC approach is that the rate of discount depends on the rate of growth of consumption per head, b, but b will in turn depend upon the distribution of investment over time, which in turn will depend upon the chosen rate of discount. This problem is not a serious one as long as we remember that the projects in question are *marginal* and will therefore have only an insignificant effect upon the overall rate of growth of consumption.[2]

It should also be obvious that the DMUC approach will be highly sensitive to the value of $-e$, the elasticity of the marginal utility function. This raises the problem of whether e is an observable entity or not. If it is, then the choice of e is not an insuperable problem. If, on the other hand, the DMUC approach is taken as being totally normative, then the choice of e becomes entirely a matter of value judgement. The question then arises as to *who* is to assess the most desirable elasticity, an issue which raises the same problem as that noted when talking about the distributive effects of policies in Chapter 2. It has been suggested [16] that the rate of discount, and hence, by implication, the elasticity, can be inferred from past government decisions. The problems involved are the same as those in adopting any implied government welfare judgement from past decisions (see Chapter 2).

[1] More extended derivations are given in Eckstein [11] and Feldstein [12]. r^* is derived in a slightly different way in Arrow [13]. The work on 'natural' rates of interest stems from the seminal work of Ramsey [14].

[2] Hirschleifer [15] regards the objection as decisive, however: 'The rate of discount adopted for investment decisions will affect the rate of growth of income (consumption in our case), which cannot therefore be taken as a datum in determining a "social rate of discount" ' (p. 496).

6.3 THE OPPORTUNITY COST RATE OF DISCOUNT: SOCIAL OPPORTUNITY COST

A second school of thought argues that the STPR is not relevant to public investment decisions, although their arguments do not imply that a positive STPR does not exist. The fundamental argument is straightforward.

Since capital funds are not unlimited, a public investment will involve the sacrifice of some other project. The forgone project is usually thought of as being in the private sector of the economy, a context which fits the American experience where public and private agencies do often compete for the right to undertake a certain project. Even where no direct competition of this kind exists, as is mainly the case in the United Kingdom and in underdeveloped countries, the government can still be thought of as competing in the capital market for funds which would otherwise go to private investments. It would seem obvious that, if the alternative investment could yield a rate of return of, say, p per cent, then the public investment must secure a rate of return of at least p per cent. Hence, the present value of the benefits, B, stemming from the alternative investment, A, is

$$\text{PV}(A) = \sum_t \frac{B(A)_t}{(1+p)^t}.$$

It follows that the public investment should achieve at least p per cent, otherwise resources are better utilised in the alternative project, the p per cent reflecting society's valuation of the returns obtained. Equivalently, p is a suitable rate of discount for public projects.

To underline the argument, imagine that the rate of return on the marginal project in the private sector is 10 per cent, and the government is using a rate of 5 per cent for public projects, the rate being based on some calculation of time preference. Then, public projects yielding just over 5 per cent in the public sector will be adopted, whereas the resources they utilise could have earned 10 per cent in the private sector.

Clearly, there are a number of problems. First, are the marginal internal rates of return (MIRRs) on alternative projects observable? On the face of it they are, since market rates of return are widely quoted. The proponents of the opportunity cost argument generally appear to presume that observable market rates reflect the relevant MIRR,[1] the widely differing rates that can be observed being due to

[1] See Hirschleifer *et al.* [17]; Hirschleifer [15]. For actual estimates of MIRR in the United States economy, see Stockfisch [18].

differences in risk (Hirschleifer [17]). Others suggest that the differing rates partly reflect risk differentials and partly reflect disequilibrium in the economy (Stockfisch [18] p. 193), though they
regard the disequilibrium aspect as not very significant. Even if
market rates do reflect MIRR, there is a problem of choosing which
market rate to use. Since public projects tend to be low-risk
projects, in advanced economies at any rate, the MIRR must be
calculated on a similar low-risk project in the private sector.[1]

Further, if a public investment is to be judged on its *social*
returns, market rates will not necessarily reflect social returns from
private industry investments, i.e. the appropriate discount rate
would require that market rates be adjusted for any external effects,
inequality between shadow and market prices and consumers'
surplus elements. Instead of MIRR, we require the *social* MIRR
(SMIRR) on the forgone project.

Lastly, and most significant, does social time preference have any
role to play in the opportunity cost argument? In a perfectly competitive world, as the next section shows, there is no incompatibility
between the two approaches since, in equilibrium, the two rates
would be equal. It seems apparent, however, that the social time
preference rate, however it is calculated, is below the MIRR on
forgone projects. In short, imperfections in the capital market and
other factors entail a disequilibrium situation in which the two rates
are not equal. It is precisely because of this that a number of
attempts have been made to combine the two approaches – i.e. to
derive some rule which incorporates both the STPR and the MIRR.
It seems fair to say, however, that the opportunity cost school of
thought, described in this section, ignores the STPR in disequilibrium situations. Stockfisch [18] acknowledges that a situation
in which $r < p$ may indicate that the *total* level of investment is too
low, but is emphatic that 'it does not follow that the government
should employ, for evaluating its projects, an interest rate that is
lower than the rate of return prevailing in the private sector of the
economy' (p. 191). The same role of the STPR – as an indicator of
the overall level of investment required – is acknowledged by Arrow
[21] and Nichols [22], but, whereas Arrow brings the STPR back
into the picture [13], Nichols argues that this role can 'in no sense

[1] The opportunity cost argument is the one which underlies the initial
choice of an 8 per cent discount rate, subsequently raised to 10 per cent,
for United Kingdom nationalised industries investments. See the White
Paper on Nationalised Industries [19]. For a useful approach to calculating the relevant opportunity cost rate in the United Kingdom, see
Alfred [20].

authorise the government to use the time preference rate for costing government projects' (pp. 910–11).

The strict version of the opportunity cost argument, then, does not dismiss the STPR as an entity, but it does eliminate its relevance to any derivation of a social discount rate.

6.4 EQUILIBRIUM, SOCIAL TIME PREFERENCE AND SOCIAL OPPORTUNITY COST

It is useful to demonstrate that the problem of deciding which rate to choose arises because capital markets are not perfect and because the overall rate of investment is non-optimal. A simple diagram illustrates the essential points. In Fig. 6.4.1 the two axes show con-

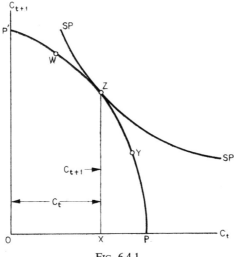

FIG. 6.4.1

sumption in two periods t and $t+1$. The curve $P'P$ represents the transformation function between the two periods – i.e. the rate at which consumption in period t can be transformed into consumption in period 2 through the medium of investment. If investment is PX, for example (reading backwards along the horizontal axis, from P to X), then consumption in period t is OX. But the investment of PX is transformed into consumption in period $t+1$, to an amount XZ. Clearly, if all resources were allocated to investment, there would be zero consumption in t and OP' consumption in $t+1$.

Similarly, OP consumption in t would leave no resources for investment, so that there would be zero consumption in period $t+1$. The
example is obviously highly simplified, since investments in periods
before t will have consumption 'throw-offs' in $t+1$, and investment
in t will not all accrue in $t+1$. However, for convenience these
problems are left aside.

The curve PP' shows the marginal net productivity of capital,
any investment giving greater gains in (undiscounted) consumption
in the future compared to the forgone consumption in the present
period. But movements up the curve from P to P' show diminishing
returns to scale. Now the slope of PP' is

$$\frac{C_{t+1}}{I_t}$$

i.e. the consumption yield in $t+1$ divided by investment in period t.
Now C_{t+1} will exceed I_t by an amount which defines the marginal
net productivity of capital, MNP_k, so that

$$\text{slope of } PP' = \frac{C_{t+1}}{I_t} = \text{MNP}_k + 1.$$

Hence,[1] $\text{MNP}_k = \text{slope of } PP' - 1.$

The marginal net productivity of capital can also be thought of as
the marginal efficiency of investment, or the marginal internal rate
of return.

Now the curve SP shows society's preferences for future as
opposed to present consumption. It is in fact a social indifference
curve. In other words, SP reflects the various elements of social
time preference. The slope of SP will show the marginal rate of
substitution between present and future consumption; i.e.

$$\text{slope of } SP = \frac{U'(C_t)}{U'(C_{t+1})}$$

which has already been found to be equal to $1+r$, the STPR (see
section 6.2).
    Thus
$$\text{STPR} = \text{slope of } SP - 1.$$

Now, the optimal amount of investment in Fig. 6.4.1 is PX, since
this takes the community to the highest possible indifference curve

---

[1] The reader will have to imagine Fig. 6.4.1 as a magnification of a
small section of a larger diagram, otherwise it would be wrong to equate
the slope of PP' with C_{t+1}/I_t.

(other indifference curves can be imagined lying above and below *SP*). But, if society reaches point *Z*, the 'bliss' point from the standpoint of intertemporal utility maximisation, it can be seen that the slope of *SP* is equal to the slope of *PP'*. From the previous results it follows that, at *Z*,

$$\text{MNP}_k = \text{STPR}.$$

Clearly, this demonstration is simplistic because of the use of intertemporal indifference curves, and the restriction to two periods only.[1] However, it should serve to demonstrate that, under the appropriate conditions, the way in which a social rate of discount is derived is immaterial. They should be equal. In practice, however, the two are observed to be different. If the STPR is observed, or thought, to be less than the opportunity cost rate, this is equivalent to saying that the economy is at a point like *Y* in Fig. 6.4.1. In this case, investment is below its optimal level *PX*. If, by any chance, the STPR exceeded the opportunity cost rate, the economy would be at a point like *W*, with over-investment. There is a general consensus that the first situation is more likely, even in advanced economies. It certainly describes the context of underdeveloped economies. Notice that, as investment increases, the discrepancy between the two rates is reduced – i.e. the slopes of the two curves converge. Over time, then, one might expect the degree of under-investment to fall.

These two observations, that investment is less than optimal, and that the degree of non-optimality will fall over time, are the clue to the reconciliation of the two approaches to deriving a social discount rate.

6.5 SOCIAL TIME PREFERENCE, SOCIAL OPPORTUNITY COST AND THE SHADOW PRICE OF SAVINGS

As section 6.4 and the remarks of Nichols and Stockfisch in section 6.3 indicated, if the STPR is constantly less than the opportunity cost rate, society is effectively expressing a preference for more investment. The use of an opportunity cost rate in these circumstances will fulfil one efficiency criterion, that no investment should be undertaken that does not yield as much as an alternative investment in the private sector. But it also suggests that the *total* amount of

---

[1] See also Feldstein [23]. This diagrammatic approach was used effectively for an analysis of private investment decisions by Hirschleifer [24].

investment is constrained in some way. If the constraint is immovable, then the existence of two rates of discount, one for the
public sector and one for the private, would lead to anomalies, with
low-rate projects being undertaken at the cost of high-rate projects.
Thus we revert to the opportunity cost school of thought arguments.
But if the constraint is not immovable, then government has a clear
directive to increase the amount of investment, either by voting
more capital funds to the private sector (making it easier to borrow,
etc.) or by voting itself more funds. One strategy would be to raise
government funds by taxation which is likely to be directly at the
expense of consumption, rather than by the issuing of bonds which
are likely to compete with private investment funds.

An alternative approach to CBA in the presence of a constraint
on investment is to use shadow prices. It has been assumed so far
that investments merely 'throw off' consumption benefits. In practice, both consumption and savings are likely to be yielded. Since
savings become investment, and there is under-investment *ex
hypothesi*, investment is taking place under a savings constraint.
This suggests in turn that any savings throw-off should be valued
more highly than any consumption throw-off. In short, we attach a
'shadow price' to savings to reflect their higher valuation in terms
of society's intertemporal welfare function.

Suppose an investment yields returns in year t, of which part (C_t)
is consumed, and part (S_t) is saved. Then, from our previous argument, S_t must be weighted more heavily than C_t. Let the weight be
a_t, so that, in terms of consumption units, the relevant present value
expression is

$$a_0 = \sum_t (C_t + a_t S_t) d^t \qquad (6.13)$$

where $d^t = 1/(1+r)^t$, r being the STPR.

Next, as the previous section argued, a_t is likely to fall over time
as the divergence between the two rates narrows. Eventually the
'optimal mix' of savings and consumption is reached at Z in Fig.
6.4.1. Exactly when the optimal mix has been reached is not easy
for a government to decide. Since it was argued that tax policies
could be used to raise the overall rate of investment, one rule of
thumb, suggested by Little and Mirrlees, is that the optimal path is
reached when a government feels it can begin to return some of its
tax revenue to consumers ([25] p. 164).[1]

[1] Little and Mirrlees develop a considerably more complex model
based essentially upon a shadow price for savings. Their model relates the
'accounting rate of interest' (our social rate of discount) to the shadow
price of labour in the context of the Indian economy.

Let the rate of fall of a_t be constant at a rate g, so that

$$a_t = a_0(1-g)^t. \tag{6.14}$$

Dividing equation (6.13) by a_t, expanding d^t and substituting equation (6.14) in equation (6.13) gives

$$1 = \sum_t \left(\frac{C_t}{a_t} + S_t\right)\left(\frac{1-g}{1+r}\right)^t. \tag{6.15}$$

The expression $\frac{1-g}{1+r}$ can be written as $\frac{1}{1+p}$ so that (6.15) becomes

$$1 = \sum_t \left(\frac{C_t}{a_t} + S_t\right)\left(\frac{1}{1+p}\right)^t. \tag{6.16}$$

In (6.16), p is the 'internal rate of return' – i.e. the rate of discount which will make the right-hand side of equation (6.16) equal to the left-hand side (see Chapter 7 for a full discussion of internal rates of return).

Thus

$$\frac{1-g}{1+r} = \frac{1}{1+p}$$

so that
$$g = 1 - \frac{1+r}{1+p}. \tag{6.17}$$

Now, if marginal internal rates of return in alternative projects are known, and r is known, it is possible to estimate g, the rate at which the savings constraint falls over time. Given a derived estimate of g it is possible to estimate a_0, the initial shadow price of savings. Suppose we estimate that in T years the optimal consumption–investment mix will have been achieved, then the savings constraint will be eliminated and the shadow price of savings will be the same as for consumption, unity. Hence

$$a_0(1-g)^T = 1. \tag{6.18}$$

Given estimates of g and T, a magnitude for a_0 can be calculated. Clearly, once a_0 is estimated, the values of a_1 to a_{T-1} can be derived from equation (6.14).

Effectively, then, this procedure uses the STPR and SOC rates to derive a shadow price of savings. This shadow price can be used to derive a modified decision rule, as follows.

The rule so far discussed is

$$\sum_t \frac{B_t}{(1+i)^t} > K \tag{6.19}$$

where i is the rate of discount to be determined and K is the cost of the project. For convenience, the capital cost is assumed to occur at the start of the project, operating costs being reflected in the value of B_t. In view of the savings constraint, however, it is necessary to distinguish consumption and savings 'throw-offs' from the investment. Savings are multiplied by the shadow price a_t, so that (6.19) becomes

$$\sum_t \frac{C_t + a_t \cdot S_t}{(1+r)^t} > K. \qquad (6.20)$$

The relevant discount rate is now the STPR, since all benefits are expressed in 'consumption units'. Equation (6.20) can be expanded to

$$\sum_t \frac{C_t}{(1+r)^t} + \sum_t \frac{a_t \cdot S_t}{(1+r)^t} > K \qquad (6.21)$$

and, by equation (6.14), this becomes

$$\sum_t \frac{C_t}{(1+r)^t} + \sum_t \frac{a_0 \cdot S_t(1-g)^t}{(1+r)^t} > K \qquad (6.22)$$

which in turn becomes, by equation (6.17),

$$\sum_t \frac{C_t}{(1+r)^t} + \sum_t \frac{a_0 S_t \cdot 1}{(1+p)^t} > K. \qquad (6.23)$$

If C_t and S_t could be assumed constant per time period, and if t is made sufficiently large, equation (6.23) would simplify to

$$\frac{C_t}{r} + \frac{S_t a_0}{p} > K. \qquad (6.24)$$

Thus, the existence of a savings constraint requires that consumption benefits be discounted at the STPR, r, and that savings benefits should be 'shadow priced' and then discounted by the MIRR, p.

6.6 Alternative Sources of Funds

Suppose that a public investment yields only consumption benefits, so that the formula for a decision rule in the previous section reduces to

$$\sum_t \frac{B_t}{(1+r)^t} > Q. \qquad (6.25)$$

Considerable attention has been paid in the literature to the true opportunity costs of any public projects (Marglin [1, 26, 27]). Given the existence of inadequate (or too much) investment in non-optimal situations, it is necessary to see what is sacrificed in undertaking a public investment. If the forgone expenditure consists entirely of a private investment, then there is a forgone rate of return of p. The true opportunity cost is therefore the value to society of this forgone rate of return, which will be, for a perpetuity,

$$Q = I \cdot \frac{p}{r} \qquad (6.26)$$

where Q is the forgone amount of expenditure, and I is the amount of investment forgone.[1]

If the same simplifying assumptions as in section 6.5 are employed – constant benefits per time period, and a high value of t – then equation (6.25) becomes

$$B_t \cdot \frac{1}{r} > I \cdot \frac{p}{r}$$

which is easily simplified to

$$\frac{B_t}{I} > p. \qquad (6.27)$$

In short, the benefit-per-unit-of-investment cost must exceed the MIRR, a restatement of the opportunity cost theory of section 6.3. The appropriate social discount rate is the MIRR.

Now suppose that, in seeking funds for the public investment, the government raises revenue partly by taxation and partly by the issue of bonds. Then it is reasonable to suppose that the true opportunity cost consists of some forgone investment (I) and some forgone consumption (C). In other words, dealing in perpetuities again, we would have

$$Q = I \cdot \frac{p}{r} + C \qquad (6.28)$$

so that the decision rule would become, with simplification,

$$\frac{B_t}{r} > I \cdot \frac{p}{r} + C \qquad (6.29)$$

or $\qquad B_t > I \cdot p + C \cdot r. \qquad (6.30)$

[1] We saw in Chapter 1 that 'cost' K really refers to the WTP for the forgone project. It follows that the opportunity cost of a project need not be equal to its capital cost. One of the attractions of Marglin's analysis is the explicit allowance made for this factor. For expositional convenience, however, the reader may find it more convenient to equate Q with K.

Thus the benefits of any project would have to exceed the forgone investment, compounded at its MIRR, plus the forgone consumption, compounded at the STPR.

Equation (6.30) describes the essential aspects of Marglin's model. It is fairly simple to expand the model, as Marglin does, to include allowance for the fact that some benefits will accrue in 'reinvestable' form, while others will not, accruing as pure consumption. Let the reinvestable proportion of each £1 of benefit be b. Let the rate which can be earned on reinvestable funds be p, the MIRR. The present value of £1 of benefit is

$$\frac{b \cdot p}{r} + (1 - b) \tag{6.31}$$

assuming that the discount rate is the STPR. (If the discount rate is the MIRR, then clearly the expression reduces to $b + (1 - b) = 1$; i.e. reinvestment is irrelevant.)

Substituting the expression in (6.31) in (6.29) gives

$$B_t > \frac{I \cdot p + C \cdot r}{b \cdot p + (1 - b)r}. \tag{6.32}$$

Objectors to the opportunity cost formulation above point to the apparent oddity of distinguishing forgone investment from forgone consumption. The argument here is that the forgone consumption stream *could* have been invested at rate p, so that equation (6.29) would become

$$\frac{B_t}{r} > I \cdot \frac{p}{r} + \frac{C \cdot p}{r}$$

i.e. $\frac{B_t}{p} > C + I$. In this way, the opportunity cost formulation is restored (Mishan [28], Carr [29]). Baumol [6] also remarks that 'consumers implicitly but very definitely indicate how they feel about this forgone consumption through a rate of return they are currently providing to business firms' (p. 792). The implication is that the *method* of financing an investment is irrelevant, but this is surely not so. The sacrifice of consumption does involve more of a cost to present society compared to a sacrifice of investment: the use of consumption-sacrificing methods of finance (such as taxation) means that the present generation is effectively shifting a *larger* volume of resources to the future than if investment-sacrificing policies are used. It seems correct, therefore, to distinguish the types of expenditure which are sacrificed.

6.7 INSTITUTIONAL BARRIERS TO EQUILIBRIUM

In the presence of non-optimality it has so far been suggested that some combination of social time preference and social opportunity cost rates is required for discounting purposes. Separate rates can be used for the types of throw-off and the types of opportunity cost, or some 'synthetic' rate, reflecting all the considerations, can be derived.[1] The basis of these arguments has been a savings constraint which it is assumed will diminish with time. It has recently been suggested, however, that the equilibrating process cannot be reached because of the existence of institutional barriers (Baumol [6]). The argument is as follows.

Suppose the government has a borrowing rate of r per cent, and let there be a tax rate of t per cent on private industry profits. In a riskless world, then, firms must issue dividends of r per cent to their shareholders, in which case they must earn a gross return of $r/1-t$, this gross return reflecting consumers' willingness to pay for the product of the private firms. The MIRR can therefore be thought of as $r/1-t$, which will clearly be larger than r if there is a positive tax rate. Now society's time preference rate cannot exceed r per cent, so the argument goes, because society is willing to lend to the government at r per cent. It follows that the STPR of r per cent will be less than the MIRR, simply because of taxation. The result, according to this argument, is an essential 'indeterminacy' in the choice of rates, and it is implicit in the analysis that 'synthetic' rates will not overcome the problem because, as long as the institutional barrier exists, so will the divergence between the two rates. The choice then is between STPR and MIRR, once again coming full circle to the arguments set out in sections 6.1 and 6.2.

Despite this argument it still seems that a process of adjustment will operate, bringing the two rates together. For, as more investment is undertaken, we would expect the social time preference rate to rise (as future generations become richer) at a faster rate. In face of the process of convergence it is difficult to avoid the conclusion that some combination of the two rates is required.

[1] Thus Marglin reduces his 'social-rate-cum-opportunity-cost' criterion to a single rate which is, in effect, some weighted average of the STPR and the MIRR.

6.8 SUMMARY

The discount rate was introduced as an accounting price which reflects society's 'trade-off' of present against future benefits. Essentially, this definition required the use of a 'social time preference rate' and various approaches to the derivation of such a rate were discussed. Of these, the 'utilitarian' approach, based on the hypothesis of diminishing marginal utility of consumption, appeared the most satisfactory. Although in theory this approach should not produce results different from those obtained by considering the 'opportunity cost' of public investments, various imperfections were seen to prevent the equilibrating mechanism operating. As such, several approaches which combine the STPR and SOC concepts were discussed and it was concluded that the derivation of a 'synthetic' rate, reflecting STPR and SOC considerations, provided the best means of choosing an operational discount rate.

Part Three
Decision Formulae

7 Formulae for Project Choice

So far, it has been shown that cost–benefit analysis proceeds on the explicit basis that a project or policy be deemed socially worth while if its benefits exceed the costs it generates. The appropriate formula for expressing the social worth of a project has not been discussed in detail, nor have guidelines been offered for assisting with the choice *between* alternative projects. Lastly, constraints on the objective function have not been incorporated.[1] This chapter looks in some detail at each of these problems, with the major assumption that costs and benefits are known with certainty. Chapter 8 relaxes the latter assumption.

7.1 The Choice Context

The necessary condition for the adoption of a project is that dis-counted benefits should exceed discounted costs. This rule can be stated as:

$$\text{GPV}(B) > \text{GPV}(K)$$

or
$$\text{NPV}(B) > 0$$

where $\text{GPV}(B)$ refers to the 'gross present value' of benefits, and $\text{NPV}(B)$ refers to the '*net* present value' of benefits, so that

$$\text{NPV}(B) = \text{GPV}(B) - \text{GPV}(K).$$

The present values are calculated at the relevant social discount rate. Formulated in this way, the 'worth' of a project is expressible as a unique absolute magnitude, with costs and benefits measured in the same units. In practice, however, the rule will require some modification in the presence of constraints on the objective function and in the light of allowances for risk and uncertainty.

---

[1] Although the problem of 'second best' is essentially a problem of maximising the objective function subject to the constraint that the appropriate 'first-best' shadow prices are not operative for large parts of the economy. Second-best theorems are therefore theorems about con-strained optimisation.

The types of choice facing the decision-maker can be classified as follows:

(i) *Accept–reject*. Faced with a set of independent projects and no constraint on the number which can be undertaken, the decision-maker must decide which, if any, is worth while. The decision rule should enable him to accept or reject each individual project.

(ii) *Ranking*. If some input, such as capital, is limited in supply it may well be that all 'acceptable' projects cannot be undertaken. In this case, projects must be ranked or ordered in terms of the objective function. The decision rule for accept–reject situations cannot be easily generalised to cover these situations.

(iii) *Choosing between exclusive projects*. Frequently, projects are not independent of each other. One form of interdependence exists when one project can only be undertaken to the exclusion of another project – e.g. two different ways of achieving the same objective. The projects are then 'mutually exclusive' and the decision rule must enable the decision-maker to choose between the alternatives.

A special case of mutual exclusion exists when any given project can be undertaken now or in a later period. There is a problem of choosing the optimal point in time to start the project. This is the problem of 'time-phasing' and, once again, the decision rule should offer guidance on this issue.

7.2 NET PRESENT VALUE AND INPUT CONSTRAINTS

Since constraints on the resource available for investment are always present in the public sector, it is worth looking a little closer at the effect of such constraints on the net present value rule. The problem is to rank projects in order of preference and to select the optimal combination of projects such that the total combined cost exhausts the budget. It is tempting to think that ranking by NPVs will achieve this result, but it does not. Consider the following simple example.

Table 7.2.1

Project	Cost (K)	Benefits (B)	B−K	B/K
X	100	200	100	2·0
Y	50	110	60	2·2
Z	50	120	70	2·4

Suppose a capital constraint of 100 exists and that the constraint operates *only for the one year in which capital expenditure is incurred*. Ranking by NPV gives the ordering X, Z, Y so that X would be the only project selected, net benefits being 100 and the budget being exhausted. But inspection of the table shows that Y *and* Z could be adopted, with a combined NPV of 130 for the same cost.

To avoid this problem, projects should be ranked by their benefit–cost *ratios* – i.e. by GPV/K, at the predetermined discount rate. The proof of this requirement is fairly straightforward.[1]

The aim is maximise

$$\sum_i B(i), \text{ subject to } \sum_i K(i) = K$$

where i refers to the ith project, and K is the capital constraint. This requires the maximisation of the expression

$$L = \sum_i B(i) + \lambda[\sum_i K(i) - K].$$

Setting the partial derivatives equal to zero gives

$$(a) \ B(i) = \lambda \cdot K(i), \text{ or } \frac{B(i)}{K(i)} = \lambda$$

and

$$(b) \sum_i K(i) = K.$$

Condition (a) requires that projects be ranked by their benefit–cost ratios, each project being selected as long as the ratio exceeds λ. Indeed, λ is no more than the shadow price of the budget, indicating the 'trade-off' between small changes in the budget constraint and the resulting change in overall net benefits.

In the simple example in Table 7.2.1 it can be seen that ranking by benefit–cost ratios secures the correct combination of projects, namely Y and Z. Thus, for single-period rationing we derive the rule that projects be ranked by their benefit–cost ratios. The decision-maker then works down the list until the budget is exhausted. This is equivalent to selecting all projects with ratios greater than or equal to the shadow price of the budget.[2]

The presence of multi-period rationing involves some complex problems which are only effectively solved by the use of

---

[1] The reader who is unfamiliar with differentiation and Lagrangean multipliers will nonetheless gain the sense of the solution without working through the problem.

[2] The rule is advanced by Hirschleifer *et al.* [1] and had been proposed earlier in J. H. Lorie and L. J. Savage, 'Three Problems in Rationing Capital', *Journal of Business* (Oct 1955).

F

programming techniques. Useful discussions can be found in Marglin [2] and Weingartner [3]. Similarly, where projects are 'lumpy' (i.e. indivisible), programming techniques of the integer kind are required (Weingartner [3]).

7.3 OPTIMAL TIME-PHASING

The issue of time-phasing is a little easier to illustrate. A solution to the time-phasing problem tells us *when* to introduce the investment. In many cases this aspect of investment planning is ignored, timing being a matter of arbitrary rules. It can be shown, however, that the net present value of a project can sometimes be increased by delaying implementation of the project, and even that projects which are judged not worth while now can be worth while later on. This illustrates the dangers of looking at the project from a 'static' rather than a 'dynamic' viewpoint.

Suppose a project is initially considered for construction in year 0, and that it has a capital cost K which is the same whether it is built in year 0, 1, 2 or whenever. Assume too that it has a 'life' of n years. No other costs are associated with the project. If the project is postponed by one year, there will be a saving of interest on K. Essentially, the present value in year 0 of the capital outlay in year 1 will be $K/1+r$:

$$\text{savings in capital cost} = K - \frac{K}{1+r} = \frac{rK}{1+r}$$

where r is the rate which can be earned on capital. On the benefit side, however, there will be a *loss* of benefits in year 1 equal to $\frac{B_1}{1+r}$ (assuming r is applied to both benefits and costs). On the other hand, the project will still last n years, so that there will be a *gain* in year $n+1$ of $\frac{B_{n+1}}{(1+r)^{n+1}}$. The overall net gains from postponement are therefore

$$\left[\frac{rK}{1+r} + \frac{B_{n+1}}{(1+r)^{n+1}}\right] - \left[\frac{B_1}{1+r}\right].$$

This calculation can be repeated for each possible length of delay. The year in which the gains from postponement are greatest is the 'optimal' year for implementing the project. Or, what is the same thing, the optimal year will be that in which the net benefits of the project are maximised.

Of course, in practice the procedure is complicated by various factors. Capital costs are likely to vary with postponement and will not be known with certainty; interest rates may well vary with time; economies of scale may well be present so that projects with large amounts of excess capacity may well be justified if the costs of excess capacity are less than the economies of scale; and, most frequently, there will be political and other reasons in favour of 'early starts' (as with the race in the 1960s over supersonic commercial aircraft), and so on.[1]

7.4 INTERNAL RATE OF RETURN

The present value rule requires the use of some predetermined social discount rate to discount future benefits and costs. An alternative rule is to calculate the discount rate which would give the project a NPV of zero and then to compare this 'solution rate' with the predetermined social discount rate. In other words, the benefit and cost streams are presented in *equation* form:

$$\sum_t \frac{B_t}{(1+i)^t} = K_0$$

where i is the rate of discount which solves the equation, and we continue to assume that all capital costs are incurred in the initial period.

The rate i is given various names: the 'solution rate', the 'yield', the 'internal rate of return' and the 'marginal efficiency of investment' (or of capital, though the latter is confusing given that we are dealing with changes in the capital stock). Once i is determined, the rule for accept–reject and for ranking is to adopt any project which has an internal rate of return in excess of the predetermined social discount rate. As with the NPV rule, then, it remains essential to choose some acceptable discount rate.

One minor drawback of the IRR approach is that the solution rate cannot be computed quickly. The reason is simply that the IRR is the solution to a polynomial equation. Thus, if the 'life' of the project is T years, the problem is to find i in the equation

$$\frac{B_1}{1+i} + \frac{B_2}{(1+i)^2} + \cdots + \frac{B_n}{(1+i)^T} = K_0.$$

[1] Dynamic criteria are discussed extensively in Marglin [2]. A detailed analysis of the economies of scale problem in relation to time-phasing, which includes case studies, is to be found in A. S. Manne, *Investments for Capacity Expansion: Size, Location and Time-Phasing* (London, 1967).

Solutions will not be obvious and the usual approach is to proceed in an 'iterative' fashion, guessing at the likely rate and entering various rates into the equation until the two sides of the equation are equal.

The IRR is further complicated when used to compare mutually exclusive projects. It is not necessarily the case that the best project is the one with the highest IRR. Consider the two projects in Table 7.4.1, X and Y, each with a life of ten years.[1]

Table 7.4.1

Project	Cost	Benefits (p.a.)	IRR	NPV at 8%
X	1	0·2	15%	0·34
Y	2	0·36	12%	0·42
'Y−X'	1	0·16	9%	—

On the IRR rule, X is preferred to Y, but on the NPV rule, Y is preferred to X. The IRR rule is misleading here since it discriminates against Y because of the size of the capital outlay. To avoid this problem it is necessary to calculate the rate of return on the hypothetical project 'Y−X' – i.e. on the difference between the capital outlays. Since the IRR on Y−X is in excess of the subjective rate of 8 per cent, used in the example, the larger project is to be preferred to the former.

Thus the mutually exclusive context requires a two-part rule to the effect that a project Y be accepted if and only if

$$i_Y > r$$

and

$$i_{(Y-X)} > r$$

where i is the IRR and r the predetermined rate. The rule is usually described as the 'incremental yield' approach, or Fisher's 'rate of return over cost', originating, as so much of investment theory has, with Irving Fisher's *The Theory of Interest* (Alchian [5]).

7.5 PRESENT VALUE VERSUS INTERNAL RATE OF RETURN

A very considerable literature has been devoted to the relative merits of the two approaches so far described. The consensus appears to favour the adoption of present value rules, at least for public investment decisions. The reasons for dissatisfaction with the IRR approach are numerous:

---

[1] The example is adapted from Henderson [4].

(i) *Sensitivity to economic life.* Where projects with different economic lives are being compared, the IRR approach will possibly inflate the desirability of a short-life project, the IRR being a function both of the time periods involved *and* the size of capital outlay. NPV, on the other hand, is not affected by absolute magnitudes of outlay. Thus, £1 invested now has an IRR of 100 per cent if it cumulates to £2 at the end of the year. Compare this to a £10 investment which cumulates to £15: i.e. an IRR of 50 per cent, but a NPV of £5. The IRR rule would rank the former project above the latter.

(ii) *Sensitivity to time-phasing of benefits.* Frequently projects may not yield benefits for many years (dams, nuclear power stations) – they have long 'gestation' periods. The IRR will tend to be lower on such projects when compared to projects with a fairly even distribution of benefits over time, even though the NPV of the former project may be larger. The problem here is essentially the same as that in (i) above: IRR will give high ranking to projects which 'bunch' the benefits into the early part of their economic lives relative to other projects.

(iii) *Mutual exclusivity.* It has already been noted that IRR needs to be supplemented by an additional rule in situations of mutual exclusion.

(iv) *Administrative acceptability.* The argument is sometimes advanced against NPV and in favour of IRR that decision-makers are familiar with the *idea* of a rate-of-return, even if they were previously used to wrong concepts, such as undiscounted returns-to-cost percentage ratios. This problem is not a serious one, however, and can be overcome by suitable expositional aids for decision-makers. A similar problem arises with allowances for risk. The appropriate procedures are dealt with in Chapter 8, but suffice it to say here that the IRR can be adjusted to incorporate risk factors and can still appear as a single figure. The NPV rule, on the other hand, may require that a *range* of NPVs be indicated, corresponding to the range of probabilities. Clearly, decision-makers in search of unique answers may find the prospect more frustrating.

(v) *Multiple roots.* In computing the IRR it is quite possible to obtain more than one solution rate. The reason for this is simple, once it is realised that the IRR is the solution to a polynomial equation. If the polynomial is of degree n, there will be n roots, i.e. n solution rates. Clearly, if a project has two solutions, say 10 per cent and 15 per cent, and the social discount rate is 12 per cent, there appears to be no clear-cut criterion for acceptance or rejection. This objection is considered by many to preclude the use of IRR as a decision rule.

The only roots of the polynomial equation which are of interest are these with positive and real values.[1] Thus, although an IRR of −2 per cent is conceivable, it has no relevant economic meaning and can be ignored. Imaginary numbers (such as $\sqrt{-2}$) are without significance and can similarly be ignored. The number of positive roots can be found by Descartes' 'Rule of Signs'. If the decision formula is expressed as an equation in i, the IRR, the positive roots can be indicated. Thus, in the simple two-period case we have

$$\frac{B_1}{1+i}+\frac{B_2}{(1+i)^2} = K$$

or $\qquad -K \cdot i^2+(B_1-2K)i+(K+B_1+B_2) = 0$

so that the sequence of signs before the terms in i is −, +. There is only *one change* of sign, so there is one positive root. If the equation was of a higher order, the same rule would apply. The sequence −, −, +, +, for example, still has only one change and hence one positive root. The sequence −, +, −, however, has two changes and hence two positive roots. This last sequence is perhaps the one most common to public investment projects. The initial expenditure (−) is followed by positive returns (+) and then by negative returns (−) as the project ages, possibly costing money to dismantle and scrap.

This sequence is illustrated in Fig. 7.5.1 below.

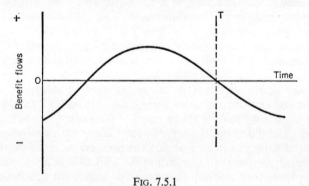

FIG. 7.5.1

The proposed modifications to the IRR rule to allow for multiple roots are numerous. It has been suggested (Soper [6]) that the project be terminated at point T in Fig. 7.5.1 – i.e. the second

[1] Real numbers consist of any integers (1, 2, 3, . . .), any ratios of integers (fractions) and any 'irrational' numbers, i.e. numbers in the integer continuum but which cannot be expressed as integer ratios.

change of sign is not permitted, and a unique rate is preserved. In addition, such a procedure seems to be common sense because there is little point in carrying on with a project that yields negative returns. The problem here is that the negative returns usually reflect costs of closure, removal or dismantling costs which cannot be avoided.

Others have suggested rules by which 'valid' IRRs can be distinguished from 'invalid' ones. In the $-$, $+$, $-$ case a useful rule has been proposed by Wright [7]. Essentially, Wright's rule observes the two roots resulting from this particular benefit flow, calls them i_1 and i_2 and formulates the following rules ($i_2 > i_1$):

(*a*) if $i_1 < e < i_2$, accept the project;
(*b*) if $e < i_1$, reject the project;
(*c*) if $e > i_2$, reject the project;

where e is the social rate of discount in our case. Notice that Wright's rule permits – case (*a*) – the lower internal rates of return to be *less* than the social discount rate, so long as the higher rate exceeds the social rate. This rule is correct, but unfortunately has application only to the $-$, $+$, $-$ flow indicated; it cannot be generalised beyond this. It is possible to develop further rules, but these increase in complexity and do not embrace all possible cases. Thus, while the multiple roots problem is not perhaps as serious as some commentators would suggest, it remains a slightly awkward obstacle to the confident use of the internal rate of return rule.

(vi) *Changes in the discount rates.* It has been argued (Feldstein and Flemming [8]) that the social discount rate may change over time. The calculation of a unique IRR in these circumstances would not permit of an easy comparison. Thus the IRR may be 15 per cent, with the social discount rate rising from, say, 12 to 18 per cent over the project life. No simple criterion of acceptability exists in these circumstances. The NPV rule, however, does enable discount-rate changes to be incorporated easily into the calculation.

(vii) *Non-uniqueness of the Fisher rule.* Feldstein and Flemming [8] further point out that the Fisher 'extended yield' method may yield non-unique solutions. If there are two projects, *X* and *Y*, it is necessary to calculate $X - Y$, the hypothetical 'incremental' project. But, depending on the phasing of benefits of the two projects, it is perfectly possible to obtain a stream of benefits for the incremental project which itself has several changes of sign. In other words, the incremental project could have multiple solutions, preventing an unequivocal rule being laid down.

Overall, then, the balance of favour is with the net present value rule for deciding upon projects. The circumstances in which rate of return rules are misleading may not be many or widespread, but they are significant enough to indicate that the problems are best avoided by the use of the more straightforward present value criterion.

7.6 OTHER CRITERIA

Although most practical cost–benefit analyses use the IRR or NPV normalisation procedure, it is sometimes the case that alternative approaches are used. This section looks briefly at these rules.

(i) *Annual value*, or 'annuity' approach. Given a stream of money benefits $B_1, B_2, \ldots, B_n$, these benefits have a present value, $PV(B)$. Corresponding to the stream of benefits will be an annuity, A_B, which, when discounted, will have the same present value as $B_1+B_2 \ldots +B_n$, so that $PV(A_B) = PV(B)$. Similarly, there will be an annuity corresponding to the stream of costs, A_K, so that the decision rule is: rank by A_B-A_K. Clearly, from the definition of the annuity, the result cannot differ from the present value rule.

An example of this approach can be found in Krutilla and Eckstein [9]. In their assessment of the Hells Canyon dams, benefits (in the form of hydroelectricity, flood control and navigation) and costs were transformed to constant absolute amounts over time, as required by the annuity approach.

(ii) *Payback*,[1] a rule which has little or nothing to recommend it but which is still widely used, especially in private industry. The rule is simple. Establish some maximum acceptable time horizon, T^*, by which, if benefit flows do not cover all cost flows in the period, the project is rejected: i.e. accept it if

$$\sum_{t=0}^{t=T^*} (B_t-C_t) > 0.$$

Clearly, the rule makes no allowance for projects with long gestation periods, the selection of T^* usually being arbitrary. The failure to discount net benefit flows ignores the argument for social discount rates. Indeed, payback implies a zero discount rate to T^* and an infinite rate thereafter. The rule has sometimes been used in Soviet planning under the name 'recoupment period'. Under certain highly restrictive conditions it does give the same answers as the NPV rule (Gordon [10]), but in general it will not do so.

[1] See also Chapter 8.

(iii) *Terminal value.* The use of terminal value procedures has gained some increased respectability in recent contributions to cost–benefit analysis (Mishan [11]). A terminal value is obtained by *compounding* benefits and costs forward in time to the terminal period (usually the end of the project's economic life), and the resulting rule is: rank by

$$TV(B)-TV(K).$$

Formulated in this way, the terminal value approach is formally equivalent to the present value rule. Mishan [11] has, however, suggested added modifications which appear to make the terminal value approach more appealing. His 'normalisation' rules are:

(*a*) Compound all consumption benefits at the STPR, *r*.
(*b*) Compound any reinvestable surpluses and any costs at the opportunity cost rate, *p*.
(*c*) Select a common terminal period, *T*, for all investments.
(*d*) 'Equalise' cost outlays across projects, so that each project has the same present value of costs.

An example shows the results. Table 7.6.1 shows three hypo-

Table 7.6.1

Project	t_0	t_1	t_2	t_3	t_4	PV(B)	PV(K)	NPV	IRR
A	−20	15	16	.	.	28·8	20	6·8	0·34
B	−100	.	.	160	.	117·2	100	17·2	0·17
C	−45	351	−402	.	.	319·1	377·3	−58·2	0·46 and 4·56

Source: Taken from Mishan ([11] p. 785), with corrections to the calculations.

thetical projects, *A*, *B*, *C*, and their associated benefit streams. Present values are calculated, and ranking by NPV gives *B*, *A*, *C*. Ranking by IRR, however, gives *C*, *A*, *B*, project *C* having two internal rates, the benefit flow being −, +, −.

Now suppose terminal values are calculated and Mishan's rules are adopted. First, expenditures have to be equalised. The cost of *A* is therefore multiplied by 5, and *C* is *divided* by 3 since there is a negative benefit flow in period 2 which, when discounted at *p* and added to the capital cost of *C* (15 in the new table), equals 100, the common outlay. Next, reinvestment is allowed for: the 16 in period 2 for project A is reinvestable at p, say 20 per cent, and the 160 in period 3 for project B is reinvestable at some rate higher than p. The 117 in period 1 for project C is reinvested at p. The final table becomes that shown in 7.6.2.

Table 7.6.2

Project	t_0	t_1	t_2	t_3	t_4	$TV(B)$	$TV(K)$	NTV	λ
A	-100	75	.	.	115	215	207·4	$+7·6$	0·207
B	-100	.	.	.	210	210	207·4	$+2·6$	0·203
C	-15	117	-134	.	.	202	207·4	$-5·4$	0·192

The new rankings, by NTV, are A, B, C. In addition, a 'normalised' IRR, λ, is computed, and this is seen to give an identical ranking. The normalised IRR (IRR*) is defined as the discount rate which makes the *terminal* value of the benefits equal to the *present* value of the expenditures; i.e.

$$\text{IRR}^* = \sqrt[n]{\frac{\text{TV}(B)}{\text{PV}(K)}} - 1$$

where n is the number of years to the selected terminal period, and $\text{PV}(K)$ is calculated at the rate p.

The attributes of this approach are claimed to be:

(i) Identical rankings whatever rule is used: i.e. NTVs, NPVs, IRRs or benefit–cost ratio will all yield the same rankings *provided* they are expressed in normalised form.

(ii) Expressed in normalised form, benefits may be discounted at *any* rate of interest to obtain a normalised present value.

(iii) The normalised internal rate of return 'accords with the popular conception of an internal rate, as an average rate of growth over the relevant period' ([11] p. 788).

(iv) The multiple roots solution to project C in Table 7.6.1 disappears in Table 7.6.2.

The procedure is interesting in so far as it does place the various decision formulae on a comparable basis and in such a way as to ensure equivalent rankings. Without in any way decrying the ingenuity with which the approach has been developed (those with a preference for rates of return approaches, for example, would find the 'normalised' IRR trouble-free), it remains true that net present value approaches, with due allowance being made for reinvestment (see Chapter 6), will achieve the same results. The principle of Occam's razor might therefore be usefully applied.

(iv) *Benefit–cost ratios.* One of the most popular decision rules, particularly in the early years of applied cost–benefit analysis, was the use of benefit–cost ratios. The general rules become:

(i) Accept a project if $\dfrac{\text{GPV}(B)}{K} > 1.$

(ii) In face of rationing, rank by the ratio $\text{GPV}(B)/K$.

(iii) In choosing between mutually exclusive projects, select the project with the highest ratio.

There are numerous difficulties with this rule. One fundamental point is that no rule should be sensitive to the classification of a project effect as a cost rather than a benefit, and vice versa. Thus, all costs can be treated as negative benefits and all benefits as negative costs. For the NPV rule it should be obvious that the outcome will be the same however the division is made. But the benefit–cost ratio rule *will* be affected by this division since it will affect the magnitudes which are entered as denominator and as numerator. Thus, if a project has (discounted) benefits of 10, 20 and 30 units, and costs of 10 and 20, the benefit–cost ratio is 2·0. But if the cost of 10 is treated as negative benefit, the ratio becomes $50/20 = 2·5$. On the other hand, benefits *minus* costs (i.e. NPV) remains the same, at 30 units, regardless of the transfer.

Apart from being sensitive to the classification of costs and benefits, the ratio rule is incorrect when applied to mutually exclusive contexts. Thus, a project costing 100 units, with discounted benefits of 130, has a NPV of 30. This is to be preferred to a project costing 40 with benefits of 60, a NPV of 20. But in ratio terms, *B* is preferred since *B* has a ratio of 1·5 compared to *A*'s 1·3.

In general, there is no defence for the use of benefit–cost ratios as a decision rule outside of the rationing context discussed in section 7.2.

7.7 NON-FINANCIAL CONSTRAINTS

As one writer has remarked, 'Economic policy is rarely concerned with the attainment of the best of all possible worlds. Rather, it seeks to improve economic welfare in the face of constraints' (Eckstein [12]).

Public investments are usually subject to constraints other than purely budgetary ones. Clearly, any public investment agency works with a limited overall budget, and this in turn is constrained in part by the total public expenditure budget. The latter can be altered by changes in general policy concerning the investment–consumption allocation pattern, and will itself be constrained by anti-cyclical policies, measures to deal with the balance of payments, and so on. The allocation to departments will depend upon the social priorities established by the government of the day, so that budgetary constraints can themselves be thought of as being largely politically determined. In short, a government social welfare function will be in operation in respect of the allocation of funds to departments. If this welfare function is well defined, the cost–benefit analyst need not be suboptimising when dealing with project selection within a budget constraint. Thus, investment in a new hospital may have as its opportunity cost a new education establishment. If funds have been 'properly' allocated, however, there should be no possibility of the hospital displacing a school with a higher social value than the hospital. In practice, of course, government welfare functions are not so well defined, nor could they be in the absence of unique measures of comparability between diverse outcomes such as 'health' and 'education'.

At the level of ranking projects within a sub-budget, however, political constraints still operate. Some projects may never come to the attention of the analyst because they have been 'screened out' for political reasons. This screening process may be perfectly 'efficient' if it reflects higher-level political objectives such as income–class equity, or regional balance. It seems a useful rule then to require that 'constraints . . . should be determined at an appropriately high political level' (Henderson [4] p. 144). Effectively, what happens then is that the constraints become part of the objective function which is no longer defined solely in terms of 'efficiency benefits'. But there may be a tendency to accept unquestioningly constraints imposed at lower levels of the political hierarchy. The reason for acceptance is usually that it greatly simplifies the problem, often eliminating complete directions of policy. Several writers have warned against this danger of overacceptance (Henderson [4, 13], Eckstein [12], Maass [14]). The problem, however, is that once the analyst himself questions the constraints he appears to be overstepping the bounds of his predefined function. This is the problem met before – with equity considerations, with normative discount rates and now with the acceptance or otherwise of political constraints. It is the general problem of defining the limits of advice, of finding the dividing line between adviser and decision-maker. Value judgements are involved, and at least one writer has remarked that 'in most cases the economist should try to formulate the maximand and at least some constraints himself and explain to his employer why he should accept them' (Turvey [15] p. 96). Others prefer the 'highbrow agnosticism' of which Turvey complains, while still others steer the middle way and warn that 'by demonstrating that they know their place, economists may hope to ensure that it is not filled by others' (Henderson [13] p. 314).

7.8 SUMMARY

The correct criterion for reducing benefits and costs to a unique value is the present value criterion. The correct *rule* is to adopt any project with positive NPVs and to rank projects by their NPVs. When budget constraints exist, however, the criteria become more complex. Single-period constraints are dealt with by a benefit–cost ratio ranking procedure. Multi-period constraints can only be allowed for with a general programming model which has as its objective function the maximisation of the combined NPV, subject to the relevant constraints.

8 Risk and Uncertainty

8.1 THE RELEVANCE OF RISK AND UNCERTAINTY

So far we have assumed that the private costs and benefits of projects are known in advance. The question that we have been concerned with is, in essence, how far these provide an adequate basis for *social* policy.

In many cases, the assumption that costs and benefits of projects under consideration are more or less definitely known is reasonable. For industrial projects, persons with experience of the field can generally provide reasonable estimates of the costs and value of production. Difficulties arise when there is less accumulated experience to draw on, e.g. for multi-purpose river-valley projects in developing countries; however, even in such cases feasibility studies carried out by economists and engineers often provide the basic information.

Nevertheless, there are valid reasons for giving special consideration to risk and uncertainty in cost–benefit analysis.

Firstly, data for estimating future benefits and costs may not always be available, or may not be available without special research directed towards this aim.[1] Such research may be costly.

Secondly, there are projects where there is an inherent tendency for benefits or costs to vary substantially from year to year, e.g. the benefits of a flood-control project in a particular year will depend on whether or not a flood occurs.

Thirdly, we may want to compare a project whose outcome is relatively certain with one which involves a high degree of uncertainty: one project may be regarded as 'a sure thing' while the other might, so to speak, lead either to triumph or disaster. Conceptual problems are involved in making these comparable to each other.

---

[1] Cf. Keynes ([1] p. 164): 'Frankly, we must admit that in order to estimate the profits on a railroad ten years or even five years hence or those of a copper mine, a textile mill, a brand of drugs, a transatlantic steamer or a building in London, the available data boil down to very little and sometimes to absolutely nothing.' The position has improved since this was written, but the problem remains.

In its most general sense, the problem of uncertainty in economic life arises when decision-makers do not know exactly what the consequences of their decisions will be.

In the context of cost–benefit analysis the existence of uncertainty implies that the outcomes (consequences) of policies (projects) are not uniquely determined. This means, firstly, that the outcomes in any time-period depend not only on the policies adopted but on other circumstances as well. In the literature on decision-making under uncertainty, these 'other circumstances' are often given the generic name 'states of nature'.

Secondly, it means that exact knowledge about the time-pattern of relevant states of nature over the life of the project is lacking.

Uncertainty in project evaluation can be classified according to the source from which it arises. Thus, for example, one important source could be changes in consumer tastes with their corresponding effects on future benefits. Changes in tastes of foreign consumers are generally regarded as particularly important both because there is usually less knowledge about what determines their behaviour patterns and because of the special importance of export markets for countries with balance of payments problems.

Secondly, uncertainty may arise from technological change. In practice, this is likely to be important in relatively new industries (e.g. aerospace, electronics) in which the pace of technical change is particularly rapid, and in 'old' industries where structural transformation has so far been delayed (e.g. introduction of high-yielding varieties of wheat in a traditional agricultural system, or the substitution of coal-based methods by atomic energy for the generation of electricity).

Yet another type of uncertainty is connected with the reactions of individuals affected by the choice of projects, reactions which may themselves make a difference to project costs or benefits. This can be a problem, for instance, in evaluating the benefits of an irrigation project. The net increment in output due to such a project will depend on the type of response made by farmers in the region – whether or how fast they make appropriate adjustments in cropping patterns, sowing practice, land and water use and the use of complementary inputs such as chemical fertilisers and high-yielding varieties.[1]

This classification of uncertainty by source is of course far from exhaustive. Its only purpose is to draw attention to some of the

[1] See, in this connection, Heady and Dillon [2] and Sovani and Rath [3].

more important cases where the presence of uncertainty may require standard methods of cost–benefit analysis to be modified.

A knowledge of the sources of uncertainty does not in itself tell us what to do about it. For this purpose, the more relevant classification is by the degree of available information about the outcomes of policies. Here the crucial question is: is there enough information to justify the assignment of probabilities to different outcomes? If there is, the situation is described as 'risky'. If not, it is said to be 'uncertain' in the strict sense of the term.[1] While the distinction is not as rigid as has sometimes been supposed, it provides a convenient point of departure for our present discussion; for the adjustments required in cost–benefit analysis in the two types of situations are likely to be different.

8.2 'OBJECTIVE' PROBABILITY AND THE EXPECTED UTILITY RULE

The concept of probability can be approached in a number of different ways. The two main approaches are (i) the 'objective' (or 'frequency' or 'classical') approach, and (ii) the 'subjective' (or 'degrees of belief' or Bayes[2]) approach.

We start by considering the implications of the 'objective' approach to probability for cost–benefit analysis under risk.

The objective approach is concerned with repetitive events. The probability of a repeated event is defined as the limiting value of the relative frequency with which the event occurs in the long run. The standard example is the probability of a head turning up when a coin is tossed repeatedly: if the number of trials is large enough, the ratio of the number of heads to the total number of trials will approach 1/2, which is defined to be the corresponding probability.

Next, consider how risk affects cost–benefit analysis. Essentially,

[1] This distinction goes back to Knight [4]: In the context of welfare economics, it was emphasised by Graaff ([5] p. 116); 'Uncertainty is not to be thought of as a quantitative thing like the chance or numerical probability of a coin showing heads when tossed a large number of times. It refers to something qualitative. . . . It arises whenever one has incomplete information on which to act.' There are some other writers who use 'uncertainty' as the general term and 'risk' as a particular kind of it, differing to this extent from the definitions cited above.

[2] After Thomas Bayes, who raised some fundamental questions about probability in [6]. An excellent non-technical discussion of the foundations of subjective probability is given in Ramsey [7].

risk means that the outcome of a particular decision depends on the circumstances ('states of nature') which might prevail. The decision-maker does not know in advance what, at any future time, the circumstances will be. However, if the circumstances in question are events that occur repeatedly, the probability that particular kinds of circumstances will prevail (that the states of nature will be such and such) can in principle be computed from past experience – the probability of a state of nature being defined as the proportion of cases in which nature turns out to be in the given state. Thus, a 'probability distribution' of the states of nature can be computed.

Assuming that the decision-maker knows exactly what the outcome of each decision would be for given states of nature, the probability distribution of states of nature can be used to derive a probability distribution of outcomes for each decision. If he knows also how each outcome is to be valued, the corresponding probability distribution of utilities can be derived.

The choice as between different decisions then reduces to a choice as between the probability distributions of (social) utilities to which the decisions lead.

However, it would make little sense to 'choose between' two given probability distributions as such. The only possible basis for choice is provided by certain statistical characteristics of the distributions concerned. For example, the 'moments' of various order of the probability distributions of outcome can provide such a basis. These are defined as follows.

Let μ_i be the value (utility) attributed to the ith possible outcome and p_i be the probability of its occurrence if a particular decision is made. Then $\sum_i p_i\mu_i = \mu$, say, is defined as the first moment of the probability distribution of utilities for this decision. The second moment is defined as $\sum_i p_i(\mu_i-\mu)^2$; and, in general, the rth moment is defined as

$$\sum_i p_i(\mu_i-\mu)^r.$$

In practice, for most probability distributions, the information contained in the first two moments provides a sufficient basis for comparison. Now, the first moment of a probability distribution, which is essentially a measure of central tendency, is also called its *arithmetic mean* or *expected value*. On the other hand, the second moment is a measure of the dispersion or spread of the probability distribution around its central value and is more familiar as the concept of *variance*.[1] The question on which discussion has centred is whether, in choosing between decisions on the basis of probability distributions of outcomes associated with them, it is in fact legitimate to neglect variance, i.e. to confine one's attention to the expected value alone.

The answer will vary depending on whether the point of view is that of the individual decision-maker or that of society as a whole. For the former, there might indeed be good reason to consider variance as well as expected values. On the other hand, the goal of CBA, as we have been at pains to emphasise, is primarily to consider the impact of policies on social welfare. For society as a whole, a relevant consideration is that there normally exists a large number of independent but broadly similar risky projects, each making a relatively small contribution to total national income and consumption. In any given year, for some such projects the net benefit will fall short of its expected value; for others, net benefit will exceed expected value. Looking at all such projects together, the dispersions from expected value of individual project benefits will thus tend to cancel out to some extent. Hence the dispersion from expected value of the total gain to society from all such projects will be much smaller than the dispersion for an individual project. This 'pooling of risks' is what justifies the 'expected utility' approach to the social choice of risky projects.

Formally, this argument rests in the last analysis on the statistical 'Law of Large Numbers'. In the present context this law can be expressed as follows.

Let the random variable $\mu_i(i = 1, \ldots, n)$ represent the social gain per year from the ith project. Let $S_n = \sum_{i=1}^{n} \mu_i$ and let $E(S_n)$ be the mathematical expectation of S_n.[2] Assume that each μ_i is bounded above, i.e. it cannot be infinitely large.

Then the Law of Large Numbers states that, provided n is large,

---

[1] It is almost always the case that moments higher than the first and the second are ignored in practical analysis. This amounts to saying that the expected value and variance provide sufficient information for decision criteria. It should not be assumed, however, that higher moments can always be ignored.

[2] By a random variable we mean, simply, a variable with probabilities attached to it. For more rigorous definitions the reader is referred to almost any text on statistics, e.g. Hoel [8]. The mathematical expectation is simply the sum of the values of each outcome, with each outcome being multiplied by its probability of occurrence.

$E(S_n n)$ can be taken as an approximation to $S_n n$ with an error which, except in extremely few cases, will be at most of order 1_n.

Provided there are a large number of *independent* projects which yield returns of a comparable order of magnitude, this justifies the use of the expected utility criterion for project choice.

From the point of view of cost–benefit analysis, the main result of our discussion so far can be described as follows.

If the probability distribution for the returns from a risky project can be estimated and the conditions for the Law of Large Numbers to apply are satisfied, the expected utility criterion gives the correct decision rule. The procedure to be applied is as follows.

From the probability distribution of returns, calculate the expected annual benefit of the project using accounting prices for inputs and outputs. The present value of this time-stream of expected benefits over the period of the project's life is then calculated using an appropriate rate of discount (see Chapter 6). This provides a measure of what the project is worth to society.

In principle, the probability distribution of the return from a project may itself be regarded as varying from year to year. In this case, the expected returns and hence expected social benefits are calculated separately for each year of project life, using the probability distribution relating to the year concerned. The present value is then calculated in the usual way.

The expected utility approach has a long intellectual history, going at least as far back as Bernoulli. It also has a strong intuitive appeal: what it essentially requires is that *all* possible circumstances that may influence the performance of a project (rather than the most favourable ones, for example) are given some weight in assessing its worth. The use of the expected utility rule for project choice rewards projects that are flexible and is easily adapted to a wide variety of possible future developments that could occur.

8.3 'SUBJECTIVE' PROBABILITY AND THE EXPECTED UTILITY RULE

Concepts of probability based on the frequency approach may not always be applicable in economic life.

Firstly, the use of frequency distributions based on past experience to derive the probability of an event may not be possible because there is no past experience to draw on. The lack of experience may arise from the nature of the events in question. Thus, the frequency approach to probability is, by definition, concerned with repetitive events. But some events are rare rather than repetitive. Indeed, if they are sufficiently rare they are regarded as 'totally new' or 'unique'. For decisions that depend on such events, the frequency approach to probability is inappropriate.

The difficulty may also simply be the lack of availability of information, i.e. even if the event in question is repetitive, the number of observations on which data are available to the decision-maker may be too small for the frequency approach to be applicable.

Thirdly, information may vary in quality. Decision-making on economic policies often involves an element of guessing which may be based on 'opinions', 'hunch', 'intuition', 'rumour' or even 'prejudice'. These in various ways amount to subjective estimates about likelihood that are influenced by many different kinds of information. The relative weights to be attached implicitly or otherwise to these different kinds of information is itself an important part of the problem.

Such considerations cannot be included within the framework of a frequency theory of probability. On the frequency approach, 'information' has an all-or-nothing character: either information relating to a sufficiently large number of repetitions of an event is available or it is not. In the former case the language of probability is relevant; in the latter it does not apply.

The point of departure for the theory of subjective probability is that some events or propositions may be considered more likely ('probable') than others without necessarily implying a frequency or statistical interpretation of probability. On this approach probability is interpreted rather as the 'degree of belief' – i.e. the degree of confidence that one has in the occurrence of some event or in the truth of a stated proposition.

As far as its intuitive basis is concerned, the subjective interpretation of probability appears to be as old as the notion of probability itself. However, the *idea* of subjective probability as such does not necessarily lead to an operationally meaningful theory. In order that this may be possible, it is essential that subjective probability be measurable. This in turn implies a conceptual framework in terms of which numerical values could be assigned to degrees of belief in a systematic manner.

Specifically, such a conceptual framework must include the following elements. Firstly, the concept of a degree of belief must be made operational by being linked to action. Thus, from an intuitive point of view, the degree of a belief is naturally interpreted as the extent to which one is prepared to act on it. Indeed, it could reasonably be argued that the kind of measurement of belief which is relevant from the point of view of probability theory is precisely measurement of belief as a basis for action.[1]

Traditionally, betting has been regarded as the kind for action to which degrees of belief are naturally related. Thus one might try to measure the degree of someone's belief in a certain event by proposing a bet on the occurrence of this event and finding out the lowest odds that he will accept. The 'probability' of 1/3 is thus related to that degree of belief which would lead to a bet of 2 to 1. Accepting or rejecting such bets may then be described as choosing between 'uncertain prospects' or between 'gambles'.

This approach suffers from two main limitations. In the first place, a bet is normally fixed in terms of money; the degree of belief, on the other hand, should, in principle, be related to the relative evaluation ('utilities') of the possible consequences which follow if the event on which one has bet occurs or does not occur. But the symmetry as between a gain of £1 and a loss of £1 does not imply the equivalence of the corresponding gain or loss of utility. Indeed; the disutility of a loss of £1 is often regarded as of greater magnitude than the utility of a gain of £1, i.e. it is assumed that money has diminishing marginal utility. Hence, in order to derive a measure of the degree of belief from betting, the bet should in principle be related to utility rather than money. Alternatively, the latter procedure may be regarded as approximately correct provided the stake is relatively small so that the marginal utility of money may be assumed to be constant.

The other limitation arises from the possibility of a person deriving a positive or negative utility from the act of gambling as such. The implications of this for decision-making will be considered later. At this stage we shall simply neglect this possibility.

We are now in a position to introduce the second basic requirement for building an operationally useful theory of subjective probability. This consists of a system of axioms for consistent choice between uncertain prospects. Such systems, which are broadly similar but differ from one another in detail, have been provided by a number of authors, including Ramsey [7], von Neumann and Morgenstern [9], Savage [10] and Marschak [11].

[1] See Ramsey ([7] pp. 169–70). Ramsey considers, for example, an alternative approach to measuring belief which states that beliefs differ in the intensity of feeling with which they are accompanied and the degree of belief is the intensity of this feeling ('belief-feeling' or feeling of conviction). Against this, Ramsey argues *inter alia* that beliefs which we hold most strongly are often accompanied by no feeling at all but are simply taken for granted.

The beauty of the axiomatic approach is that once some fairly weak consistency conditions are imposed on the decision-maker, both his numerical probabilities (degrees of belief) and his utility indices become simultaneously determined. Further, these numerical probabilities are found to satisfy the same algebraic laws as are satisfied (for quite different reasons) when the theory of probability is based on the frequency approach, while the numerical utility indices are unique except for scale and origin.

What are the implications of the theory of subjective probability for cost–benefit analysis?

The most important implication is that even if the decision-maker lacks enough information to be able to use statistical probabilities, he would still be justified in choosing risky projects according to the expected utility criterion. This basic result (Marschak [11], Massé [12]) can be stated as follows:

Let A denote the set of possible outcomes of the decisions made by the economic agent. Let a_{ij} $(i = 1, 2, \ldots, m; j = 1, 2, \ldots, n)$ equal the element of A associated with the ith state of the world and the jth decision of the agent. If the agent behaves 'as he should',[1] there is a unique set of non-negative numbers p_i, whose sum equals 1, and a numerical function $u(a_{ij}) = u_{ij}$ such that one decision (for example, the jth decision) is preferred to another (for example, the kth), if, and only if,

$$\sum_{i=1}^{m} p_i u_{ij} > \sum_{i=1}^{m} p_i u_{ik}.$$

The numbers p_i are called subjective probabilities. The function u is called the utility function. The sums appearing in the two terms of the above inequality are the expectations of utility associated with the jth and the kth decision, respectively.

The subjective probability approach thus leads to the same decision rule as was derived from the Law of Large Numbers for the frequency probability analysis: choose the project with the highest expected utility.

However, a justification for the expected utility criterion for project choice which rests on subjective probability raises some special difficulties, which we consider below.

Firstly, the axioms on which the subjective probability approach

---

[1] That is, according to certain axioms. These can be formulated in a number of different ways, for example as described in section 1.4 above in the context of cardinal measures of utility.

leads to the expected utility rule exclude the love or hatred of gambling as such (cf. section 1.4 above). This exclusion may not always be justified. Thus, the love of danger, hence of 'gambling', could, in certain circumstances, be a relevant element in individual decision-making under uncertainty.[1]

Secondly, there is the following basic problem. Subjective probability is defined in terms of an individual decision-maker's degrees of belief. On the other hand, cost–benefit analysis is concerned with project choice from the point of view of society as a whole. How, then, is one justified in using a subjective probability approach in the context of cost–benefit analysis?

One possible answer is that social attitudes towards uncertainty should reflect individual attitudes towards it. Hence, if individuals are consistent in the sense that they obey the 'rationality axioms' required by the theory of subjective probability (and hence act as if they maximised expected utility), society should behave in the same way. The argument may thus be regarded as an application to choices involving uncertainty of the principles of 'individualistic ethics' for constructing a social welfare function, viz. the principle that social choice should reflect individual values (see Chapter 3). The difficulties involved are also broadly similar to those that arise in that context.

Thus, one important difficulty is that subjective probabilities, i.e. degrees of belief, *are* subjective. An individual's degrees of belief in the occurrence of an event depend, no doubt, on the amount of information concerning the event that he has. However, it will also depend on the way he assesses the information available, e.g. how he sorts out 'rumour' from 'hard' evidence and combines them to arrive at an overall judgement. Such 'weighing up of evidence' depends on the individual decision-maker: his intuition, his experience, his life-style, his training in logical thought, his personality as a whole. Given exactly the same information concerning an event, individuals may thus differ in their degrees of belief as to its occurrence. Hence, even though the degrees of belief of a 'consistent' individual will obey the usual rules of probability, two such consistent individuals may not necessarily derive the same probability

---

[1] Cf. Marschak ([13] p. 138): 'The danger of loss including ruin, though probably shunned in the conservative code or cant of business, has quite possibly added to the zest and desirability of many an historically important venture, in the career of the leaders of mercenary armies, in the financing of great geographic discoveries or, closer to our time, in the financing of inventions and theater plays, and in stock and commodity speculation.'

measures of events even if they consider their respective beliefs on the same data. Whose beliefs, then, are to be believed?

That the problem is similar in principle to the more familiar problem considered earlier (whose value judgements are to be used for social choice?) will be readily seen. Moreover, on the subjective probability approach, the probability numbers and the utility numbers are determined *together*. Hence, given the axioms, and sufficient data to measure subjective probability, the rules for project choice are completely determined. The subjective element in the assessment of probability can thus be of crucial importance.

The force of this criticism of the subjective probability approach as a basis for project choice is limited by the following considerations.

Firstly, from one point of view, the subjective element involved in this approach may be regarded as an element of strength rather than of weakness. The evaluation of risky projects necessarily involves elements of personal judgement. The subjective probability approach has the virtue of making such judgements explicit.

Secondly, to hold that individual judgements of probability are subjective does not necessarily imply the view that standards by which such judgements can be compared are totally absent. The concept of a 'right-thinking' person whose degrees of belief provide such a standard may be of some use in this context. It is easy enough to criticise such a concept as 'idealised' or 'abstract'. Yet experience suggests that the degrees of belief of an individual with training, special knowledge or sound judgement are frequently 'better', i.e. correspond more closely to what actually happens. The suggested interpretation provides a formal way of recognising the value of such qualities for wise project choice.

The other main criticism of the subjective probability approach is concerned with the axioms on which this approach is based. Specifically, the question is: assuming that the axioms hold for individuals, does it necessarily follow that they hold for society as a whole?

In our earlier discussion of the choice of a social welfare function, we have already dealt with the same question in a different form, namely, given utility indices for all individuals which have been derived on the basis of a set of axioms relating to their choice as between uncertain prospects, can these indices be aggregated into an index of social choice? It was pointed out that, in general, this cannot be done without interpersonal comparisons of utility involving fairly specialised value judgements.

To sum up, from the point of view of the methodology of cost–benefit analysis, an appeal to the subjective probability analysis turns out to be a rather mixed blessing. While it appears to justify the use of the expected utility rule even if 'hard' data on relative frequencies are lacking, it does so only by letting in various types of value judgements 'through the back door'. A study of the literature suggests that the exact implications of the value judgements in question are yet far from clear.

8.4 RISK AVERSION

Our argument in section 8.2 that it is appropriate to judge a project by its expected social utility alone assumes that there are a large number of projects, each contributing a relatively small proportion to social welfare. It is this that justifies the 'cancelling of risks' from individual projects. If this assumption fails to be satisfied, the expected utility criterion is no longer decisive. Some account will then have to be taken of the variance as well as the expectation of the probability distribution of the utility due to the project.

Thus, as between two projects which differ in their variance, but have an equal expected utility, it may be desirable to penalise the project with a greater variance. This can be regarded as constituting society's adjustment for 'risk aversion'.

There are two possible circumstances where such considerations are likely to be important. Firstly, a particular project may, in fact, be large in relation to the total national income. This could occur, for example, in a small underdeveloped country with one main crop or mineral product.

Secondly, regional objectives, rather than national income alone, could be important. For example, the failure of a project might have particularly damaging consequences for the region where it is located.

In either case, it appears reasonable, up to a point, to reward projects with a relatively certain outcome (i.e. with a small variance), even if they lead to reduced expected income (hence lower expected utility). The expected utility criterion is no longer adequate.

One suggested method for dealing with such cases is to make the merit of a project depend both on the expectation and the variance of its returns. Thus let μ and V denote expected return and the variance of returns respectively. The suggested criterion is:

$$\text{maximise } U = \mu - \lambda V$$

where λ is some positive constant between 0 and 1. The higher λ is, the higher the aversion to risk.[1]

On the basis of this approach, attempts have been made to derive indifference curves between μ and σ where σ denotes standard deviation (the square root of variance). These are sometimes referred to in the literature as 'gamblers' indifference curves'. Given λ, one can then, in principle, read off the trade-off between μ and σ, i.e. the rate at which expected income must increase in order to compensate for increase in standard deviation. By varying λ, one can also study the implications of the extent of risk aversion for project choice.

While the use of such an approach can sometimes lead to useful insights, in general it is not to be recommended. For not only is it impossible to derive the indifference curves without making restrictive assumptions, but the quadratic form of the utility function also leads to paradoxical results. Thus, for example, as Arrow and others have shown, it implies that as an individual (or a nation) becomes wealthier, the amount of risky investments will tend to diminish. Both experience and intuition suggest the contrary.[2]

There is as yet no generally accepted method for dealing with risk aversion in cost–benefit analysis in a systematic way. Hence, the only feasible alternative is to estimate the expected social utility of a project in the usual way and then reduce this by a certain percentage depending on the extent of risk aversion thought to be appropriate.

A more precise analysis of the concept of 'a socially appropriate degree of risk aversion' is an extremely difficult task, which we shall not attempt to undertake. However, some general comments are in order.

Firstly, the appropriate degree of risk aversion must depend on the general levels of prosperity. Richer communities can afford to take more risks – for example, to undertake more research which tends to involve a very high variance of outcomes.

Secondly, both for an individual and a society, the appropriate-

---

[1] In effect, this implies the use of a quadratic utility function for choosing between projects. This follows from the definition of variance. We saw that, for a variable x and mean μ, we can write $V = E(x-\mu)^2$, where E denotes expectation. It follows that the equation above becomes

$$U = \mu - \lambda E(x-\mu)^2$$

which is a quadratic equation in x.

[2] The paradoxical implications of a quadratic utility function are discussed in Arrow [14].

ness of the degree of risk aversion depends on whether the existing liquidity position is regarded as satisfactory. A society with large accumulated foreign exchange reserves may, for example, have a different attitude to the riskiness of an export project than one with a low level of reserves and a persistent balance of payments problem. Such considerations should be reflected in cost–benefit analysis.

Thirdly, the degree of risk aversion may be influenced by religious or moral values. A strong aversion to risky undertakings may for example be associated with the prevalence of a puritanical ethic.

To conclude, the problem of properly assessing risk aversion is a difficult one. However, its practical importance for cost–benefit analysis should not be exaggerated.

In a great many cases, the Law of Large Numbers will hold. The expected utility rule will then be applicable.

As far as the exceptions are concerned, consider again the two main cases we mentioned as examples. In one case, a single project accounts for a significant share of national income. In the other, objectives of policy which cannot be subsumed under national income are important.

In neither case can standard methods of cost–benefit analysis be easily applied. Hence, more traditional approaches to decision-making will, in any event, be necessary to deal with them.

8.5 UNCERTAINTY AND DECISION CRITERIA

Situations may exist where the decision-maker cannot assign any probabilities at all (whether of the objective or the subjective variety) to the various events that could affect the results of his actions. In such situations, often described in the literature as situations of 'complete ignorance', the expected utility criterion for project choice cannot be applied.

The decision problem in situations of this type can, in principle, be attacked by using tools similar to those used in the theory of games. It is assumed that the decision-maker knows his possible actions, the possible states of nature and the utility (pay-off) to him of the results of his actions under each such state; in other words, he knows his pay-off matrix.[1]

A number of different decision criteria based on this approach have been proposed in the literature. The most important are

[1] To this extent the description of such situations as involving 'complete ignorance' is inaccurate.

described below. An example is then given, illustrating the application of each rule.

1. *The Maximin Pay-off (Wald) Criterion*

The logic of the maximin approach lies in the quest for security. By assumption, probabilities of different states of nature do not exist. Hence, it is agreed, the prudent man should guard against the *worst* possible outcome from each strategy. This leads to the following rule:

For each strategy consider the minimum pay-off it could give.

Choose the strategy with the highest minimum pay-off.[1] In an alternative statement of the same rule, pay-offs (utility) are replaced by 'loss' (disutility or real cost). The rule becomes: Choose the strategy with the lowest maximum loss. In this form the rule is called the minimax loss criterion.

2. *The Minimax Regret Criterion (Savage)*

The criterion can be derived from the minimax loss principle if one redefines the 'loss' corresponding to each strategy for each state of nature as the difference between the disutility actually incurred and that which would have been incurred had the state of nature been correctly forecast, and the appropriate (minimum-cost) strategy for that state of nature adopted. The rule is as follows:

For each entry in the pay-off matrix, subtract the actual pay-off (i.e. the entry itself) from the potential pay-off (the amount that *could* have been obtained had nature's strategy been known in advance). This difference is taken to measure 'regret'. For each strategy pick out the maximum regret that it could involve. Then choose the strategy with the lowest maximum regret.

3. *The Index of Pessimism Criterion (Hurwicz)*

Both the maximin pay-off (Wald) and the minimax regret (Savage) criteria are concerned exclusively with maximising security. They differ only in offering different concepts of what maximum security means. The Wald criterion identifies maximum security with the

---

[1] The logic of the maximin approach is well described in A. E. Housman's lines:

> Then face it as a wise man would
> And plan for ill and not for good.

highest floor level for pay-off; the Savage criterion regards it as the lowest maximum regret. Both favour ultra-conservative decisions, since only the worst consequences are taken into account.

Hurwicz proposed instead that decisions be based on both the 'worst' and the 'best' outcomes, the relative weights to be assigned to these depending on the degree of pessimism of the decision-maker. This leads to the following rule:

Let a fixed number α between 0 and 1 represent the 'index of pessimism' of the decision-maker.

Let m_i and M_i be respectively the minimum and the maximum of the pay-offs corresponding to strategy i ($i = 1, 2, \ldots$).

For each i compute the index $\alpha m_i + (1-\alpha)M_i$, i.e. the weighted average of the lowest and the highest pay-offs that could result from the ith strategy, weighted by α and $1-\alpha$ respectively. Let this be called the α-index for strategy. Then choose the strategy with the highest α-index.

4. The Principle of Insufficient Reason (*Laplace, Bayes*)

According to the Principle of Insufficient Reason, which was first stated by Bernoulli, a decision-maker under 'complete ignorance' should assume that all possible states of nature are equally likely. This leads naturally to the following rule:

Assume that all the states of nature under consideration are equiprobable. From the pay-off matrix derive the expected pay-off for each strategy. Then choose the strategy with the highest expected pay-off.

A numerical example may help to illustrate how the various decision criteria are applied. Assume that the decision-maker has four strategies to choose from. There are four possible states of nature. The pay-off matrix, representing the utility levels of the decision-maker in the various possible cases, is as follows:

	States of nature			
Strategies	1	2	3	4
1	2	2	0	1
2	1	1	1	1
3	0	4	0	0
4	1	3	0	0

To apply the 'maximin utility' criterion we simply look at the minimum utility for each strategy. These are:

Strategies	Minimum utility
1	0
2	1
3	0
4	0

According to this criterion, strategy 2, which gives a higher minimum level of utility than the others, should be chosen.

To apply the minimax regret criterion we must first derive the regret matrix corresponding to the given pay-off matrix. Consider, for example, the column of regrets if the true state of nature is 1. If the decision-maker had known in advance that this was so, his correct choice would be strategy 1, which gives him a higher utility than other strategies for that state of nature. Hence the implied regret for strategy 1, under state of nature 1, is $2-2 = 0$; that for strategies 2, 3 and 4 are $2-1 = 1$, $2-0 = 2$ and $2-1 = 1$ respectively. The regrets when other states of nature prevail can be calculated in the same way.

The regret matrix is:

	States of nature			
Strategies	1	2	3	4
1	0	2	1	0
2	1	3	0	0
3	2	0	1	1
4	1	1	1	1

By looking at the regrets for each strategy, it is clear that strategy 4 has the lowest maximum regret. Hence the minimax regret criterion recommends strategy 4.

To apply the Hurwicz criterion, we pick out for each strategy i ($i = 1, 2, 3, 4$) the lowest pay-off (m_i) and the highest pay-off (M_i) and compute their weighted average, $\alpha m_i + (1-\alpha)M_i$, α being the index of pessimism.

Strategy (i)	m_i	M_i	$\alpha m_i + (1-\alpha)M_i$
1	0	2	$2-2\alpha$
2	1	1	1
3	0	4	$4-4\alpha$
4	0	3	$3-3\alpha$

According to this criterion, which strategy should be chosen depends on the degree of pessimism as measured by α. However, it is clear that according to this criterion, strategy 4 is preferable to strategies 1 and 3 for all α less than 1 and is also preferable to strategy 2 for all α less than $\frac{3}{4}$. Hence as long as the index of pessimism is below $\frac{3}{4}$, the Hurwicz criterion recommends strategy 4 as optimal.

Finally, to apply the Bayes–Laplace criterion we assume that all four strategies of nature are equiprobable so that each has the probability $\frac{1}{4}$. On this basis, the expected utilities of the various strategies are found to be 5/4 for strategy 1, and 1 for each of the others. Hence the Bayes–Laplace criterion recommends strategy 1.

In addition to the criteria described above, a number of others which are too complex to be included in this study have also been proposed in the literature.[1] Clearly, there is no dearth of decision criteria for dealing with 'pure uncertainty'. Unfortunately, none of them appears to be particularly satisfactory.

The basic limitation of the maximin (Wald) criterion is that it utilises only a small part of the information provided in the pay-off matrix, namely, that relating to the 'worst' outcome for each choice of strategy. It thus leads to a conservative bias which, if adopted for the social choice of projects, might well inhibit long-run growth and development.

The minimax regret (Savage) criterion suffers equally from the limitation mentioned – a conservative bias. In addition, it suffers from two other serious limitations.

Firstly, the appropriateness of measuring 'regret' by the difference between actual and potential utility is open to question. Thus, suppose in one case the actual (utility) pay-off is 30 while the potential (utility) pay-off is 32. The differences in the two cases will necessarily imply an equivalent 'regret' only if utility is *cardinally* measurable (cf. section 1.4 above).

Secondly, the criterion need not be independent of irrelevant alternatives,[2] as is easily seen from the following example.

Let the matrix of utility pay-offs with three states of nature and two strategies open to the decision-maker be as follows:

	States of nature		
Strategies	1	2	3
1	2	12	6
2	7	4	12

[1] See, for example, Luce and Raiffa [15].
[2] Cf. above, p. 79, for a definition of the independence of irrelevant alternatives. The influence of such alternatives on maximin principles is discussed in Dorfman [16].

The corresponding 'regret' matrix is

		States of nature	
	1	2	3
Strategies			
1	5	0	6
2	0	8	0

The minimax regret criterion would then recommend strategy 1 in preference to strategy 2 since the maximum regret for this strategy is lower than that for strategy 2.

Now suppose a third strategy becomes available to the decision-maker so that the pay-off matrix becomes:

		States of nature	
	1	2	3
Strategies			
1	2	12	6
2	7	4	12
3	12	7	3

The regret matrix corresponding to the new pay-off matrix is:

		States of nature	
	1	2	3
Strategies			
1	10	0	6
2	5	8	0
3	0	5	9

Hence, according to the minimax regret criterion, strategy 2 is now preferred both to strategy 1 and to strategy 3 since strategy 2 involves the lowest maximum regret.

The Bayes–Laplace criterion has been criticised as being based on a contradiction, for it attempts to bring back probability, which a situation of complete ignorance is supposed by definition to exclude.

In order to legitimise the attempt, appeal is made to the Principle of Insufficient Reason. However, this principle itself is of doubtful validity since knowledge, including knowledge of equiprobability, cannot be inferred from ignorance.

One consequence of this basic weakness is that the choice of strategy according to the Bayes–Laplace criterion may vary with the classification of states of nature which are to be regarded as equiprobable. For example, in evaluating different schemes of flood control the states of nature could conceivably be classified as 'flood' and 'no flood', or as 'severe flood', 'moderate flood' and 'no flood'. With the former classification the probability of the non-occurrence of floods is regarded as $\frac{1}{2}$; with the latter it is $\frac{1}{4}$. The expected utility of various policies, and hence project choice, will tend to vary in the two cases.

The Index of Pessimism (Hurwicz) criterion has much intuitive appeal. It is also perhaps rather less open to some of the more serious objections that have been raised against other proposed criteria for decision-making under 'complete ignorance'.

Thus, the Hurwicz criterion explicitly introduces a psychological variable (α, the degree of pessimism) into the decision-making process. This has the effect of making the criterion not only more realistic but also more general. Thus, for $\alpha = 1$ ('complete' pessimism), the criterion reduces to the maximin rule; for $\alpha = \frac{1}{2}$ it is equivalent to the Bayes–Laplace criterion.

However, this greater generality of the Hurwicz criterion has its own disadvantage, which is that the value of α is left undefined. One suggested way of estimating α is to infer it from an observed decision under conditions where complete ignorance appears to prevail. Thus, for example, suppose the pay-off matrix in utility numbers is:

	State of nature	
Strategy	1	2
1	0	4
2	3	3

If the decision-maker chooses strategy 1, one could infer that $0\alpha+4(1-\alpha)$ exceeds $3\alpha+3(1-\alpha)$, i.e. α is less than $\frac{1}{4}$. If the decision-maker professes to be indifferent between the two courses of action, $\alpha = \frac{1}{4}$. The value of α inferred from observations could then be used in other cases, so as to ensure consistent choice.

One difficulty with this procedure is that it fails to distinguish between 'is' and 'ought'; for the decision to use 'existing' values of α must itself imply a value judgement. This is indeed a difficulty of all decision criteria, whether or not uncertainty is important (cf. Chapter 3 above).

An alternative and less ambitious approach would be to carry out a 'sensitivity analysis', using the Hurwicz criterion with varying values of α. This will not of course tell us which α *should* be used for social choice of projects. It will, however, give the decision-maker under uncertainty some insight into what such decision involves. It may even help him to adopt such value judgements as may be necessary in a consistent and systematic rather than in a haphazard and subjective way.

G

Finally, one must concede that the Hurwicz criterion, even though it is more general than some other proposed criteria, is still not general enough; for it is based on two extreme values of outcomes, the best and the worst only, all intermediate outcomes being excluded from consideration.

8.6 SOME RULES OF THUMB

The techniques for dealing with risk and uncertainty in cost–benefit analysis that we have been discussing so far are relatively sophisticated. On the other hand, in practice such adjustments, if they are made at all, tend to be conventional rules of thumb of a very simple type. For example, the following three methods were suggested in the *Green Book* [17]:

(a) Adding a risk premium to the 'pure' rate of discount in cal-culating present values.

(b) Raising those items of costs or reducing those items of benefits that appear to be uncertain, by a certain percentage.

(c) Using a project life less than the formal economic life for comparable but relatively riskless projects.

We shall comment briefly on each of these.

(a) The question of the appropriate rate of discount to be used in project evaluation formed the subject-matter of Chapter 6. How-ever, the problems arising from risk and uncertainty were not specifically discussed in that context. Essentially, adding a risk premium to the discount rate makes the discount factor $d_t = \dfrac{1}{(1+i+j)^t}$ instead of $\dfrac{1}{(1+i)^t}$, where j is the risk premium.

It follows that using a risk premium implies that the risks involved increase at a compound rate with time. For most of the risks to which a project is normally subject, this does not appear to be the case.

The 'common-sense' argument in favour of the use of a risk premium, viz. that the more distant in time an item is, the greater is the uncertainty involved, appears to confuse uncertainty with underestimation. What the risk-premium argument implies, for example, is that the extent of underestimation of costs (or over-estimation of benefits) involved in a project design increases mono-tonically with time. But in most cases things may turn out better *or* worse than expected.

There is one important exception to this conclusion. This arises if the risks concerned consist solely in the possibility that the project may fail at any time (i.e. its net benefit may become zero from that time onwards), the probabilities of failure in different periods being equal and mutually independent.

In such a case, a risk premium equal to the probability of failure will indeed provide a correct method of calculating present values; it will also be formally equivalent to the 'expected utility' criterion (see sections 8.2 and 8.3). This can be seen as follows.

Suppose that for each year of operation of the project there are only two possibilities to be considered, namely:

(i) 'success', i.e. a level of production whose benefit is assessed at V; and
(ii) 'failure', i.e. going out of production, leading to zero benefit from that year onwards.

Let the probability of failure in any given year be j. Consider the mathematical expectation of the benefit due to the project in the first year. This equals

$$(1-j)V+p \cdot 0 = (1-j)V.$$

To calculate the expected benefit in the second year we have to take into account three mutually exclusive events:

(i) that the project has already failed in the first year;
(ii) that the project has not failed in the first year but fails in the second; and
(iii) that the project does not fail in the first two years.

For items (i) and (ii) the contribution to expected benefit is 0. Also, the probability of item (iii) is $(1-j)^2$. Hence the expected benefit for year 2 is $(1-j)^2 V$. A similar argument shows that the expected benefit in year 3 is $(1-j)^3 V$, and so on.

Thus the project leads to the time stream of expected benefits:

$$(1-j)V, \quad (1-j)^2 V, \quad (1-j)^3 V, \ldots.$$

The present value of this is equivalent to that of a time stream of 'riskless' benefits of V per year over project life at a rate of discount which is increased approximately by j.[1]

Consider next the second type of adjustment mentioned above:

[1] This follows from the consideration that for relatively small p,
$$\sum_t (1-p)^t = \sum_t \frac{1}{(1+p)^t} \text{ aproximately.}$$

applying a premium or a discount on estimates of costs and benefits respectively so as to provide a safety margin. This device can be rationalised as follows. Experience suggests that estimates by technicians and engineers, which provide the basis for project analysis, tend to be over-optimistic. This is probably because such estimates are based on 'ideal' conditions which may not, in fact, prevail. A well-known example is the frequency with which the actual construction costs of a project exceed figures specified in the design. The discrepancy is then attributed to delays in getting the work started, costs of materials being higher than expected and other unforeseen contingencies. Similarly, the increases in crop yields resulting from the use of some new input (e.g. chemical fertilisers) are often found to be less than agronomic experiments carried out in 'model farms' tend to suggest. In such cases, the use of a safety margin would help to provide a corrective.

To this extent, it helps in making forecasts of project performance, and hence cost–benefit analysis itself, more accurate. However, the method has serious limitations.

Firstly, *ad hoc* adjustments to initial estimates of costs and benefits are not an adequate substitute for a thoroughgoing and systematic assessment. Such an assessment, based both on past experience and on expert knowledge of the field, must in any case form an essential part of project evaluation.

Secondly, there are many kinds of risks other than that of over-optimism. The method in question provides little help in dealing with these.

Hence, the usefulness of the method as a *general* adjustment for risk and uncertainty is rather limited. On the other hand, as noted earlier, the use of a safety margin can provide an adjustment for risk aversion. Hence, in situations where for various reasons the expected utility rule does not apply, it has a useful role to play.

The third alternative suggested by the *Green Book* [17] amounts to using an underestimate of project life. This can be regarded as an alternative way of applying a safety margin and hence as a crude adjustment for risk aversion. It has also the effect of removing from consideration the benefits and costs of a project in its later years. To this extent it is similar to a risk premium.

Closely related to this method is the use of the so-called 'pay-off period'. This is defined as a fixed and relatively short time-period within which any project in order to be acceptable must break even. Again, the method is very crude and has little to recommend it.

To sum up, the use of rough adjustments such as these can be better understood as a reflection of the force of inertia in management practices rather than as a reasoned attempt to adjust for risk and uncertainty. Their replacement by methods with a firm foundation in economic theory can confidently be predicted as cost–benefit analysis gets under way.

Before concluding the chapter, a word of warning is in order. This chapter has been concerned with the appropriate adjustments to be made in evaluating projects that involve uncertainty. For projects with relatively certain costs or benefits, such adjustments are unnecessary. However, this in itself does not provide a reason for society preferring 'certain' to 'uncertain' projects *per se*. The theory of decision-making carries no implication whatever that only decisions made under certainty are worthy or justified.[1] Indeed, one of the points to emerge from our discussion is the irrationality of some rules of thumb in common use (e.g. a risk premium on the rate of discount) which may have the effect of unduly discouraging investment in uncertain projects.

8.7 SUMMARY

This chapter has been concerned with the complex issue of risk and uncertainty. Two main approaches were distinguished, the first based on the idea of 'expected utility' and the second on explicit attempts to account for risk aversion. Within the former category it was noted that, where probabilities could be attached to outcomes, these probabilities might be 'objective' – i.e. based on the observation of repeated past events – or 'subjective' – based on the 'degree of belief' of the decision-maker. Objections to both approaches were noted, although it was concluded that the expected utility approach was applicable in many cases. The problem of additional value judgements was raised in respect of subjective probabilities, since there is clearly a problem of deciding *whose* assessments are to count.

Where the expected utility approach was not applicable, and

---

[1] The fallacy of insisting on certain knowledge is vividly illustrated by the conversation that takes place among the chorus in *Agamemnon* while Agamemnon is being murdered:

11. Wait; not too fast. What is our evidence? Those groans?
   Are we to prophesy from them that the king's dead?
12. We must be certain; this excitement's premature.
   Guessing and certain knowledge are two different things.

The Oresteian Trilogy (trans. Philip Vellacott)

probabilities could still be attached, it was concluded that the attempt to use a utility function incorporating both expected values and variance foundered on several objections. The state of play as regards the theory of risk aversion in the context of cost–benefit analysis was therefore seen to be unsatisfactory.

Where probabilities cannot be attached to outcomes at all, the context was dubbed one of 'uncertainty' and well-established decision rules were considered. Criticisms of each approach were noted, but it was shown that, perhaps rather surprisingly, rules for dealing with uncertainty were better established than rules for dealing with risky situations.

Finally, it was recognised that, in practice, either no rules are applied to deal with risk/uncertainty, or that certain 'rules of thumb' were used. The most celebrated of the latter is the 'risk premium' approach which was discussed in some detail. With some exceptions it was shown to be a misleading approach to dealing with risk and uncertainty.

Part Four
Case Studies

9 The Siting of London's Third Airport

LONDON is already served by two airports, at Heathrow and Gatwick. In December 1970 a Government-appointed Commission, under the chairmanship of Mr Justice Roskill, recommended that a third airport should be built at Cublington in Buckinghamshire, some 45 miles from the centre of London (see Fig. 9.0.1), and that the first of the airport's proposed four runways should be built in 1980. The recommendation was the outcome of a lengthy inquiry into a number of possible sites, of which four were short-listed for detailed analysis. Of the seven members of the Commission, only one, Professor Colin Buchanan, dissented from the majority view.[1]

At an early stage, the Commission established a Research Team whose primary function was to carry out a detailed 'cost–benefit' analysis of the four sites. The analysis was published in January 1970 and showed Cublington to be the least disadvantageous site on the basis of the assumptions and shadow prices devised by the Research Team.[2]

This cost–benefit analysis, and the modifications to it, undoubtedly played a dominant role in determining the Commission's majority recommendation. Thus the majority recommendation declares that 'Recognising, as we always have, both the strengths and limitations of cost–benefit analysis, we used it to assist in the short-list selection and, as is well known, the Research Team used it in the work which we published in January 1970. Nothing has happened to make us regret our decision. No one has yet suggested

[1] The United Kingdom Government was not bound by the recommendation of the Roskill Commission. At the time of writing the United Kingdom Government has announced its intention to reject the Commission's majority recommendation and to build the airport at Foulness. The background and nature of the Commission's proceedings are outlined in Pearce [1].

[2] This report comprised vol. VII of the Commission's *Papers and Proceedings*, hereafter referred to as CTLA, vol. VII [2]. The Commission's final Report was published in January 1971 and is referred to here as CTLA, *Report* [3]. At no stage was it easy to distinguish the division of responsibilities between the Commission and their Research Team for the published work, and no attempt is made to do so here.

a better alternative' (CTLA, *Report*, para. 3.13). And later, '. . . we know that its results must be treated with reserve, not only because of doubts attaching to the results but also because of the many items which the analysis cannot reflect' (ibid., para. 3.16).

Fig. 9.0.1 below shows the relative positions of the four short-listed sites, Cublington, Thurleigh, Nuthampstead and Foulness,

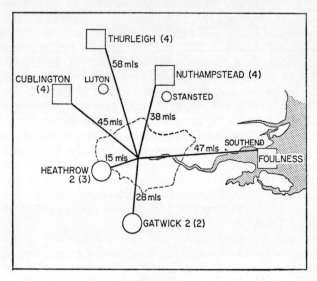

FIG. 9.0.1

and their travel distances from the centre of London. Several smaller airports are also shown. The unbracketed figures by the airport sites on the map show the number of existing runways, and the bracketed figures show proposed or possible runways. Clearly, the timing of the third London Airport (TLA) will depend on the extent to which the capacity of the other airports is expanded. The third runway at Heathrow is very much conjecture: the site there is between the M4 motorway and the A4 main road and, while it is possible to develop the site for a full-scale runway, it has generally been considered suitable only for a short- or vertical-take-off aircraft. The second runway at Gatwick is very much more likely, but was excluded from the Commission's final set of assumptions as far as determining the opening date of the TLA was concerned. The choice of Foulness would have enabled Luton airport to remain open, and possibly expand from one to two runways. The choice of any of the inland sites would involve the closure of Luton airport, because of air traffic management difficulties.

9.1 THE COST-BENEFIT ANALYSIS: AN OVERVIEW

The 'cost–benefit analysis', published in January 1970, was unusual in several respects: first, because of the absence of a valuation of the benefits of the airport, and second, because it attempted to value some disamenity effects previously omitted from cost–benefit studies because of the practical difficulties involved. Since benefits were not valued, the decision rule implied in the analysis was to select the site with the lowest total of social costs. It was argued, however, that the unmeasured benefits not only exceeded the costs, but were equal for all the four sites, so that what appears to be an exercise in cost minimisation is formally equivalent to maximising net social benefits (see below, section 9.3).

A shortened version of the final social cost table is given in Table 9.1.1. 1982 was selected as base since it was considered to be the most likely opening date for the TLA.[1] Cost streams were all discounted at a uniform rate of discount of 10 per cent, the rate used by the United Kingdom Government for nationalised industries' investment procedures.

The items of interest in Table 9.1.1 are the airspace movement costs (AMCs), the passenger user costs (PUCs) and the noise costs.

Fig. 9.1.1 on p. 205 shows the four sites, plus Heathrow (H) and the centre of London (L). The circle shows a hypothetical boundary embracing all the sites, London and Heathrow. Suppose now that an aircraft arrives at point A on the boundary, and the airport is sited at Cublington (C). Then it has to fly the distance AC (assuming, for simplicity, crow's-flight distances) and, on disembarking, passengers have to travel by surface transport the distance CL, assuming their destination is London. If the airport was at Thurleigh (T), the relevant distances would be AT and TL. The same analysis applies for entry points such as B, D and E.

Essentially, the costs associated with the distances AC, BC, AT, BT, etc., are the 'airspace movement costs', while the costs associated with surface access – i.e. the distances CL, TL, NL, etc. – are the 'passenger user costs'. Since the exercise is one of *comparative evaluation*, it is the differences in these costs between the sites that

---

[1] In other words, 1982 was thought to be the optimal time-phasing of the project. The date was selected on the basis of the procedure outlined in section 7.3 above.

will matter. However, not only will the costs for any one passenger (and the airlines) differ according to which site is used for the TLA, but each site may 'attract' a different *amount* of traffic. That is, there must be some way of forecasting the total number of persons, and commercial interests, with a 'propensity to fly' in each year of the relevant planning period, and their likely allocation between airports. Thus, if Foulness is the chosen site it is necessary to find out

Table 9.1.1 *Summary Cost–Benefit Analysis*
(1968 prices, discounted to 1982, £million)

	Cublington	Foulness	Nut-hampstead	Thurleigh
Airspace movement costs	1685–1899	1690–1906	1716–1934	1711–1929
Passenger user costs	1743–2883	1910–3090	1778–2924	1765–2922
Other costs, including capital costs	614–638	612–625	626–639	641–653
Noise costs	23	10	72	16
Total costs	4065–5433	4222–5631	4192–5569	4133–5520
Differences in cost compared to lowest-cost site	0	157–198	127–136	68–87

Source: Abstracted from component tables in Appendix 20 and Appendix 22, CTLA, *Report*. Ranges of values reflect low and high values of travelling time respectively (see below, pp. 218–20).

whether (*a*) the total number of passengers using *all* airports would be the same as if, say, Thurleigh was chosen, and (*b*) of the total who do fly, how many passengers would prefer to use Foulness, how many Heathrow and how many would use other airports such as Manchester. It will be seen that these two considerations were of paramount importance in producing differences in the total costs between the sites. The predicted choices of passengers in choosing airports was based upon a 'gravity model'. In addition, one aspect of the gravity model – the 'accessibility index' – was to modify the forecasts of total passengers.

The noise costs consisted of an evaluation of the welfare losses due to noise nuisance on residents in the 'noise zone' surrounding the airport, including disturbance to hospitals, schools and to recreational activities. Essentially, the principle used for evaluating the noise nuisance was that of hypothetical compensation, i.e.

estimating the lump-sum figure which would be required to compensate those who suffer from noise nuisance in such a way as to leave them as well off as they were before. As will be seen, the actual procedure used for estimating these compensatory sums relied upon a theoretical assumption that the price of any unit of property reflects not just the bricks and mortar embodied in the property, but also the surrounding amenity (or disamenity), accessibility to town

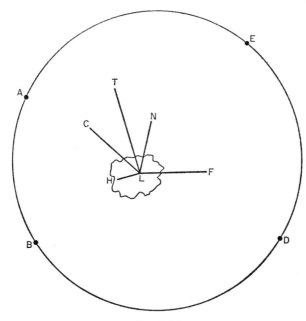

FIG. 9.1.1

centres, countryside, etc. On this assumption, any change in the surrounding amenity will, other things being equal, result in a change in the price of the property. Price changes alone would not reflect the full value of the welfare loss, however, since consumers may well attach a subjective value to their property which is in excess of the market price: there will be an element of consumer's surplus. In so far as any resident moves *because of* the airport, then he sustains a loss equal to this consumer's surplus and the price depreciation on his property. The resulting totals are shown in the 'noise costs' row of Table 9.1.1.

9.2 Assumptions and Terms of Reference

In any analysis where costs and benefits are projected over a lengthy time horizon, it is necessary to make assumptions about the state of technology in that period, and even about political change. The relevance of this kind of uncertainty was noted in Chapter 8. Significant among the many assumptions made by the Research Team, and by the Commission, were the following:

1. The possibility of a Channel Tunnel. The effect of the tunnel, if it were built, would clearly be to divert some proportion of European air traffic to surface transport, thus affecting the forecasts of total air passengers and their allocation between airports. In a note to the CTLA the Board of Trade stated that some 14 per cent of all passenger air traffic used routes which could be affected by the Channel Tunnel. This proportion was expected to fall to about 8 per cent in 1980. (See 'Further Research Team Work', Document 25.) In the final *Report*, the Commission estimated that, at best, some 5 million air journeys would be lost to the Tunnel in 1981, representing a one-year delay in the timing of the airport since passengers at London area airports are forecast to grow at approximately this rate each year. The effect was therefore thought to be 'too small to justify any further revision of the . . . traffic forecasts' (*Report*, Appendix 6, p. 194).

2. No realistic commercial development of vertical-take-off and short-take-off (VTOL/STOL) aircraft. The development of these aircraft for carrying passengers would mean that (*a*) the capacity of Heathrow and Gatwick could be expanded, (*b*) the smaller airports such as Luton, Southend and Stansted could be used and (*c*) other local airports serving passengers outside the London zone could be more intensively used. However, the Commission argued in their *Report* that 'a complete system of suitable airports might have to be available not only at cities in this country but also at destinations in Western Europe' (*Report*, para. 5.20). Exactly what the Commission had in mind here is not clear, but the implication is that VTOL/STOL services would be dependent 'upon the provision by Government or by industry of very large sums of money – an event which cannot be taken for granted'.

3. No national airports policy. No integrated plan of development for United Kingdom airports exists. The cost–benefit study was therefore carried out in a vacuum as far as the development of certain other airports is concerned. In its final report, the Commission re-emphasised that, as far as the developments of other airports were concerned, 'it is no part of our task to advise upon

them' (*Report*, para. 5.12). Nonetheless, they saw it as an integral part of their task to 'make reasonable assumptions about what is likely to take place at other airports which though outside our immediate responsibility could nonetheless affect our conclusions. The capacity of other airports thus becomes a matter of assumption or prediction in the light of the evidence before us *but not the outcome of an elaborate optimisation of the entire system*' (our italics). The Commission cannot be faulted for staying within their terms of reference, which appeared to imply consideration of a TLA to serve a regional rather than a national need. But it does mean that the exercise was one of unnecessary suboptimisation. Furthermore, the Commission was forced to consider travel demand from areas outside the South-east region in order to assess the overall traffic at the TLA. But this demand is affected by the availability of services from other existing airports. A complete analysis would therefore have amounted to an exercise in a national airports policy – global optimisation. The Commission's compromise between its terms of reference and the need to consider airport demand outside the South-east was effected by assuming a total *status quo* in terms of airport capacity at all other airports. Indeed, in the analysis preceding the final *Report*, several important airports outside the South-east region were excluded from consideration altogether. This issue is raised again when the 'gravity model' is discussed.

4. No 'advanced passenger train' – i.e. no development of trains capable of average speeds over 150 m.p.h. The effects of improved rail travel of this kind are twofold. Firstly, such rail links would compete with intra-United Kingdom air traffic, altering the amount of air traffic, and the distribution of the remaining traffic between airports. Secondly, it would affect substantially the 'accessibility' of the TLA sites, with differential effects if some sites are served by the link and others are not.

9.3 THE ABSENCE OF MEASURED BENEFITS

In cost–benefit analysis both costs and benefits are measured, and the objective function is most frequently taken to be the maximisation of net benefits. In the CTLA study, however, two types of benefit were distinguished, one of which was measured and the other of which was not. First, certain 'user benefits' were assessed. In forecasting the number of passengers likely to use the TLA, the Research Team argued that certain sites were likely to attract fewer passengers than other sites. By definition of passenger user costs and airspace movement costs, it follows that the site with the highest number of passengers would accumulate artificially high social costs. But 'it would be paradoxical that the most accessible site should have to carry such a debit',[1] so that the extra passengers at the more accessible sites were credited as *benefits* to those sites, the least accessible site being taken as 'base'. In this way, the different traffic loads at each site were 'equalised' in the sense of having these user benefits entered into the analysis as negative costs.

Second, a 'base load' of benefits was presumed for each site. These consisted of:

(i) the extra demand for air travel, which indicates an increased desire (and hence willingness to pay) for air travel;
(ii) the role of business air travel as a 'lubricant' to international trade;
(iii) the role of business air travel in spreading scientific and technological advances throughout the world;
(iv) the generation of income in the country where the airport is sited.[2]

These benefits were not assessed in monetary terms, nor is it easy to see how they could have been. For the procedure of selecting the site with lowest social cost to be correct, however, two propositions must hold:

(a) the 'base load' of benefits must exceed the social costs at the chosen site; and
(b) the 'base load' of benefits must be exactly the same at all four sites.

If proposition (a) does not hold, then the appropriate course of action is not to build the TLA at all (unless there is some other compelling reason for its construction, not allowed for in the cost–benefit analysis). If proposition (b) does not hold, then the social cost analysis will not produce the same results as a cost–benefit analysis.[3]

[1] CTLA, vol. VII, para. 1.5, p. 30.

[2] This list is a summary of paras. 5.8 to 5.12 in CTLA, vol. VII.

[3] In a revealing statement, the Research Team stated that the 'base load of benefits is *approximately* the same for all four sites' (CTLA, vol. VII, para. 5.2). But, as argued above, the base load of benefits must be *exactly* the same for the cost-minimisation analysis to be logically equivalent to a cost–benefit appraisal. Of course, the lowest-cost site might also have the highest base load of benefits, a view which could be held if the Research Team's traffic forecasts were correct (showing larger traffic volumes at the inland sites), and if their procedures for valuing air travellers' costs and disamenity costs are accepted.

9.4 THE FORECASTS OF PASSENGERS

In order to calculate the costs to air travellers it was necessary to forecast the total demand for air travel over the thirty-year planning horizon. The way in which this demand was expected to be 'allocated' between airports in the future is dealt with later on.

The first move was to estimate the total 'propensity to fly' (PTF) of the relevant classes of air travel users – British leisure passengers, British business passengers and non-British passengers.[1] In addition, air cargo traffic had also to be predicted.

The forecasting procedure for British leisure passengers *only* is outlined below. An air passenger survey carried out in 1969 produced a breakdown of air passengers by income of head of household. Thus it was possible to compare the number of persons in the total population, classified by income group, with the numbers of air passengers in each group. For example, the number of persons in the income group £1000 to £1500 in 1969 was 15 million, of which 1·21 million undertook air journeys. Hence the total 'propensity to fly' of this group was $1 \cdot 21/15 = 0 \cdot 08$. A total of 5·2 million journeys were undertaken in all. When these 'propensities to fly' were applied to the income distribution for the whole population in 1962, the result was an expected total of journeys of 4·0 million. In fact, only some 2·9 million journeys took place in 1962 (or *probably* took place: the estimate is not certain). Thus, the total increase in air journeys over the period 1962–9 was

$$(5 \cdot 2 - 2 \cdot 9) = 2 \cdot 3 \text{ million,}$$

of which $(5 \cdot 2 - 4 \cdot 0) = 1 \cdot 2$ million is accounted for by changes in the numbers of persons in the income groups, and

$$(4 \cdot 0 - 2 \cdot 9) = 1 \cdot 1$$ million is accounted for by an increase in the propensity to fly *within* income groups. Effectively, the 1·1 million can be thought of as a 'substitution' effect.

Now, in order to forecast the growth of British leisure traffic to

---

[1] Leisure and business passengers were distinguished because of the different values which these categories of passenger were supposed to attach to travel time (see below, pp. 218–20). Non-British passengers were distinguished partly because the method of predicting their demand for air travel was different, and partly because cost–benefit analyses frequently omit benefits and costs to foreign persons. The Research Team was therefore prepared to indicate the extent to which their inclusion or omission would alter the final cost figures. There is no particularly good reason for cost–benefit analyses to be 'nationalistic', but enormous problems can arise in identifying the gains and losses to foreign residents.

the year 2006 (giving a thirty-one-year time-horizon from 1975 but involving projections of thirty-seven years), it was necessary to know

(i) the future population to 2006;
(ii) the distribution of that population by income group;
(iii) any change in the propensity to fly *within* income groups.

By assuming a 3 per cent per annum rate of growth of real incomes and by supposing that the total distribution by income groups was increased at the same rate as the average income level, the Research Team overcame problem (ii). But, as the 1962–9 analysis showed, much of the increase in air travel was due to a changed propensity to fly within income groups, and there was no obvious way of estimating any likely changes in this variable over time. The result was that the 4·7 per cent per annum increase in 1962–9 was assumed to continue for all income groups. However, a 'ceiling' of three journeys was arbitrarily fixed to allow for the otherwise improbable number of journeys being made by certain income groups in the year 2006.

The change in the PTF was clearly central to the forecasts of passengers. The 1962–9 growth of traffic was thought to be explained by falls in the real cost of air travel, growth of charter traffic and other factors which made air travel more attractive. These factors were thought to be 'likely to continue to obtain in the future' (CTLA, vol. VII, para. 4.14). It is difficult to see how else the forecasts could have been made, but the most striking thing about them is the lack of any concrete information upon which to estimate the growth of demand, and the fact that substantial revisions were made even to the data for 1962–9.

The resulting forecasts for British non-business and other passengers are shown below.

The forecasts in Table 9.4.1 did not allow for the effect of choosing a particular site for the TLA. It was thought that the *accessibility* of the TLA site to the centres of population would affect the numbers using all airports. It was argued, however, that British leisure passengers *only* would be affected by the differences in accessibility. The growth of tourist traffic to Britain, for example, was assumed to be affected by 'the tour operators' methods of handling visitors rather than [by] the choice of one of the four possible sites . . .' (CTLA, vol. VII, para. 4.38). Business passengers were assumed to make the flight whatever the site (their demand being centred at Heathrow). In order to discover the effect of the TLA's accessibility on the total of British leisure traffic, an analysis was carried out to discover the relationship between passenger demand for travel at Heathrow and Gatwick and the accessibility of the passengers' points of origin to those airports. The results were of some importance, since they were designed to test the extent to which airport accessibility determined the demand for air travel.

Table 9.4.1 *Forecasts of Air Terminal Passengers at Heathrow,*
Gatwick and the TLA
(million journeys)

	British non-business	Total
1969	5·2	17·1
1975	9·3	33·2
1981	15·8	55·8
1991	43·9	122·5
2006	132·4	259·9

Firstly, those parts of Great Britain likely to be a source of demand for London's airports were divided into twenty-nine 'zones'. The income distribution and demographic grouping of each zone was estimated and the numbers in each group were multiplied by the national propensity to fly as previously derived to obtain a figure for 'expected passengers' from each zone. These *expected* numbers were compared to the *actual* numbers. In general, the ratio of actual to expected passengers was greatest in zones near to the airports, as one would expect if accessibility was at all important.

Secondly, it was necessary to measure the accessibility of each zone to each airport. An 'accessibility index' was calculated as

$$A_i = \frac{\sum_j D_j \cdot F_{ij}}{\sum_j D_j}$$

where i is the zone, j is the airport, D_j is the total number of passengers flying from airport j and F_{ij} is the 'cost' (yet to be defined) of getting from i to j. The point of the A_i index was to suggest that accessibility was determined by the cost of travelling from i to j – higher costs would mean lower accessibility – and by the range of services provided at airport j. Since no measure exists for the range of services, D_j is assumed to reflect this aspect.

Thirdly, given the ratio of actual to expected flights from each zone i, and given the index A_i, the regression equation

$$\frac{\text{Actual flights}}{\text{Expected flights}} = a + b \cdot A_i$$

was computed (a and b are constants). The exercise was carried out for Heathrow, Gatwick, Luton, Southend and Southampton airports, and produced a correlation coefficient (r^2) of 0·79 for regions in the South-east and 0·86 for regions outside the South-east.[1] This relationship suggested that the various factors explaining the 'propensity to fly' were not the total explanation: accessibility to airports played some role in generating traffic. Thus, the A_i indices for each TLA site were computed and were used to revise the forecasts of British leisure passengers.

Table 9.4.2   *Passenger Forecasts, Year 2000*
(million journeys)

	Cublington	Foulness	Nut-hampstead	Thurleigh
1. British leisure passengers	107·5	92·6	102·4	106·9
2. Other passengers	103·2	103·2	103·2	103·2
3. Total passengers	210·7	195·8	205·6	210·1

Source: Adapted from CTLA, *Report*, Appendix 20, Table 7. It should be noted that, although the totals in row 3 are not significantly different from those given in CTLA, vol. vii (Table 13.10 and para. 13.52), the component items show substantial changes. For example, the previous forecasts for British leisure passengers (row 1) were 132·7, 121·8, 127·8 and 131·5 respectively. The influence of the accessibility index is not shown in the revised data. Its importance can be gauged from the unrevised (vol. vii) estimates, however. The figures for British leisure passengers, year 2000, were:

	C	F	N	T
without accessibility index:	129·2	129·2	129·2	129·2
with accessibility index:	132·7	121·8	127·8	131·5

The above equation can be rewritten as

$$\text{Actual flights} = (a + bA_i) \text{ Expected flights.}$$

Now, for future periods, expected flights were known from the

[1] In CTLA, vol. vii, the exercise had been carried out for Heathrow and Gatwick only, producing an (unreported) coefficient of approximately 0·7. The revised analysis can be found in *Further Research Team Work*, Document No. 10, and in the final *Report*, p. 192.

analysis of the total propensity to fly. The accessibility index for each TLA site could be estimated, including possible changes in it over time, and the parameters a and b were estimated from the initial observations of South-east airports. Hence, future 'actual' flights (AF) could be estimated so that, for any time-period t,

$$AF_t = (a+bA_{i,t}) . EF_t.$$

The expression $a+bA_i$ is the 'generation factor', the amount by which 'expected' flights must be multiplied to get estimated future flights.

The resulting forecasts are shown in Table 9.4.2. Each column relates to the number of passengers using an airport *system* with (a) Cublington as TLA, (b) Foulness as TLA, (c) Nuthampstead as TLA, (d) Thurleigh as TLA.

So far, then, estimates of total passengers using the airport 'system' as a whole have been obtained.

9.5 Predicting the Allocation of Passengers to Airports

The choice prediction model was a 'gravity model', a construct which contains two major elements – an 'attractiveness factor' pulling passengers towards a particular airport, and a 'deterrence factor' pushing them away. In this case the attraction was defined in terms of the numbers of persons using the airports (D_i). In the forecasts, however, the numbers using each airport were not known, so that 'for future years, the number of passengers used were the capacities in the case of Heathrow and Gatwick and a best estimate of the numbers using the third London airport' (CTLA, vol. VII, para. 13.24).

The deterrent in each case was the cost of reaching the airport (F_{ij}). The relevant costs here are *behavioural* costs, the costs as perceived by the traveller, so that, if he places some value on his travelling time, he is likely to regard a longer journey (in terms of time) as being 'more expensive' than a shorter journey. Now these costs may vary according to the *mode* of travel. In their analysis, the Research Team distinguish public and private transport, so that F_{ij} became a function of these two types of costs. In turn, of course, the costs to all passengers will depend upon how many use public and how many private transport, i.e. upon the *modal split*. The modal split is likely to vary between sites according to the availability of different modes of transport at the different sites. Hence it becomes necessary to predict the nature of transport facilities between zones and airports, and between airports and likely destinations.

The model actually used in the passenger allocation forecasts was similar to the following.

Let j refer to the jth airport
   i refer to the ith passenger zone
   T refer to trips
   D refer to the number of passengers using airports
   P refer to the attractiveness of airports
   F refer to the behavioural costs of travelling.

Then, by definition,

$$\sum_j T_{ij} \equiv D_i \equiv 0_i \qquad (9.1)$$

i.e. the total number of trips from i to all airports is 0_i. For convenience, let

$$\frac{X_{ij}}{\sum_j X_{ij}} = \frac{T_{ij}}{\sum_j T_{ij}} \qquad (9.2)$$

where $\qquad X_{ij} = P_j \cdot F_{ij} \qquad (9.3)$

so that multiplying (9.2) by T_{ij} gives

$$T_{ij} = \frac{X_{ij}}{\sum_j X_{ij}} \cdot \sum_j T_{ij}.$$

Substituting (9.1), $\qquad T_{ij} = \frac{X_{ij}}{\sum_j X_{ij}} \cdot 0_i.$

Substituting (9.3), $\qquad T_{ij} = \frac{P_j F_{ij} \cdot 0_i}{\sum_j P_j \cdot F_{ij}}. \qquad (9.4)$

Equation (9.4) relates to a specific mode and purpose of travel. Thus, the complete gravity model estimates (9.4) with respect to public and private modes of surface travel, and to leisure and business travel.

The 'attractiveness' factor (P) was estimated by the number of trips (D), so that, if no further modifications were made, equation (9.4) would become

$$\frac{D_j \cdot F_{ij} \cdot 0_i}{\sum_j D_j \cdot F_{ij}} \qquad (9.5)$$

which is the equation in CTLA, vol. VII.[1]

---

[1] See vol. VII, chap. 13, Appendix 1, p. 271.

The constraints imposed upon the model were several, but the most important related to the effects of congestion at any one airport. As long as the number of trips predicted by the model for airport j is less than the capacity of the airport, then the attraction of the airport is measured by

$$P_j = V_j = \sum_i T_{ij} \qquad (9.6)$$

i.e. by the trips from all zones (i) to the airport (j). Thus the condition is

$$(V_j \leqslant K_i) \Rightarrow (P_j = V_j = \sum_j T_{ij}) \qquad (9.7)$$

where K is the trip capacity of airport j. Use of V_j as a measure of P_j for all airports, however, produced a situation in which trips to some airports exceeded the capacity of those airports, which is not possible. Therefore the model incorporated a 'congestion penalty' to any airport in which $V_j > K_j$ in such a way as to adjust P_j downwards to meet condition (9.7). This congestion factor was obviously relevant to Heathrow and Gatwick which would, on the Commission's assumptions, soon reach their capacity.

The forecast 'allocation' of passengers to each TLA site were as shown in Table 9.5.1. It can be seen that the inland sites (a) generate

Table 9.5.1 *Passengers, Year 2000*
(million journeys)

	Cublington	Foulness	Nut-hampstead	Thurleigh
Total, all passengers	211	196	206	210
TLA site	110–113	81–85	105–108	108–112
Residual	98–101	111–115	98–101	98–102

Source: CTLA, *Report*, Table 10.4.

a greater total amount of traffic compared to Foulness, and (b) secure a larger proportion of the total compared to Foulness. The 'residual' row indicates the numbers of passengers who would have to be absorbed by airports other than the TLA.

9.6 USER BENEFITS

The difference between the totals of the PUCs in Table 9.1.1 is the 'user benefits' credited to the inland sites. These arise because of

(a) the existence of the 'generated' trips accruing to the inland sites; and

(b) the fact that passengers who would use any of the TLA sites will achieve some resource savings by using an airport which has cheaper travel costs.

Generated trips were assumed to be a benefit to a site because of the apparent paradox that, since costs only were being measured, a site attracting more passengers would be debited with higher costs simply because it is more accessible. The component parts of the user benefits were

(i) $\frac{1}{2}(T_2 - T_1)(C_1 - C_2)$ – the 'consumers' surplus' element,

where the subscript 1 refers to trips and costs in a system of airports with Foulness as TLA, and subscript 2 to a system with an inland site as TLA. T refers to numbers of trips and C to 'behavioural costs' – the costs perceived by the traveller, including fares and time valuations if the travel is by public transport, and operating costs and time valuations for private transport. Thus, expression (i) relates to the trips 'generated' by the inland site $(T_2 - T_1)$, and the difference in behavioural costs for passengers. It was argued that some travellers would just prefer site 2 to not travelling at all, so that their net benefit would be nearly zero, while others would travel to site 2 and would very nearly have been persuaded to go to site 1, so that their net benefits are $C_1 - C_2$. The 'average' generated traveller is therefore assumed to have net benefits of $\frac{1}{2}(C_1 - C_2)$.

(ii) $(T_2 - T_1)(C_2 - R_2)$ – the 'operator's surplus',

where R_2 are the travel resource costs at the inland site. Resource costs are the value of resources used up in travelling. The difference between C_2 and R_2 will therefore be profit to the transport undertaking (e.g. fares minus costs of providing the service), and tax revenue to governments. Thus, (ii) represents the gains from generated traffic to transport undertakings and the Government.

(iii) $T_1(R_1 - R_2)$ – resource cost savings to traffic which would use any TLA site.

Clearly, most passengers will travel whether the airport system contains Foulness or an inland site as the TLA. However, if the site is 2 rather than 1, some people may secure savings (and others, costs) by utilising the inland site.

Thus, the overall 'user benefits' were

$$\frac{1}{2}\sum (T_2 - T_1)(C_1 - C_2) + \sum (T_2 - T_1)(C_2 - R_2) + \sum T_1(R_1 - R_2)$$

which can be rearranged as

$$\sum T_1 R_1 - \sum T_2 R_2 + \frac{1}{2}\sum (C_1 + C_2)(T_2 - T_1)$$

where the final term reflects the benefits to generated traffic, these benefits being measured by the average of the traveller's costs in one system and those in another. An example, taken from CTLA, vol. VII, Table 13.15, will illustrate the principle. The figures are illustrative in so far as they do not reflect any of the revisions in the final *Report*.

Table 9.6.1   *User Benefits, Cublington 1991*

	Heath-row	Gat-wick	Man-chester	TLA	Luton	Total
(a) $\sum T_1 R_1$	86·0	31·4	30·5	91·4	18·0	257
(b) $\sum T_2 R_2$	87·0	32·4	2·8	115·1	22·1	259
(c) $\frac{1}{2}\sum (C_1+C_2)(T_2-T_1)$	3·1	2·0	−35·7	63·6	5·8	39
Net user benefits						
= (a)−(b)+(c)	2·3	0·9	−7·8	39·7	1·7	37

The table relates to a sample year, 1991. Row (a) shows the resource costs of travelling to each of the listed airports *assuming Foulness is the site of the TLA*. Row (b) shows the total resource costs of travelling to each airport *assuming Cublington is the TLA site*. Row (c) shows the number of generated trips multiplied by an average of the behavioural costs at each site. The costs are aggregated in the final column. Since Luton would be closed if Cublington was the TLA site (because of air traffic control difficulties), the Luton column entry (£22·1 million) is credited to Cublington. By making a similar estimate for the year 2000, and interpolating figures for 1981 to 1990 and 1992 to 1999, the undiscounted net user benefits accruing to each inland site were estimated.

Thus, given the total number of passengers and their allocation to airports over the relevant time-period, given the likely modal split and behavioural and resource costs, and given the manner in which net user benefits were calculated, the end result is the figures for passenger user costs shown in Table 9.6.2 below.

Table 9.6.2   *PUCs: 1968 prices, 1982 as base*
(£ million)

	Cublington	Foulness	Nut-hampstead	Thurleigh
PUCs	1743–2883	1910–3090	1778–2924	1765–2922
Net user benefits*	167–207	0	132–166	145–168

* That is, NUB = PUC (Foulness)−PUC (inland site). These figures relate to ranges for the value of travelling time, and to the 'middle' estimate of rail fares for London to TLA site rail links. See final *Report*, Appendix 20, Table 14, p. 253.

9.7 THE VALUE OF TIME

In the gravity model, behavioural costs (C) were crucial variables while both behavioural and resource costs (R) were extremely important in assessing user benefits. Behavioural costs relate to the sacrifice of the alternative use of time spent travelling as a passenger. Thus, the leisure passenger is assumed to attach some 'cost' to his travelling time because he sacrifices some alternative use of that time and that alternative use has a value to him. Resource costs relate to the 'factor costs' of economics, and will therefore include the apparent 'loss' of working time by businessmen. If they spend an hour travelling it is at the expense of output they could otherwise have produced.

If it can be assumed that working time is 'lost' when business people travel, and if it can be assumed that each employee is paid a wage/salary equal to his marginal revenue product, then the employee's gross income (i.e. before tax, etc.) represents an approximation of this lost time. In addition, each employee's work entails the existence of some 'overhead' costs in the form of accommodation and equipment. The employee's absence from work therefore appears to entail some 'cost' in the form of unutilised capital equipment. Accordingly, some percentage of gross income was added to the figure already derived. The 'gross income plus overheads' approach reflects a standard procedure used by the Ministry of Transport.

Thus, as an example of the approach used, consider the value per hour attached to business time in 1969. Average incomes of business air passengers were found to be £3100. To these were added £1525 (i.e. nearly 50 per cent 'mark-up' compared to the standard Ministry of Transport figure of 10 per cent)[1] for 'overheads'. The total value is therefore £4625 which, assuming a 40-hour week (=2000 hours per annum), gives an hourly rate of 555d (£2·31). Since the real value of marginal product is expected to rise over time, higher values were obtained for future years.

In order to obtain 'values' for leisure time, the Research Team referred to a number of studies concerning the behaviour of travellers when faced with 'modal' or route choices. Thus, a person choosing to travel by taxi at 10s (50p) for 10 minutes compared to a 4s (20p) rail journey of 30 minutes appears implicitly to value 20 minutes 'saved' time at (10−4) = 6 shillings (30p). This suggests an hourly rate of 18s (90p). One oddity of this particular study was the

[1] Due to the considerably higher average incomes of air travellers compared to the national average.

absence of a survey (by the Commission's Research Team, anyway – see below) of *air* passengers. It was assumed that the values obtained in other studies, mainly of commuter traffic, were applicable without modification to air passengers. A number of the studies suggested that the value of leisure time was a *constant* proportion of the leisure passenger's income. These estimates, when averaged, suggested 25 per cent as the appropriate proportion.

Thus, in 1969 leisure air passengers were found to have an average income of £1820.[1] Using the 2000-hour working year, this suggests 220d (92p) per hour gross income, 25 per cent of which is 55d (23p). The figure of 55d was used in the analysis.

Various figures were attached to time values of persons accompanying leisure passengers, to taxi drivers, to children,[2] so that all travellers were included. Table 9.7.1 below shows the values of time used in CTLA, vol. VII.

Table 9.7.1
(old pence per hour)

	Business	Leisure	Children	Adult accompanying	Paid drivers
1968	555	55	13	39	128
1981	747	80	19	57	194
1991	849	92	26	77	267
2000	867	100	33	100	356

Source: CTLA, vol. VII, Table 11.3.

The rising values of time over time reflect rising real income trends. Business incomes were assumed to rise at 3·25 per cent per annum, in line with projected productivity increases, and non-business incomes at 3 per cent per annum. Allowing for this differential between productivity and income rates, business incomes were assumed to maintain a constant ratio to leisure incomes throughout the entire period (see Table 4.18 of vol. VII).

To obtain resource costs (R) it was necessary to estimate costs per unit of time (e.g. business time) and costs per unit of distance (e.g. vehicle operating costs). The result was a 'composite' resource cost for any journey of

[1] The income data were secured from the Air Passenger Survey of 1969 carried out at Heathrow and Gatwick. Other surveys produced different average income figures, some higher, some lower.

[2] Originally at one-third the adult accompanying passenger rate but reduced to 6d (2½p) per hour in the final *Report* (p. 242). Both values appear to have been obtained in an entirely arbitrary fashion.

(Cost per minute × Journey time)

+(Cost per mile × Journey distance).

Composite behavioural costs were obtained in the same way. Some behavioural costs were considered a function of distance – e.g. operating costs for private car users. Behavioural costs also varied with mode of travel. Thus 4·5d (1·8p) per mile was assumed as a behavioural operating cost for existing rail links, and 6d (2½p) for new links – in each case reflecting the fares charged (or which would be charged).

In this way, composite resource and behavioural costs were broken down by

(a) type of passenger – business/leisure;
(b) road and rail;
(c) new and 'old' rail links;
(d) time (minutes) and distance (miles).[1]

9.8 NOISE COSTS

It was noted earlier that the costs attributed to noise nuisance appeared as an extremely small item compared to the heavy costs debited by the analysis to air passengers. The noise model is therefore of some interest, partly because of the intuitively surprising result (in view of the political and social pressure being brought on governments to reduce noise nuisance), and partly because it represents a major effort to value a disamenity which hitherto had evaded most attempts at quantification.[2]

Noise levels were measured by the 'Noise and Number Index' (NNI), an index reflecting both the noise level emanating from any one aircraft and the number of aircraft in a given time period. In order to calculate noise costs over time it was therefore necessary to estimate the change in the NNI boundaries over time. Neither the Commission nor the Research Team considered that significant reductions in noise levels per aircraft were likely before 1985, even allowing for the possibility of introducing noise-suppression techniques. Unfortunately, the use of NNI indices has been subjected to severe criticism and it is extremely questionable whether they have any reliable operational use.

[1] See Tables 11.11 and 11.12 in CTLA, vol. VII.
[2] In a different context, the problems of valuing disamenity of this kind led several writers to suppose that the errors of estimation were too large for the analysis to be very reliable See, for example, Ridker [4].

The social survey which was frequently quoted in evidence and in the CTLA papers had attempted to correlate social reactions to noise levels at Heathrow throughout twenty-four-hour periods.[1] On this basis, the Commission argued that the 'NNI did give a valid measure of the nuisance experienced in situations where the ratio of night to day aircraft movements was the same as had existed at Heathrow' (*Report*, para. 7.17). But night noise is essentially different from daytime noise owing to interference with sleep, and no night-time flying restrictions are proposed for the TLA. The absence of an appropriate weighting for night noise nuisance is therefore a defect of the approach adopted by the Commission and Research Team.

The essential argument in the Commission's analysis was that noise disamenity would be reflected in property prices. If prices fell and residents moved *because* of the airport, hypothetical compensation was assessed in terms of the price depreciation and the lost consumer's surplus. Other residents were treated in a different fashion. The groups concerned were distinguished as follows.

Group	Type	Social costs (Research Team's symbols)
(a) Moving because of airport		$S+R+D$
(b) Moving anyway		D
(c) Remaining		N
(d) New entrants		Zero

where R = removal costs

S = consumer's surplus

D = change in market price

N = 'sum of money which would just compensate . . . [the house owner] . . . for the nuisance suffered and make him as well off as he was before' (CTLA, vol. VII, para. 20.3, p. 366).

On this analysis, then, the main variables to be measured were D, N and S, and the number of households affected (H).

The numbers of households affected were recalculated several times during the proceedings. In their final report, the Commission produced the following estimates of the numbers of households within the 35 NNI contour (regarded as the noise level which begins to cause nuisance) in the year 2006.[2]

[1] *Noise: Final Report*, Cmnd 2056 (H.M.S.O., London, 1963).

[2] *Report*, Table 7.1. The figure for Foulness is substantially greater than that reported in CTLA, vol. VII. The explanation appears to lie in a

Cublington	29,400
Foulness	20,300
Nuthampstead	94,800
Thurleigh	25,600
Luton	13,600

D represents the depreciation in the house price, or the difference between the rate of growth of house prices in a noisy area compared to a non-noisy area. Thus, 'the price at which noisy property is placed on the market must also be such as to make it as attractive for the average buyer as property in a quieter neighbourhood' (para. 20.10). Property prices should, on this argument, reflect the value placed on the noise. Further, this differential will reflect the noise disamenity over future time-periods as well, since 'people buying a house affected by aircraft noise would be very naïve if they did not expect an increase in the noise at least for the next ten years or so' (CTLA, vol. VII, para. 20.12). In order to obtain values of *D* it was first necessary to estimate the house prices in the noise-affected zones of each of the four TLA sites. This was done by finding rateable values for each sub-district of the zones. Then, a sample area was selected and estate agents and valuers were asked to put market valuations on the sample properties. A relationship was then established between market price and rateable value in the form

$$P = a + bV,$$

where *P* is market values, *V* is rateable value and *a* and *b* are constants. (The correlation coefficient was not reported so that the reliability of the equation is not known.) The resulting ratio was applied to the rateable values in the affected zones. To obtain *D* it was then necessary to estimate the effect of noise on house prices. The Gatwick environment was thought to be similar to that of the TLA sites, and, after rejecting a number of approaches, estate agents in the Gatwick area were themselves asked to assess the likely depreciation due to noise (i.e. they had to abstract from all other factors). The results were expressed as percentage depreciation rates and were applied to the values of *P* derived for the affected zones. Thus, highly-priced houses were thought by estate agents to depreciate by between 12½ and 50 per cent in the noisy zones of

---

revision of the Foulness NNI contours due in turn to revisions of the air traffic forecasts – see para. 7.15 of the report. Luton figures are included because of the Research Team's argument that, if Foulness was chosen, Luton should stay open.

Gatwick (noise areas being defined in terms of Noise and Number Indexes), so that an average of 20 per cent was used in the analysis of the TLA sites for this noise zone and for these high-priced houses. Depreciation rates on high-priced houses were thought to be higher than on lower-priced houses. This implies that higher income groups value peace and quiet more highly than do lower income groups. Here again, if the figures can be trusted, we have an instance of willingness to pay being dependent upon ability to pay. The noise *nuisance* suffered by both householders may be identical, but the differences in income prevent the lower income group from expressing values as high as those of high income groups. The only acknowledgement by the Commission of this aspect of the analysis was their willingness to allow depreciation rates to rise at 5 per cent per annum, since 'as society as a whole gets richer, higher values should be placed on residential quiet' (*Report*, Appendix 22, p. 267).

The value of N was derived as follows.[1] It is possible to measure people's attitude to noise by a 'noise annoyance score', scaled 1 to 5. In the no-airport situation a given population will have a particular distribution showing population against the noise annoyance score. The median of this distribution is selected. Then the depreciation on the house in this category is assessed, assuming an airport is now built. Thus the median annoyance score is related to a particular depreciation figure. The assumption is then that the person occupying this median position would be just willing to pay the value D in order to buy his previously quieter environment. People with annoyance scores *above* the median value are assumed to be willing to pay *more* than D, but they can in fact buy 'quiet' for D only. So, the argument goes, they will move. Those with annoyance scores below the median will stay because they are not willing to pay D to move. The model is slightly more complicated because of the existence of consumers' surplus lost by moving, and because of the existence of removal costs. These will in fact mean that the true cost of buying 'quiet' will be greater than the value D, so that a further proportion of the distribution will not move. Some will move, however (at least, they will according to this model), and the value of D associated with the median annoyance score is the value attached to all those *remaining* – i.e. D for the median group $= N$. At the same time, the approach predicts the numbers moving *because* of noise. In fact, the assumption that average values of D

[1] This outline owes more to the explanation provided by Professor A. Walters on day 8 of the noise discussion during the stage v proceedings than to vol. vii. The transcript reference is 54, pp. 86–91. (A similar explanation is given in CTLA, *Report*, Appendix 22.)

corresponded to the median of the noise annoyance distribution was never tested, and the final *Report* contains some sensitivity analyses.

The value of S, the consumers' surplus attached to property, was obtained by questionnaire techniques. The critical question asked: 'Suppose that your house was wanted to form part of a large development scheme and the developer offered to buy it from you, what price would be just high enough to compensate you for leaving this house and moving to another area?'[1] In the sample, 8 per cent of respondents said they would not sell, implying that there was no price which would compensate them. The initial 'average' of 39 per cent 'consumer surplus' was subsequently admitted to have been derived from these respondents who quoted a figure. In their amendments, the Research Team imposed a new limit of 200 per cent of consumers' surplus on those who would not name a price. The resulting average consumers' surplus figure was 52 per cent, which, with a 16 per cent allowance for disturbance expenses (R), made a total of 68 per cent.[2] The values of S and R were assumed to rise at a rate of 3 per cent per annum.

The categorisation of residents was carried out by estimating total residential population, plus likely new entrants. Those likely to move whether there was an airport or not were estimated on the basis of data on natural migration (of about 4 per cent of the population per annum).

9.9 SOME SOURCES OF CRITICISM

(a) Cost Minimisation versus Net Benefit Maximisation
Section 9.3 detailed the arguments necessary for these two approaches to be identical. The only real argument put forward to justify the presumption that any of the sites would show net *benefits* to the nation is that the expected revenue from air passengers would be sufficient to meet all the construction costs of the TLA *plus* the 'non-recoverable' costs of noise, relocating defence institutions, etc. (Other costs are 'recoverable' – e.g. rail costs are recovered through the charging of rail fares, and so on.) Taking an average of the costs of the four sites, the Research Team suggested in CTLA, vol. VII, that the construction and non-recoverable costs total some £290 million (1975 as base), whereas existing landing fees would

[1] The survey is outlined in *Further Research Team Work*, Document No. 4, and is discussed in the CTLA *Report*, Appendix 23.
[2] See *Further Research Team Work*, Document No. 4.

result in a revenue of only £145 million. For revenues to cover the relevant costs, landing fees would have to be increased by 125 per cent (allowing for any lost traffic that would result). The argument is that raising the 'price' of using the airport in this way would have a negligible effect on the growth of air traffic and would easily meet the 'non-recoverable' cost element.[1] This still leaves the nation with the other benefits (increased national income, etc.) so that the argument that benefits exceed costs is, on this view, easily accommodated.

Of course, the whole argument is contingent upon the assumption that the non-recoverable costs, such as noise and disamenity, have been properly valued in the first place. Also, an increase in real national income, generated by the TLA, will itself impose further external diseconomies in the form of pollution, noise and disamenity, so that the value of the gain in national product is not itself a measure of the welfare gain. To assess the likely magnitude of this gain (a 'secondary benefit' as it is called in the *Report*), it would in turn be necessary to value these 'second-round' externalities. If the low values placed on disamenity in the Research Team's analysis are thought to be correct and are applied to these further costs, then it will almost certainly be the case that the increase in national income will outweigh the external effects associated with that increase: the secondary benefit would be positive. But the whole argument turns upon the correct assessment of the external costs associated with (*a*) the airport itself, and (*b*) the generated national income. The arguments for supposing that these costs have been undervalued are presented below (pp. 230–2).

(*b*) *Passenger Forecasts*
It is useful to note some of the possible criticisms of the forecasting approach.

Firstly, the forecasts must be subject to wide margins of error owing to the dubious assumptions about the 'propensity to fly' and its behaviour to the year 2006. Of course, if the errors are distributed in the same way for each TLA site this will not be a serious problem.

Secondly, accessibility was assumed to affect only British leisure passengers, whereas the airlines were concerned to argue that foreign tourist traffic at least might be affected by the choice of site.

Thirdly, the index A_i has no real foundation in economic theory and hence no foundation in a theory of rational choice. The use of the A_i index tells us that some people will not travel by air *at all* because airports are relatively inaccessible. It has been shown, how-

[1] CTLA, vol. VII, paras. 5.4 to 5.9 and 5.13 to 5.16.

H

ever, that if the A_i index for an airport in the system tends to zero (the airport becomes less and less accessible), so the demand at that airport will increase such that it tends towards the demand for airports with unchanged accessibility – which is a perverse result indeed.[1] However, the Commission and the Research Team declared that 'The accessibility model appears to us to pass the test of being understandable and does appear to fit the facts better than any alternative model which we have examined' (*Report*, Appendix 14, p. 221).

Fourthly, the regression equation linking actual and expected flights to accessibility related to airports in the South-east. It was then used to forecast passengers on the assumption that the parameters '*a*' and '*b*' would be constant over time. But there is no particular reason why this should be so, since the values of '*a*' and '*b*' are derived from a point estimate in time: there is no second or third observation to provide a check. Hence the forecasts of 'accessibility-generated traffic' could be seriously in error. There is no way of telling.

(c) *Passenger Allocation Model*

The defects of gravity models as explanations of future behaviour are numerous, though generally very technical.[2] The primary problem is that although they purport to explain economic behaviour (the choice between airports, for example, is an economic decision subject to constraints), they have little basis in economic theory. Certainly, the TLA gravity model appears to obey at least one requirement, that a rise in the cost of travel (F_{ij}) will result in some fall in overall demand. In this case the effect operates through the accessibility index. However, the demand for air travel is not just a function of the F_{ij} and of the (rather inadequate) surrogate for the availability of services at each airport (D_j). It will also depend upon air fares and flight convenience and comfort, factors which cannot be entered into the gravity model analysis. In other words, the gravity model provides a very 'partial' picture of the determinants of demand.[3]

[1] We owe this point to Professor John Wise of Southampton University. The result is contained in his paper, 'Gravity Models in Relation to the Siting of the Third London Airport' (unpublished).

[2] A useful critique is to be found in Heggie [5].

[3] The Commission resorted to a dubious defence of the gravity model in the final *Report*, declaring that 'it has not been shown that the gravity model is inconsistent with consumer maximisation of utility' (Appendix 17).

Another anomaly arises in that the addition of other airports to the analysis of regional demand was found not to affect the results at all. Thus, in the final *Report* Birmingham and Castle Donington airports were included in the analysis (they had been omitted in the previous work). Indeed, 'the gravity model did not allocate any passengers to these airports' (*Report*, Appendix 17), which is a strange result in that it means that even passengers living in Birmingham and finding a required flight there would prefer to travel to Manchester or the TLA.

As the Commission itself declares, 'The acid test is the accuracy with which the [gravity] model predicts behaviour' (*Report*, Appendix 17). But it is precisely on this ground that the construct is so dubious. The model was indeed 'tested' against data on passenger choices concerning Heathrow and Gatwick, but was not found to be particularly successful. Heggie [5] found that gravity models in general performed dismally in terms of predicting actual behaviour. Overall, then, it is difficult to see how so much faith could be placed in their outcomes.

(d) The Valuation of Time

The values of time spent in travelling dominated the differences between the final totals obtained for AMCs and PUCs. Unfortunately, the basis of the estimates used is not a sound one. With business travel time, for example, it was assumed that (a) no businessmen used travelling time for work purposes, (b) that there were no leisure offsets to working time spent travelling and (c) that business and leisure travel are easily distinguished. Assumption (a) is clearly false in respect of air and rail travel: some work is certainly carried out by at least a proportion of business travellers. The ability to carry out work would depend upon a comfort factor, and upon the distance of the journey. No survey was carried out to discover to what extent 'work offsets' of this kind existed. The only reference to the issue is contained in the statement of methodology (para. 20) which declares that 'from common observation, it seems safe to conclude that only a small proportion of business travellers do serious work while actually travelling to and from an airport'.[1]

[1] A remark which is strangely at odds with the general disdain shown by the Commission for 'common observation' during the stage v proceedings. However, the remark is partly substantiated in the final *Report* by reference to an unpublished study, 'Report on County Hall Journey to Work Survey 1964', by C. Barnett and P. Salamans; see the final *Report*, p. 227.

Again, with respect to the possibility of securing leisure benefits during journeys, the same paragraph declares that 'such constrained activity (i.e. securing what leisure activities are available while travelling – reading newspapers, etc.) is hardly compatible with any benefits of this kind'. It is not easy to understand why this should be so. The Commission reiterates its view in the final *Report* by saying that they 'have made no allowance for the employee's own preference' (*Report*, p. 227). The correct approach assumes that it is total utility that matters, and that travellers' utility gains are therefore a proper offset against output losses. The 'output loss' approach does not view the issue from a utility standpoint and is therefore not adequate for purposes of cost–benefit.

Other objections are not difficult to find. The point of using gross business incomes was that they supposedly reflected the value of the traveller's marginal product in work. But labour market imperfections will mean that this equation does not hold. Nor is it always possible to convert time savings into resource savings, and, vice versa, time 'lost' into resource losses. Thus, an extra ten minutes travelling time may not have been used 'productively' had it been spent at work.[1] However, it was argued that small time savings and losses were not significant in explaining the differences in social costs between the sites (*Report*, p. 229).

Empirical studies of the valuation which companies appear to place on travel time during working hours are not many. Those that do exist suggest contradictory results. In a survey of major exporting firms, Essex County Council discovered that most firms were indifferent to the length of air flights by their employees.[2] In a statistical study of some sophistication, Gronau obtained a value of working time of some 40 per cent of the wage rate.[3] In short, there

---

[1] Thus, in most transport studies, including the TLA study, all time was valued, regardless of its 'length'. It has been argued several times in the literature that small time savings or losses should be ignored on the grounds that indivisibilities in the use of time prevent those time savings being used productively. See, for example, D. G. Tipping, 'Time Savings in Transport Studies', *Economic Journal* (Dec 1968).

[2] Essex County Council, Evidence to the CTLA, Document 5031. The Commission rejected this questionnaire as 'wanting' (*Report*, p. 226), preferring not to place reliance upon any questionnaire technique.

[3] R. Gronau, 'The Effect of Travelling Time on the Demand for Passenger Airline Transportation', Ph.D. thesis (Columbia University, 1967), reported in A. J. Harrison and S. J. Taylor, 'The Value of Working Time in the Appraisal of Transport Expenditure', in Ministry of Transport, *Time Research Note* 16 (London, July 1970).

is little empirical work, and the results which have been obtained are not sufficiently consistent for the 'product loss' approach to be used. Nor, indeed, is the distinction between working and non-working time easy to make in many cases – especially where business travellers have 'elastic' hours of work.

Lastly, the theory underlying the 'product loss' approach is inadequate. Economic theory suggests that firms and individuals would allocate time between uses in the same way that consumers allocate money between goods – i.e. to maximise utility. If working time is 'lost' through travelling, the result must be a disequilibrium situation to which individuals and firms will adjust. That is, the sacrifice of some leisure time for travel will mean that the marginal utility of the last hour of work can no longer be equal to the marginal utility of leisure. Theoretically, adjustment should take place in such a way as to restore equilibrium by increased working time. In practice it may be difficult to test the existence of this adjustment mechanism. In their final *Report* the Commission compromise by the use of a range of 350d to 620d (£1·46 to £2·58).

As far as the value of leisure time is concerned, the major defect in the TLA study was the absence of an empirical appraisal of air passengers' attitudes towards costs. One such study was produced during the stage v proceedings by the consultants to the British Airports Authority.[1] Several approaches were used, two of which involved questionnaires. One approach asked for the willingness to pay of leisure passengers to have their journeys reduced by one-half in terms of time. The answers produced showed some 66 per cent giving a zero valuation on time (they were not prepared to pay anything for a reduced time of travel), and the remainder producing values which averaged about 40 per cent of their salaries. The overall recorded average was therefore about 14 per cent of salary, compared to the 25 per cent used by the Ministry of Transport and the CTLA Research Team.[2] The true average could well be lower if

[1] British Airports Authority, Evidence to the CTLA, Document 5005.

[2] In a paper by G. Hoinville and R. Berthoud, 'The Application of Survey Research in Deriving Values of Time Savings and Evaluating Community Preferences', the authors suggest that such a question goes 'far beyond respondents' capacity to answer meaningfully', so that the answers based upon it would presumably be, in their view, non-significant. But their argument appears to be relevant only to business passengers who were asked to 'imagine' they were leisure passengers. It is not clear if the absurdity they think exists refers to this problem, or to some other aspect of the question. The paper is in Ministry of Transport, *Time Research Note* 16 (London, July 1970).

some of the travellers giving zero valuations in fact secured benefits from travel.

Other studies of air passengers are rare. Indeed, the 'standard' value of 25 per cent of the wage rate is borrowed from studies which were mainly concerned with commuter traffic.[1] Although journeys to and from airports have a 'commuter' aspect, there is no particular reason to suppose that the results will be the same in the case of air passengers. In their final *Report* the Commission again compromised by adopting a range of leisure time values of 27½d to 82½d (11½p to 34½p).

The real conclusion that emerges is that research into the value of business and leisure time is not sufficient to support the use of precise figures in a cost–benefit analysis relating to air travel. The adoption of ranges of values obviously overcomes some of the criticisms. It is significant, however, that the range of values for leisure time has a minimum which is still considerably in excess of the average value suggested by the one and only survey of air passengers (see above, p. 229).

(e) The Value of Noise Nuisance

The criticisms of the approach to valuing noise nuisance are several. New entrants, for example, suffer zero costs because they are assumed to enter the area if the fall in house prices provides a minimum compensation to them for noise nuisance, and of its likely growth over time. The presupposition is that, on purchase, a consumer is totally informed of the disamenities surrounding his proposed house. Further, he must be in possession of information about likely developments in the area over the next decade at least – three decades if the time horizon for the cost–benefit study in vol. VII is adopted. In practice, however, house purchasers rarely have the chance to experience the amenity conditions of an area for any length of time before actually moving in: their decision is essentially

[1] See the reviews of some fourteen studies in A. Harrison and D. Quarmby, *The Value of Time Savings in Transport Investment Appraisal* (Ministry of Transport, London, 1969). During the stage V proceedings, the Ministry of Transport reaffirmed its faith in the figure of 25 per cent and even suggested that 'the studies which have become available since then have tended to suggest that the current figure of 25 per cent is on the low side'. It was further suggested that non-commuting studies did not differ significantly from commuting studies in their valuations of leisure time. The empirical research upon which these statements rest, however, is small in amount. See *Further Research Team Work*, Document No. 15.

made under conditions of uncertainty. Because of this, market prices tend to reflect the existing market conditions and uncertainty about the future. They do not accurately reflect the future. Certainly, there can be no justifiable reason for supposing that a householder can *predict* the rate of change of a disamenity. Nor is it the case that householders are totally mobile and able to respond in the manner suggested. Indeed, in the final *Report*, the Commission acknowledge the failure of the market mechanism to operate in the manner suggested (*Report*, p. 269), but the appropriate conclusions are not drawn.

Nor does it seem very likely that the question asked with respect to the size of surplus would elicit the correct response. This question could only have been useful if it elicited the householder's subjective evaluation of the house. By prefixing the question with a hypothetical 'development plan', the question was far more likely to make many respondents think of the existing market price (in the questionnaire the respondent is asked for his estimate of the market price *before* he is asked this question) and add to it some percentage which he thinks 'the market will bear' *because of development*. Indeed, the Research Team noted that for some respondents stating a zero consumer surplus 'The motive was resignation: there was no thought of withstanding a developer and no attempt was made to estimate surplus'.[1]

At no stage did the questionnaire indicate whether the hypothetical development was a private or public one. The likely reaction of respondents is to suppose that it is the latter. Since house owners are well aware that local authority and government 'compensation' values frequently understate true market values, the element of 'resignation' was likely to be significant. It seems most likely then that at least the lower tail of the distribution of responses understates the true consumer's surplus.

Most serious of all, the respondent may not have been clear that the 'development' proposed might involve a complete move away from the area. Development plans frequently involve moves within the area that a resident considers 'local'. In the case of an airport, however, the 'noise-sensitive' resident should have been asked what compensation he requires to move right outside at least the 35 NNI area. He should also have been made aware of the fact that he might have to change his occupation.

Nor is it clear as to how the 8 per cent of the survey respondents who 'would not sell' are to be treated. Presumably, these householders do not require infinite sums to persuade them to move. In a

[1] *Further Research Team Work*, Document No. 4.

separate survey, some 43 per cent of respondents would not sell or refused to name a sum which would induce them to move.[1] As with the Research Team's survey, the distribution was arbitrarily curtailed by imposing a limit to the 'surplus' of 20 per cent of the house value. While infinite sums would seem illogical, there can be no operational rule for curtailing distributions. It may simply be the case that noise nuisance cannot be valued in this way.

Lastly, the method used could involve a serious circularity. Given the widespread increase in general noise levels, the effective choice faced by the householder is to move to another area where noise will *also* increase, though possibly not as much as the TLA site. The ability of the householder to notice noise differentials between areas is reduced, and 'so also therefore will the sum of money necessary to induce the family to move. But the disbenefit suffered from each contribution to a rising noise level is properly valued only by a sum of money large enough to compensate the family for the loss of the original low-noise situation, this being the sum that will enable them to maintain their original level of welfare' (Mishan [6]). In short, the very method of estimating noise costs involves a circularity: as noise increases, the costs of noise are likely to decrease.

In their final report, the Commission effectively introduced a new argument with respect to the apparent noise-cost differentials between the sites. The noise advantages of Foulness were argued to be 'by no means as unqualified as many people have supposed' (*Report*, para. 7.24). Apart from the fact that the choice of Foulness would enable Luton airport to stay open, inflicting noise nuisance on residents there, the Commission point out that the reduced traffic at Foulness compared to the inland sites would mean greater demands on other regional airports, imposing noise nuisance there. Since the only other airport included in the traffic forecasting model was Manchester, it must be assumed that it is the noise costs at Manchester that are being referred to. No attempt was made to assess what these would be. But the whole argument is contingent upon the accuracy of the traffic forecasts, the validity of which is dubious. For all the reasons stated, it seems likely that the noise costs of the TLA have been undervalued.

(f) Equity

In the original statement of methodology, and again in vol. VII, the CTLA Research Team refer to the issue of equity. They point out

[1] British Airports Authority, evidence presented at stage v of CTLA Proceedings, Documents 5006 A, B and C.

that 'normal' cost–benefit studies ignore the *distribution* of benefits and costs, i.e. their incidence on different income groups (or social class groups, or age groups, etc. – there is no overriding reason for selecting income). They cite two conditions under which this treatment would be justified:

(*a*) 'where the bulk of the benefits are paid for in cash by the beneficiaries, and where machinery exists for the compensation of any substantial losers' (para. 1.22);

(*b*) 'where any benefits and costs *to which the above does not apply* are spread reasonably thinly over a large number of people' (our italics).

The conclusion then was that 'in the case of the third London airport, . . . neither of these requirements appears to be met'.

Procedures for incorporating distributional issues into the objective functions were discussed in Chapter 2. In the TLA case, however, the 'solution' adopted was to reject any idea of prior weighting – i.e. of weighting gains and losses in the cost analysis itself. The final report of the Commission implied that compensation payments could be made to those who suffered noise nuisance, so that hypothetical compensation would be replaced with actual compensation. However, this solution does not meet the requirements laid down in (*a*) and (*b*) above. It is the *beneficiaries* of the airport who must pay the compensation. But the incidence of benefits is not known because not all benefits (indeed, the major part of them) were calculated. Presumably, the argument must be that, since the 'nation' benefits, compensation payments will be a legitimate demand upon taxpayers. It is difficult to avoid the conclusion, however, that air passengers are the beneficiaries and that the compensation should be paid out of increased air fares. But increased fares will mean some reduced demand for air travel, thus altering the pattern and total of demand. In short, air fares should reflect the full social costs of air travel.[1]

Even if compensation *is* paid, the distribution of income is

----

[1] Social costs which in turn may well have been underestimated. Apart from the social costs of road access mentioned earlier, other costs must be considered. Mishan [6] points to the serious consequences of 'tourist blight', encouraged by easier air travel, and to the fact that, if total air journeys at Foulness really will be fewer than those at inland sites, fewer accidents will occur. Of course, with 'standard' Ministry of Transport valuations of human life of some £9000, the last aspect would make little difference.

altered. Ground residents are supposedly no 'worse off' after receiving compensation,[1] but the general taxpayer has met the capital
costs of providing an airport for the convenience of air travellers
and, presumably, to secure the 'base load' of benefits mentioned
earlier. The existence of a progressive income tax could be put
forward as an argument for supposing that the burden is shared in
an 'equitable' fashion, but it is not a strong argument in view of the
lack of continuous progression in the United Kingdom tax system.
Thus, the general population appears to be paying for benefits
which accrue to air travellers, of whom a substantial proportion
(some 40 per cent in the year 2000, on the CTLA forecasts) will be
high-income business travellers. The question remains, therefore, as
to whether society has any preference with respect to distributional
changes of this nature. This is perhaps a political issue as long as it
is 'equity' that is being discussed. But it is an economic issue if the
objective function is *social utility* and if marginal utilities of income
differ from person to person.

Hence the confusion between 'equity' or 'distributive justice',
the distributional aspects of compensation and maximising social
utility. The payment of compensation only preserves Pareto optimality. 'Equity' obviously includes this aspect in that failure to
compensate would strike most of us as 'inequitable'. But equity is a
wider issue and is concerned with the essentially normative issue of
whether it is 'fair' to benefit one section of the community rather
than, or at the expense of, another section. No normative statements are concerned in the argument that marginal utilities of
income differ: the sole problem is the rather serious one of measuring income utilities, a problem that was discussed in Chapter 2. On
the other hand, 'maximising social utility' (e.g. by weighting all
gains and losses by income utilities) cannot in general be given a
purely objective and measurable meaning independent of value
judgements, as was shown above in Chapter 3.

[1] 'Supposedly' because of the 'circularity' of the arguments concerning
amenity, noted earlier. No one is being compensated for the reduction in
the *total amount* of amenity and landscape. Nor are non-residents the
recipients of compensation: many of us may feel worse off because of the
destruction of landscape, wherever the TLA is sited.

10 The Damodar Valley Flood Control Scheme

THE last chapter studied the application of cost–benefit analysis to the choice of site for a particular project. The present chapter is concerned with evaluating a project which is already in operation.

10.1 THE DAMODAR VALLEY SYSTEM

The Damodar river rises in the Palamau hills, Bihar (north-east India), at an elevation of about 2000 feet. It flows eastwards for about 180 miles through Bihar and enters the deltaic plains of West Bengal below the coal-mining centre of Raniganj (see Fig. 10.1.1). It continues to flow east and as it reaches the boundary of Burdwan district it is joined by the river Barakor. The enlarged river flows along the boundary of Bankura and Burdwan districts and then into the Burdwan district, passing just south of Burdwan town. About ten miles east of Burdwan town, the river abruptly changes its course and turns south. It bifurcates into the rivers Mundeswari and Damodar about two miles before entering Hooghly district. In the extreme southern part of Hooghly district, some thirty miles below Calcutta, it joins the Hooghly river which reaches the sea shortly afterwards.

The catchment area of the river at its mouth is about 8500 square miles, of which nearly 7000 square miles is the catchment area of the upper Damodar. (The confluence with Barakor river is regarded as separating the upper and the lower stretches of the Damodar.)

The topography of the Damodar valley changes from hilly and forest regions in the upper portion of the drainage area to the flat deltaic plains of the lower region. This is reflected also in the slope of the river, which is 10 feet per mile in the first 150 miles of its course, 3 feet per mile in the next 100 miles and less than 1 foot per mile in the last 90 miles.

The Damodar is a flood-prone river. Since at least as far back as 1730, it has been known to overflow its banks during the rainy season, leading to devastating floods in the lower valley.

The occurrence of floods along the Damodar river is due in the first

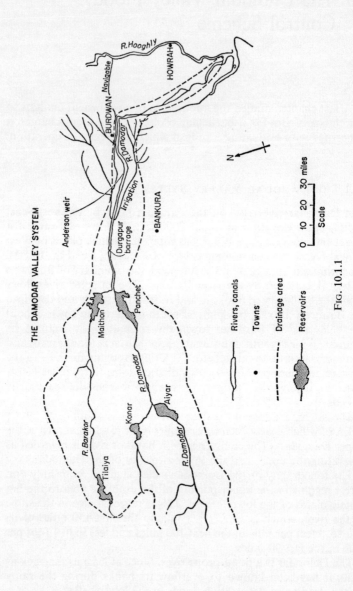

THE DAMODAR VALLEY SYSTEM

R.Hooghly

HOWRAH

Navigable

BURDWAN

R.Damodar

Irrigation

Anderson weir

Durgapur barrage

• BANKURA

Panchet

Maithon

R. Barakor

R. Damodar

Konar

Tilaiya

Aiyar

R. Damodar

N

0   10   20   30 miles
Scale

Rivers, canals

Towns

Drainage area

Reservoirs

Fig. 10.1.1

Table 10.1.1 Allocation of Storage Capacities in the D.V.C. Dams

	Tilaiya		Konar		Maithon		Panchet		Total	
	Storage capacity (in thousand acre-feet)	Percentage	Storage capacity (in thousand acre-feet)	Percentage	Storage capacity (in thousand acre-feet)	Percentage	Storage capacity (in thousand acre-feet)	Percentage	Storage capacity (in thousand acre-feet)	Percentage
Irrigation and power	115	36	179	66	496	45	185	15	975	33
Flood control	144	45	45	16	440	40	881	73	1510	52
Dead storage	61	19	49	18	168	15	148	12	426	15
To top of gate	320	100	273	100	1104	100	1214	100	2911	100

Source: D.V.C. Data Book (1966).

instance to heavy storm-rainfalls during the monsoon period, and more generally to certain characteristics of the river regime. Thus, in the earlier part of its course the river flows very rapidly, eroding land and collecting silt, a tendency which has been accelerated by deforestation in the upper reaches. In its lower reaches, the flat deltaic plains of West Bengal, it becomes a sluggish stream and discharges its flood waters and silt along its banks.

The system of dams and reservoirs designed to develop and control the waters of the Damodar valley is administered by a public corporation – the Damodar Valley Corporation (D.V.C.). The control system is generally referred to as the D.V.C. system. It consists of four dams, Tilaiya and Maithon on the Barakor, and Konar and Panchet Hill on the river Damodar (Fig. 10.1.1). Of these, Tilaiya is a concrete gravity dam while the others are earth dams with a concrete spillway. The total storage capacity of the four dams together amounts to 2·9 million acre-feet, which is allocated between the different objectives as shown in Table 10.1.1.

In addition to the four dams, the system includes a hydro power station at each of the dams except Konar; thermal power stations;

Table 10.1.2   *Classification of Area of Some Districts in the Lower Damodar Valley According to Some Characteristics, 1962–3*
(in thousand hectares)

| Characteristics | Districts (West Bengal) | | | | |
	Burdwan	Bankura	Howrah	Hooghly	Purulia
(a) Area irrigated by various canals*	259·30	118·10	24·50	109·20	78·10
(b) Area available for cultivation	542·70	507·00	118·30	251·10	446·20
(c) Area sown more than once	32·80	19·40	19·50	47·70	14·10
(d) Net area sown	495·10	346·60	95·30	239·10	236·20
(e) Area not available for cultivation†	139·80	39·30	36·80	62·60	89·30
(f) Current fallows	11·80	81·50	8·70	2·60	79·10
(g) Other uncultivated land, excluding current fallows	35·80	78·90	14·30	9·40	130·90
(h) Total area of the district	700·71	685·54	145·08	313·92	623·42

  * Relates to 1960–1.
  † Excluding forest area.

Source: Directorate of Agriculture, West Bengal.

the Durgapur barrage; and numerous irrigation canals off the barrage. Some characteristics of the lower Damodar valley are described in Table 10.1.2.
The capacity costs of the project are shown in Table 10.1.3.

Table 10.1.3   *Capacity Costs of D.V.C. Dams*

	Tilaiya	Konar	Maithon	Panchet
Storage capacity to top of gate (thousand acre-feet)	320	275	1104	1214
Total cost in million rupees	37·1	97·5*	179·3	191·4
Cost per acre-foot in rupees	116	357	162	157

* Exclusive of the costs of the hydroelectric station.

Source: Data supplied by the D.V.C.

The estimated lifetimes of the component dams are as shown in Table 10.1.4.

Table 10.1.4

Estimated Lifetime of D.V.C. Dams

Dam	Estimated lifetime in years
Tilaiya	151
Konar	219
Maithon	246
Panchet	75

Source: *D.V.C. Data Book.*

10.2 FLOOD CONTROL AND COST–BENEFIT ANALYSIS

The project studied in this chapter has considerable significance in terms of the problems discussed in Chapters 1–8, especially in the following respects. Firstly, the benefits of a flood-control project during a particular year depend on whether or not a flood occurs in that year, and this cannot be known in advance. Hence, in evaluating such a project, the problems of risk and uncertainty, considered in Chapter 8, are involved in an essential way. Our discussion in Chapter 8 reached the conclusion that under conditions of risk and uncertainty the expected utility criterion provides the most generally acceptable method of project evaluation. We shall attempt to use this approach in the present case, subject to the usual limitation that utility has to be measured in monetary units, appropriate price data being used for this purpose. In a sense, the whole of the present chapter can thus be regarded as an extended appendix to Chapter 8.

Secondly, our objective is to develop a method for evaluating the benefits not only of the project as it now stands but also of possible variants of it. The question of the potential benefits of 'complete protection' against possible floods compared to the partial protection that is currently provided by the D.V.C. project is relevant here. The D.V.C. project as originally conceived was supposed to build at least six dams and provide enough flood storage capacity to prevent *any* flood damage in the area. Subsequently it was decided to provide only partial flood protection and the number of dams was reduced to four. It has often been suggested that the storage capacity should actually be increased so that the original purpose of the project may be fulfilled. An evaluation of the social benefit of complete protection in the area is thus a matter of some practical importance and relates clearly to the problem of evaluating 'given' as opposed to 'variable scale' projects discussed in Chapter 5. We shall attempt to develop a conceptual framework which enables us to make such an evaluation.

Thirdly, we shall confine ourselves to the evaluation of benefits only. We make no attempt at a systematic analysis of costs. In particular, the existing allocation of storage capacity costs as between different objectives of the system, e.g. irrigation, power, flood control, etc., is taken as given. Since a multiple-purpose river-valley scheme such as this one can properly be regarded as an indivisible unit, such an allocation is necessarily arbitrary in some degree.

Finally, our main concern throughout is to illustrate principles rather than to deal exhaustively with all the problems that actually arise.

10.3 THE 'OFFICIAL' APPROACH TO BENEFIT ESTIMATION

While there has been a great deal of study of flood-control problems in India from the engineering and hydrological points of view, on the economic aspects of flood control little systematic research appears to have been done.

The authors of the *D.V.C. Data Book* point out that 'curves establishing relations between flood storage versus damage in the lower valley have not been worked out after a carefully planned survey of the affected regions after the occurrence of floods', and that, in consequence, the benefits of the moderation of floods achieved by the use of the D.V.C. dams have not yet been assessed

on a scientific basis. An approximate appraisal of the flood-control
benefits of D.V.C. is attempted in the *Data Book* as follows.

Firstly, the moderation of floods by the D.V.C. reservoir system
since it started operating in 1958 is described. This is shown here in
Table 10.3.1.

Table 10.3.1 *Actual Moderation of Damodar Floods, 1958–63*

Date	Peak flow (without dams) in thousand cusecs*	Moderate flow at dams in thousand cusecs*
23–24 July 1958	228	30
12–13 Aug 1958	126	32
16–17 Sept 1958	555	175
11 July 1959	134	71
21–22 July 1959	137	90
10 Sept 1959	137	101
13 Sept 1959	137	56
1–2 Oct 1959	623	288
25–26 Aug 1960	119	72
30 Aug 1960	173	104
27–28 Sept 1960	348	92
22–23 Aug 1961	110	64
10–11 Sept 1961	118	44
2–3 Oct 1961	516	161
25–26 July 1962	117	44
22–23 Sept 1962	152	45
28–29 Sept 1963	216	41
2–3 Oct 1963	451	121
24–25 Oct 1963	465	91

* A cusec is one cubic foot per second.

Source: *D.V.C. Data Book* (1966).

Secondly, the relationship between the flood discharge and the
area affected is stated to be as in Table 10.3.2.

Table 10.3.2 *Relationship between Flood Discharge and Area Affected*

Flood discharges	Region affected	Area in square miles
Less than 100,000 cusec	None	0
100,000 to 200,000 cusec	Amta–Mundeswari	300
200,000 to 300,000 cusec	Amta–Mundeswari and Raina area	500
300,000 cusec and above	Amta–Mundeswari, Raina and left-bank area	1500

Thirdly, the number of occasions when the different areas would
have been affected without dams and the number of occasions when
they were actually affected with dams are listed in Table 10.3.3.

I

Table 10.3.3

Date	Amta–Mundeswari without dams	Area with dams	Raina without dams	Area with dams	Left bank without dams	Area with dams
23–24 July 1958	*	–	*	–	–	–
12–13 Aug 1958	*	–	–	–	–	–
16–17 Sept 1958	*	*	*	–	*	–
11 July 1959	*	–	–	–	–	–
21–22 July 1959	*	–	–	–	–	–
10 Sept 1959	*	–	–	–	–	–
13 Sept 1959	*	–	–	–	–	–
1–2 Oct 1959	*	*	*	*	*	–
25–26 Aug 1960	*	–	–	–	–	–
30 Aug 1960	*	–	–	–	–	–
27–28 Sept 1960	*	–	*	–	*	–
22–23 Aug 1961	*	–	–	–	–	–
10–11 Sept 1961	*	–	–	–	–	–
2–3 Oct 1961	*	*	*	–	*	–
25–26 July 1962	*	–	–	–	–	–
22–23 Sept 1962	*	–	–	–	–	–
28–29 Sept 1963	*	–	*	–	–	–
2–3 Oct 1963	*	*	*	–	*	–
24–25 Oct 1963	*	–	*	–	*	–
Total of occasions	19	4	8	1	6	0

* shows area was affected; – shows area was not affected.

The benefits due to flood control are considered to be twofold: (i) the saving of crops, and (ii) the protection of property. The probable damage due to flood inundation is estimated from the previous data together with the further assumptions that (a) the intensity of cultivation is 80 per cent, (b) the average yield of the crop (paddy) is 25 maunds per acre (=2056 lb per acre), (c) the price of paddy is Rs 15 per maund (i.e. Rs 0·18 per lb) and (d) flooding of the left-bank area causes damage to property to the extent of about Rs 200 million, in addition to the damage to agricultural production.

On these assumptions, the losses due to damage in the Amta–Mundeswari area are put at Rs (300×0·8×640×25×15) = Rs 60 million. Similarly, the damage due to flooding in the Raina area is put at Rs 40 million and that due to flooding of the left bank at Rs 400 million.

Hence the damage that would have occurred without dams is put at Rs (19×60+8×40+6×400) million = Rs 3860 million. The damage with the dams is estimated to be Rs (4×60+40) million =

Rs 280 million. Hence the reduction in damage due to the dams is estimated as Rs 3580 million.

Since this refers to the period 1958–64, the corresponding average flood benefit per year becomes Rs $\frac{3580}{7}$ million = Rs 51 million approximately.

10.4 AN ALTERNATIVE APPROACH TO BENEFIT ESTIMATION

The method of evaluating flood-control benefits described above is based on the correct idea that these benefits consist in the reduction of flood damage that the project in question makes possible. However, the method suffers from a number of inadequacies.

Firstly, in using the sample observations during 1958–64 to derive the project benefits of flood control, the method appeals implicitly to the theory of probability; but it fails to specify a well-defined probabilistic model which can serve as a basis for prediction.

Secondly, the sample itself is too small.

Thirdly, the method does not lend itself conveniently to an analysis of the variations in project benefit corresponding to variations in the reservoir operation policy.

Fourthly, the inclusion of all flood discharges above 100,000 cusecs in a given year leads to double-counting of crop damage and hence to overestimation of flood-control benefit.

Because of these defects in the method used by the authorities of D.V.C., and as the more conventional analysis based on the 'stage-damage curve' (which relates various flood stages to the associated levels of flood damage) is ruled out by the shortage of data, we shall attempt to develop an alternative approach in terms of which the data that *are* available can best be utilised.

The basic assumption underlying our approach is that flood damage is a function of the peak flow only (cf. Maass *et al.* [1] pp. 287–8). In fact, the level of damage depends also on such considerations as the time of year (which, for example, affects the maturity of crops), the velocity of flow, the physical and chemical properties of flood waters and the depth and duration of inundation. The use of peak flow as *the* determinant of flood damage only provides a convenient first approximation.[1]

[1] By defining 'peak flow' as the yearly maximum of 'average daily flows' (rather than as 'momentary peaks'), one can also, to some extent, implicitly take duration into account (see below, pp. 248–9).

If flood damage can be regarded as related predominantly to the level of flood discharge, as is often the case, the benefits of flood control per period can be written as

$$B = \int_x p(x)\{c(x) - c(x^1)\}dx$$

where $p(x)$ denotes the probability density of peak flow x;
  $c(x)$ is the corresponding social cost ('flood damage'); and
  x^1 denotes the moderated outflow corresponding to the flood discharge level x.

In the case of a reservoir storage system of flood control, let $x^1 = \Psi(x)$ represent the reservoir operation policy. Then, substituting this equivalence into the first equation gives

$$B = \int_x p(x)\{c(x) - c(\Psi(x))\}dx.$$

Assuming a stationary probability distribution $p(x)$ over the relevant period, the present value of an annuity of B per period over the life of the project at the appropriate rate of discount gives the gross benefit of the project. By subtracting from this figure the relevant investment and operation costs similarly 'discounted' to the base year, we can get the appropriate measure of the net benefit of the project.

If $c(x^1) = 0$, we have $B = \int_x p(x) \cdot c(x) \cdot dx$ which represents the gross benefit of complete protection. The corresponding present value gives the 'expected present social value' of complete protection. A comparison of this value with the social cost involved can in principle determine whether complete protection is 'worth while'.

It is likely that the reservoir operation policies as represented by $x^1 = \Psi(x)$ will vary with the peak flow, x. Suppose they vary as follows:

If $x > x_1$,   then $x^1 = \Psi_1(x)$;
if $x_1 \leq x < x_2$, then $x^1 = \Psi_2(x)$;
. . . .

and so on.

The gross benefit of flood control becomes

$$B = \int_x p(x)c(x)dx - \left[\int_{x_1}^\infty p(x)c\{\Psi_1(x)\}dx + \int_{x_2}^{x_1} p(x)c\{\Psi_2(x)\}dx \ldots\right].$$

Given the operating policy, the probability distribution $p(x)$ and the flood damage function $c(x)$, B can be readily calculated.

10.5 AN APPLICATION OF THE ALTERNATIVE APPROACH

In this section, the principles described in section 10.4 are applied in order to evaluate flood-control policies in the Damodar Valley Project. There are two main problems: (*a*) the estimation of the probability distribution of the peak flow; and (*b*) the estimation of the peak flow/flood damage relationship. These problems are taken up in turn.

(*a*) Probability Distribution of Peak Flow

The probability distribution of the peak flow was derived from the data on the yearly maximum of average daily discharges in cusecs. These are given in Table 10.5.1 below. (The reader who is not

Table 10.5.1

Peak Flows at Rhondia, 1935–52
(thousand cusecs)

Year	Maximum of average daily discharges
1935	422·5
1936	174·5
1937	121·7
1938	61·9
1939	258·5
1940	266·5
1941	625·0
1942	375·0
1943	251·3
1944	153·5
1945	120·9
1946	313·7
1947	259·6
1948	229·7
1949	230·1
1950	245·9
1951	347·4
1952	168·3

familiar with the mathematics used can safely skip the section which derives the probability distribution.)

The statistical theory of extreme values, as developed by Gumbel [2] and others, was applied to derive the probability distribution of the peak flow. The logic of the theory can be described briefly as follows. Consider a sample containing n independent observations on a continuous variate x. We seek the probability distribution of the maximum value of x in the sample. Clearly, the probability distribution of the maximum value will depend on the probability distribution of x and on the sample size. Thus, let $f(x)$ be the probability distribution of x and let $\varphi_n(x)$ be the probability that the value x is the largest among n independent observations.

Then
$$\varphi_n(x) = \{F(x)\}^n$$

where $F(x) = \int_{-\infty}^{x} f(x)\ dx$ is the cumulative probability distribution of x.

As is usual in the analysis of flood data, we assume that the initial distribution of x is the exponential type:

$$f(x) = e^{-x}.$$

It can then be shown that

$$\lim_{n \to \infty} \varphi_n(x) = e^{-e^{-y}}$$

where y is a transform of x such that

$$y = \alpha_n(x - u_n),$$

with $1/\alpha_n$ and u_n having the same dimension as x, so that y is a pure number.

Hence, the double exponential distribution $e^{-e^{-y}}$ represents the cumulative probability distribution of the reduced variate. The derivative of this gives the corresponding probability distribution (probability density function) desired.

There are two possible approaches to the estimation of the theoretical distribution of the largest value.

Firstly, if we know the functional form of the initial distribution and the values of its parameters as well as the sample size n, then the parameters α_n and u_n can be obtained directly.

Secondly, if, as is more usual, the initial distribution is unknown, we can still estimate the parameters α_n and u_n, provided we assume that the distribution is of the exponential type. In this case, there are a number of alternative methods for estimating the parameters α_n and u_n. We shall follow the large-sample modified least squares method described by Gumbel ([2] pp. 35, 168–9).

As Gumbel shows, for large n, α_n and u_n can be estimated with a reasonable degree of approximation independently of n. The estimates depend only on the sample distribution of extreme values and are derived by the normal equations

$$\frac{1}{\alpha} = \frac{Sx}{N}$$

$$u = \bar{x} - \frac{Y_N}{\alpha}$$

where Sx, $\bar{x}$ denote respectively the standard deviation and mean of observations of the extreme values and N, Y_N are functions of the number N of extreme values observed. The values of σ_N and Y_N as functions of N have been tabulated by Gumbel ([2] p. 228).

The parameters of the theoretical distribution are now calculated for the data of Table 10.5.1. They are shown in Table 10.5.2 below.

Table 10.5.2 *Estimation of Parameters*

	Peak Flow: maximum of average daily discharges
N = Number of observations of largest value	18
$\bar{x}$ = Sample mean (thousand cusecs)	257·05
S_x = Sample standard deviation (thousand cusecs)	127·05
σ_N	1·0493
Y_N	0·5202
$\dfrac{1}{\alpha}$ (thousand cusecs) $= \dfrac{S_x}{\sigma_N}$	121·08
u (thousand cusecs) $= \bar{x} - \dfrac{Y_N}{\alpha}$	194·04

Having calculated the constants, we can now proceed to derive the observed and theoretical distributions of the largest value for each of the two types of peak-flow data considered. These are shown in Table 10.5.4.

Column 1 of Table 10.5.4 shows values of the reduced variate y at intervals of 0·25, the length of the class interval being necessarily arbitrary. Column 2 gives the corresponding values of $e^{-e^{-y}}$ as calculated from Becker's tables [3]; it gives the cumulative probability of y for each value of y tabulated in column 1. Column 3 is derived by multiplying each item in column 2 by the sample size; it gives the theoretical cumulative frequency. Column 4 gives the first differences of successive entries in column 3 and represents the theoretical frequencies in each class interval.

The peak flows x, equal to the yearly maximum of average daily discharges obtained by letting y take on the values shown in column 1, are given in column 5 $\left(x = \frac{y}{\alpha} + u; \alpha, u \text{ being found from Table} \right.$ 10.5.2 $\left. \right)$. The cumulative observed frequencies corresponding to these values of x are derived from Table 10.5.3, which gives the peak-

Table 10.5.3

Ranking of Peak Flows in Ascending Order
(peak flow = yearly maximum
of average daily discharges)

Rank	Peak flow (thousand cusecs)
1	61·9
2	120·9
3	121·7
4	153·5
5	168·3
6	174·5
7	229·7
8	230·1
9	245·9
10	251·3
11	258·5
12	259·6
13	266·5
14	313·7
15	347·4
16	375·0
17	422·5
18	625·0

flow data of Table 10.5.1 ranked in ascending order. These are given in column 6. Column 7 is obtained by taking first differences of the figures in column 6. These show the observed frequencies for the same class intervals for which the theoretical frequencies were calculated.

The cumulative frequency distributions for theoretical and observed peak flows as calculated above are graphically represented in Fig. 10.5.1 (peak flow = yearly maximum of average daily discharges). The observed and theoretical cumulative distribution show close agreement. This provides some justification for the use of the estimated distribution for the assessment of flood damage in this region.

Table 10.5.4 Theoretical and Observed Distribution of Peak Flow
(maximum of average daily discharges)

(1) Reduced variable	(2) Theoretical cumulative probability	(3) Theoretical cumulative frequency	(4) Theoretical frequency	(5) Observed peak flow $x = \frac{y}{\alpha} + u$	(6) Observed cumulative frequency	(7) Observed frequency
−1·00	0·06599	1	1	73	1	1
−0·75	0·12039	2	1	103	1	0
−0·50	0·19230	4	2	133	3	2
−0·25	0·27693	5	1	164	4	1
0·00	0·36788	7	2	194	6	2
0·25	0·45896	8	1	224	6	0
0·50	0·54524	10	2	255	10	4
0·75	0·62352	11	1	285	13	3
1·00	0·69220	13	2	315	14	1
1·25	0·75088	14	1	345	14	0
1·50	0·80001	14	0	376	16	2
1·75	0·84048	15	1	406	16	0
2·00	0·87342	16	1	436	17	1
2·25	0·89996	16	0	466	17	0
2·50	0·92119	17	1	497	17	0
2·75	0·93807	17	0	527	17	0
3·00	0·95143	17	0	557	17	0
3·25	0·96197	17	0	587	17	0
3·50	0·97025	18	1	618	17	0
3·75	0·97675	18	0	648	18	1

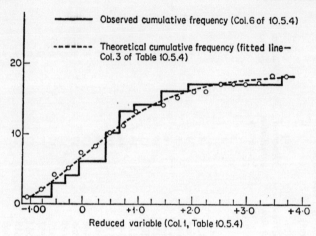

FIG. 10.5.1

(b) *The Relationship between Peak Flow and Flood Damage*

The relationship between peak flow and flood damage was derived in two stages: (1) the relationship between peak flow and area inundated, and (2) the calculation of the damage per unit area inundated.

The choice of this method was dictated by the lack of data required for more sophisticated methods of analysis. Since, in the area concerned, flood damage consists predominantly of damage to agricultural output, it is believed that the method provides reasonably satisfactory estimates of flood damage.

The relationship between the flood intensity and the area inundated was derived from the observations listed in Table 10.5.5.

Table 10.5.5

x *Discharge at Rhondia* (thousand cusecs)	*y* *Area inundated* (square miles)
150	360
200	386
250	405
300	423
400	454
500	479
600	500

Source: *Report of the Committee for the Augmentation of Water Resources of Damodar Valley Corporation* (Calcutta, 1959) p. 52.

A linear regression $y = \alpha + \beta x$ was fitted to the data by the standard least-squares method and gave the following results:

$$\alpha = 324{\cdot}930$$
$$\beta = 0{\cdot}305$$
$$r^2 = 0{\cdot}944$$
$$t = \frac{r\sqrt{5}}{\sqrt{1-r^2}} = 9{\cdot}215.$$

The function

$$y = 324{\cdot}93 + 0{\cdot}305x$$

was used for calculating the area inundated, y, for a given discharge, x. (See above for the derivation of this equation. The relationship between the theoretical and observed values suggested that a linear regression was justified.)

To calculate the damage per unit of area inundated, we made the same assumptions that were used by the D.V.C. in computing their own estimates of flood damage, namely:

(a) The intensity of cultivation is 80 per cent.
(b) Paddy is the only crop grown.
(c) The average yield of paddy is 2056 lb per acre.
(d) The average price of paddy is Rs 0·18 per lb.

The probability distribution of the peak flow together with the discharge/flood-damage relationship enable the gross benefit of flood-control policies as described in section 10.4 to be computed. For this purpose, the maximum of average daily discharges measure of the peak flow was used, since this appeared to be the concept most closely related to the data of Table 10.5.5, from which the linear regression of the area inundated on flood discharge was computed.

We then have the annual expected area inundated

$$= 324{\cdot}93 + [0{\cdot}305 \times 257{\cdot}03] = 403{\cdot}38 \text{ square miles}$$

(the sample mean $\bar{x}$ being used to estimate the population mean). On the assumptions made about the damage per unit area inundated, the value of crops lost per year is Rs 82 million.

The life of the project was assumed to be one hundred years, which is generally used for the evaluation of similar projects in India. The present value of an annuity of Rs 82 million per year for a hundred years at a 10 per cent rate of discount is Rs 820 million approximately.[1] This can be regarded as an estimate of the damage to agricultural production due to floods in the Damodar valley.

Apart from the damage to agricultural output, damage to property such as railway lines or roads on the left bank of the Damodar river may also occur if the peak flow is sufficiently high. The expected level of such damage can then be computed from our estimated probability distribution together with the relevant damage function. Similar considerations apply to the damage due to loss of life, although special difficulties are involved in evaluating such damage.

The Damodar Valley Project cannot at present provide for complete flood protection. Hence, to compute the benefits of the extent of flood protection achieved by the project, one could follow the method indicated in section 10.4, by estimating the functions $\Psi(x)$ representing the reservoir operation policies in various ranges of values of x. The benefits so computed could then be compared with the relevant costs.

10.6 A SUMMARY

We shall conclude by pointing out some of the more important limitations of the method of evaluating flood-control benefits described in this chapter.

Firstly, the estimation of the flood-damage function involves a number of serious difficulties. Thus, the relationship between flood discharge and area inundated in this region is likely to show an upward shift over time owing to the building of new structures and the silting of the river bed in the lower valley. This has in fact been happening in the deltaic regions of West Bengal, with the result that a peak flow of a given intensity now tends to produce a greater extent of inundation than in the past.

Again, the damage per unit area inundated tends to increase over time because of economic development. To the extent that such an increase in the damage factor is due to autonomous economic development, the estimation procedure may be corrected by appropriate statistical analysis (e.g. by taking trend factors into

---

[1] Within the normal range of rates of discount it actually makes very little difference whether the lifetime used is 100 years or 150 years or infinity. 10 per cent has been widely used as an accounting rate of discount in public-sector projects in India. However, this rate is used here merely to illustrate the method. The question of the appropriate social rate of discount has been discussed in Chapter 6 above.

account). On the other hand, economic development may result from the flood-control project itself. In this case, there are considerable conceptual difficulties in evaluating project benefits. These are connected with the question: do flood-control schemes lead to 'over-development' in the flood basin? Such a question cannot easily be answered within the framework of cost–benefit analysis itself (but see Renshaw [4]).

Secondly, this exercise has been confined to the flood-control component of the D.V.C. project; for this purpose, we took the allocation of storage capacity between different objectives, e.g. flood control, irrigation and power, as given. This means in effect that we accepted without question the constraints imposed on the system, viz. certain minimum levels of power, flood-control storage and so on. On the other hand, one of the aims of cost–benefit analysis of multi-purpose river-valley projects should be to examine the opportunity costs of varying the levels of different constraints. This can provide means of estimating the trade-offs between different objectives. However, the method described for estimating the benefits of flood control may itself be regarded as a first step towards making such comparisons possible. Thirdly, no attempt was made to estimate the 'secondary' benefits of flood control.

Finally, it must be stressed once more that the statistical calculations provided in this chapter must be regarded as illustrative and preliminary rather than as providing a blueprint for the project in question.

Bibliography

INTRODUCTION

[1] J. Dupuit, 'On the Measurement of the Utility of Public Works' (1844), translated from the French, in *International Economic Papers*, no. 2 (London, 1952).

[2] U.S. Government: Federal Inter-Agency River Basin Committee, Subcommittee on Benefits and Costs, *Proposed Practices for Economic Analysis of River Basin Projects* (Washington, 1950).

[3] U.S. Government: Bureau of the Budget, *Budget Circular A-47* (Washington, 1952).

[4] O. Eckstein, *Water Resource Development: The Economics of Project Evaluation* (Cambridge, Mass., 1958).

[5] R. McKean, *Efficiency in Government through System Analysis with Emphasis on Water Resources Development* (New York, 1958).

[6] J. Krutilla and O. Eckstein, *Multiple Purpose River Development: Studies in Applied Economic Analysis* (Baltimore, 1958).

[7] A. Maass *et al.*, *Design of Water Resource Systems* (London, 1962).

[8] U.S. Government: Panel of Consultants to the Bureau of the Budget, *Standards and Criteria for Formulating and Evaluating Federal Water Resources Development* (Washington, 1961).

[9] T. Coburn, M. Beesley and D. Reynolds, *The London–Birmingham Motorway: Traffic and Economics*, Road Research Laboratory, Technical Paper No. 46 (London, 1960).

[10] U.K. Government: Cmnd 3437, *Nationalised Industries: A Review of Economic and Financial Objectives* (H.M.S.O., London, 1967).

[11] I. M. D. Little and J. Mirrlees, *Manual of Industrial Project Analysis*, vol. II: *Social Cost–Benefit Analysis* (O.E.C.D., Paris, 1969).

[12] A. Seldon, in the Introduction to G. H. Peters, *Cost–Benefit Analysis and Public Expenditure*, Eaton Paper No. 8, 2nd ed. (Institute of Economic Affairs, London, 1968).

[13] W. Baumol, *Welfare Economics and the Theory of the State* (London, 1952).
[14] J. de V. Graaff, *Theoretical Welfare Economics* (Cambridge, 1957).

Chapter 1

[1] P. Newman, *Theory of Exchange* (Englewood Cliffs, N.J., 1965) pp. 23–6.
[2] W. Armstrong, 'The Determinateness of the Utility Function', *Economic Journal* (Sept 1939); and articles in *Economic Journal* (Sept 1945), *Oxford Economic Papers* (Jan 1950, Oct 1951, Oct 1953 and June 1955).
[3] J. von Neumann and O. Morgenstern, *The Theory of Games and Economic Behavior* (Princeton, 1947).
[4] J. Marschak, 'Rational Behaviour, Uncertain Prospects and Measurable Utility', *Econometrica* (Apr 1950).
[5] D. H. Robertson, *Utility and All That and Other Essays* (London, 1952).
[6] W. J. Baumol, 'The Neumann–Morgenstern Utility Index: An Ordinalist View', *Journal of Political Economy* (Feb 1951).
[7] J. Rothenberg, *The Measurement of Social Welfare* (Englewood Cliffs, N.J., 1961).
[8] P. A. Samuelson, 'Probability, Utility and the Strong Independence Axiom', *Econometrica* (Oct 1952).
[9] P. A. Samuelson, R. Dorfman and R. M. Solow, *Linear Programming and Economic Analysis* (New York, 1958).
[10] F. E. Mosteller and P. Nogee, 'An Experimental Measure of Utility', *Journal of Political Economy* (Oct 1951).
[11] H. A. Simon, *Models of Man* (New York, 1957) chap. 14.
[12] C. W. Churchman, 'Concepts without Primitives', *Philosophy of Science* (1953).
[13] D. Luce and H. Raiffa, *Games and Decisions* (New York, 1957).
[14] J. O. Wisdom, *Other Minds* (Oxford, 1952).
[15] P. F. Strawson, *Individuals* (London, 1959).
[16] C. W. Churchman, 'On the Intercomparison of Utilities', in S. Krupp (ed.), *The Structure of Economic Science* (Englewood Cliffs, N.J., 1966).
[17] R. M. Dunn, 'A Problem of Bias in Benefit–Cost Analysis: Consumer Surplus Reconsidered', *Southern Economic Journal* (Jan 1967).

[18] W. J. Stober, L. Falk and R. Ekelund, 'Cost Bias in Benefit–Cost Analysis: Comment', *Southern Economic Journal* (Apr 1967–8).

CHAPTER 2

[1] N. Kaldor, 'Welfare Comparisons of Economics and Interpersonal Comparisons of Utility', *Economic Journal* (1939). Reprinted in K. Arrow and T. Scitovsky (eds), *Readings in Welfare Economics* (London, 1969) pp. 387–9.

[2] J. R. Hicks, 'The Foundations of Welfare Economics', *Economic Journal* (1939); and 'The Valuation of Social Income', *Economica* (1940).

[3] T. Scitovsky, 'A Note on Welfare Propositions in Economics', *Review of Economic Studies* (1941–2). Reprinted in K. Arrow and T. Scitovsky (eds), *Readings in Welfare Economics* (London, 1969) pp. 390–401.

[4] J. Krutilla, 'Welfare Aspects of Benefit–Cost Analysis', *Journal of Political Economy* (June 1961).

[5] O. Eckstein, *Water Resource Development* (Cambridge, Mass., 1958) pp. 36–7.

[6] Commission on the Third London Airport, *Papers and Proceedings*, vol. VII (H.M.S.O., London, 1970).

[7] A. Maass, 'Benefit–Cost Analysis: Its Relevance to Public Investment Decisions', *Quarterly Journal of Economics* (May 1966).

[8] I. M. D. Little, *A Critique of Welfare Economics*, 2nd ed. (Oxford, 1957).

[9] R. Dorfman, 'An Economic Strategy for West Pakistan', *Asian Survey*, III (May 1963).

[10] J. T. Bonnen, 'The Distribution of Benefits from Cotton Price Supports', in S. B. Chase (ed.), *Problems in Public Expenditure Analysis* (Brookings Institution, Washington, 1968).

[11] B. Weisbrod, 'Income Redistribution Effects and Benefit–Cost Analysis', in S. Chase (ed.), *Problems in Public Expenditure Analysis* (Brookings Institution, Washington, 1968).

[12] M. McGuire and H. Garn, 'The Integration of Equity and Efficiency Criteria in Public Project Selection', *Economic Journal* (Dec 1969).

[13] J. Krutilla and O. Eckstein, *Multiple Purpose River Development* (Baltimore, 1958).

[14] C. D. Foster, 'Social Welfare Functions in Cost–Benefit

Analysis', in M. Lawrence (ed.), *Operational Research in the Social Sciences* (London, 1966).

CHAPTER 3

[1] K. J. Arrow, *Social Choice and Individual Values*, 2nd ed. (New York, 1963).

[2] A. K. Sen, *Collective Choice and Social Welfare* (London, 1970).

[3] A. Bergson, 'A Reformulation of Certain Aspects of Welfare Economics', *Quarterly Journal of Economics* (Feb 1938).

[4] A. Bergson, 'Socialist Economics', in H. S. Ellis (ed.), *A Survey of Contemporary Economics*, vol. I (Philadelphia, 1948).

[5] P. A. Samuelson, *The Foundations of Economic Analysis* (Cambridge, Mass., 1950).

[6] J. de V. Graaff, *Theoretical Welfare Economics* (Cambridge, 1957).

[7] I. M. D. Little, 'Social Choice and Individual Values', *Journal of Political Economy* (Oct 1952).

[8] A. Bergson, 'On the Concept of Social Welfare', *Quarterly Journal of Economics* (May 1954).

[9] M. C. Kemp, 'Arrow's General Possibility Theorem', *Review of Economic Studies*, XXI (1953-4).

[10] J. S. Coleman, 'The Possibility of a Social Welfare Function', *American Economic Review* (1966).

[11] C. Hildreth, 'Alternative Conditions for Social Orderings', *Econometrica* (Jan 1953).

[12] J. C. Harsanyi, 'Cardinal Utility in Welfare Economics and in the Theory of Risk-taking', *Journal of Political Economy* (Oct 1953).

[13] P. K. Pattanaik, 'Risk, Impersonality and the Social Welfare Function', *Journal of Political Economy* (May 1968).

[14] D. Black, 'On the Rationale of Group Decision Making', *Journal of Political Economy* (Feb 1948).

[15] J. M. Buchanan and G. Tullock, *The Calculus of Consent* (Ann Arbor, 1962).

[16] T. Majumdar, 'Choice and Revealed Preference', *Econometrica* (1956).

[17] I. M. D. Little, *A Critique of Welfare Economics* (Oxford, 1950).

CHAPTER 4

[1] P. Samuelson, R. Dorfman and R. Solow, *Linear Programming and Economic Analysis* (New York, 1958).

[2] R. F. Kahn, 'Some Notes on Ideal Output', *Economic Journal* (1935).

[3] L. W. McKenzie, 'Ideal Output and the Interdependence of Firms', *Economic Journal* (1951).

[4] M. Dobb, *Welfare Economics and the Economics of Socialism* (Cambridge, 1969) chap. 4.

[5] J. R. Hicks, *Value and Capital*, 2nd ed. (Oxford, 1946).

[6] S. Marglin, *Public Investment Criteria* (London, 1967) esp. chap. 2.

[7] R. McKean, 'Shadow Prices', in S. B. Chase (ed.), *Problems in Public Expenditure Analysis* (Brookings Institution, Washington, 1968).

[8] A. Prest and R. Turvey, 'Cost–Benefit Analysis: A Survey', *Economic Journal* (Dec 1965).

[9] R. L. Lipsey and K. Lancaster, 'The General Theory of Second Best', *Review of Economic Studies* (1956–7).

[10] J. Margolis, 'Comment' on McKean [7], pp. 71–7.

[11] O. Davis and A. Whinston, 'Welfare Economics and the Theory of the Second Best', *Review of Economic Studies* (1966).

[12] J. Wiseman, 'The Theory of Public Utility Price: An Empty Box', *Oxford Economic Papers* (1957).

[13] R. Turvey, *Optimal Pricing and Investment in Electricity Supply* (London, 1968) chap. 8.

[14] R. Rees, 'Second Best Rules for Public Enterprise Pricing', *Economica* (Aug 1968).

[15] C. Foster and M. Beesley, 'Estimating the Social Benefit of Constructing an Underground Railway in London', *Journal of the Royal Statistical Society*, series A (1963).

[16] H. Demsetz, 'The Exchange and Enforcement of Property Rights', *Journal of Law and Economics* (Oct 1964).

[17] D. H. Brownlee, 'User Prices *vs.* Taxes', in N.B.E.R., *Public Finances: Needs, Sources and Utilisation* (Princeton, 1961).

[18] J. Rothenberg, 'Urban Renewal Programs', in R. Dorfman (ed.), *Measuring Benefits of Government Investments* (Brookings Institution, Washington, 1965).

CHAPTER 5

[1] J. M. Buchanan and W. Stubblebine, 'Externality', *Economica* (1962), reprinted in K. Arrow and T. Scitovsky (eds), *Readings in Welfare Economics* (London, 1969).

[2] J. Duesenberry, *Income, Saving and the Theory of Consumer Behaviour* (Cambridge, Mass., 1949).

[3] M. Kemp, 'The Efficiency of Competition as an Allocator of Resources: II – External Economies of Consumption', *Canadian Journal of Economics and Political Science* (May 1955).

[4] O. Davis and A. Whinston, 'Some Notes on Equating Private and Social Cost', *Southern Economic Journal* (Oct 1965).

[5] F. T. Dolbear, 'On the Theory of Optimum Externality', *American Economic Review* (Mar 1967).

[6] E. J. Mishan, 'Reflections of Recent Developments in the Concept of External Effects', *Canadian Journal of Economics and Political Science* (Feb 1965).

[7] A. O. Hirschman, *Development Projects Observed* (Brookings Institution, Washington, 1967).

[8] E. J. Mishan, *The Costs of Economic Growth* (London, 1967).

[9] R. Turvey, 'On Divergencies between Social Cost and Private Cost', *Economica* (1965).

[10] J. G. Head, 'Public Goods and Public Policy', *Public Finance* (1962).

[11] J. M. Buchanan, 'Joint Supply, Externality and Optimality', *Economica* (Nov 1966).

[12] R. Musgrave, 'Provision for Social Goods', in J. Margolis and H. Guitton (eds), *Public Economics* (London, 1969).

[13] P. Samuelson, 'Contrast between Welfare Conditions for Joint Supply and Public Goods', *Review of Economics and Statistics* (Feb 1969).

[14] E. J. Mishan, 'The Relationship between Joint Products, Collective Goods and External Effects', *Journal of Political Economy* (May–June 1969).

[15] R. E. Millward, 'Exclusion Costs, External Economies and Market Failure', *Oxford Economic Papers* (May 1970).

[16] P. Bohm, 'An Approach to the Problem of Estimating Demand for Public Goods', *Swedish Journal of Economics* (Mar 1971).

[17] P. Bohm, 'Estimating Demand for Public Goods: An Experiment', *European Economic Review* (1971).

[18] M. Peston, *Public Goods and the Public Sector* (London, 1972).

CHAPTER 6

[1] S. Marglin, 'The Social Rate of Discount and the Optimal Rate of Investment', *Quarterly Journal of Economics* (Feb 1963).
[2] A. C. Pigou, *The Economics of Welfare*, 4th ed. (London, 1932) esp. pp. 23–30.
[3] M. Dobb, *An Essay on Economic Growth and Planning* (London, 1960).
[4] A. K. Sen, 'On Optimising the Rate of Saving', *Economic Journal* (Sept 1961).
[5] O. Eckstein, 'A Survey of the Theory of Public Expenditure Criteria', in N.B.E.R., *Public Finances: Needs, Sources and Utilisation* (Princeton, 1961).
[6] W. J. Baumol, 'On the Social Rate of Discount', *American Economic Review* (Dec 1968).
[7] G. Tullock, 'The Social Rate of Discount and the Optimal Rate of Investment: Comment', *Quarterly Journal of Economics* (May 1964).
[8] R. Frisch, 'A Complete Scheme for Computing All Direct and Cross-Demand Elasticities in a Model with Many Sectors', *Econometrica* (Apr 1959).
[9] I. F. Pearce, *A Contribution to Demand Analysis* (Oxford, 1964).
[10] J. E. Meade, *Trade and Welfare* (London, 1955) esp. chap. 6.
[11] O. Eckstein, 'Investment Criteria for Economic Development and the Theory of Intertemporal Welfare Economics', *Quarterly Journal of Economics* (Feb 1957).
[12] M. Feldstein, 'The Derivation of Social Time Preference Rates', *Kyklos*, XVIII (1965).
[13] K. Arrow, 'Discounting and Public Investment Criteria', in A. V. Kneese and S. Smith (eds), *Water Research* (Baltimore, 1966).
[14] F. P. Ramsey, 'A Mathematical Theory of Saving', *Economic Journal* (Dec 1928).
[15] J. Hirschleifer, 'Comment' to O. Eckstein [5].
[16] U.S. Bureau of the Budget, *Standards and Criteria for Formulating and Evaluating Federal Water Resources Development* (Washington, 1961).
[17] J. Hirschleifer, J. de Haven and J. Milliman, *Water Supply* (Chicago, 1960).
[18] J. A. Stockfisch, 'The Interest Rate Applicable to Government Investment Projects', in H. Hinrichs and G. Taylor (eds), *Program Budgeting and Benefit–Cost Analysis* (Pacific Palisades, Calif., 1969).

[19] *Nationalised Industries: A Review of Economic and Financial Objectives*, Cmnd 3437 (H.M.S.O., London, 1967).
[20] A. M. Alfred, 'The Correct Yardstick for State Investment', *District Bank Review* (June 1968).
[21] K. Arrow, 'Criteria for Social Investment', *Water Resources Research* (1st quarter, 1965).
[22] A. Nichols, 'On the Social Rate of Discount: Comment', *American Economic Review* (1970).
[23] M. Feldstein, 'The Social Time Preference Rate in Cost–Benefit Analysis', *Economic Journal* (June 1964).
[24] J. Hirschleifer, 'On the Theory of Optimal Investment Decision', *Journal of Political Economy* (Aug 1958), and more recently in *Investment, Interest and Capital* (Englewood Cliffs, N.J., 1970).
[25] I. M. D. Little and J. Mirrlees, *Manual of Industrial Project Analysis in Developing Countries*, vol. II: *Social Cost–Benefit Analysis* (O.E.C.D., Paris, 1969).
[26] S. Marglin, 'The Opportunity Costs of Public Investment', *Quarterly Journal of Economics* (May 1963).
[27] S. Marglin, *Public Investment Criteria* (London, 1967).
[28] E. J. Mishan, 'Criteria for Public Investment: Some Simplifying Suggestions', *Journal of Political Economy* (1967).
[29] J. L. Carr, 'Social Time Preference versus Social Opportunity Cost in Investment Criteria', *Economic Journal* (Dec 1966).

CHAPTER 7

[1] J. Hirschleifer *et al.*, *Water Supply* (Chicago, 1960).
[2] S. A. Marglin, *Approaches to Dynamic Investment Planning* (Amsterdam, 1963).
[3] H. M. Weingartner, *Mathematical Programming and the Analysis of Capital Budgeting Problems* (Englewood Cliffs, N.J., 1963).
[4] P. D. Henderson, 'Notes on Public Investment Criteria in the United Kingdom', *Bulletin of the Oxford University Institute of Statistics* (1965), reprinted and revised in R. Turvey (ed.), *Public Enterprise* (London, 1968).
[5] A. Alchian, 'The Rate of Interest, Fisher's Rate of Return over Cost, and Keynes' Internal Rate of Return', *American Economic Review* (Dec 1955).
[6] C. S. Soper, 'The Marginal Efficiency of Capital: A Further Note', *Economic Journal* (Mar 1959).

[7] J. F. Wright, 'Notes on the Marginal Efficiency of Capital', *Oxford Economic Papers* (July 1963).

[8] M. Feldstein and J. S. Flemming, 'The Problem of Time-stream Evaluation: Present Value versus Internal Rate of Return Rules', *Bulletin of the Oxford University Institute of Statistics* (Feb 1964).

[9] J. Krutilla and O. Eckstein, *Multiple Purpose River Development* (Baltimore, 1958).

[10] M. J. Gordon, 'The Payoff Period and the Rate of Profit', in C. Solomon (ed.), *The Management of Corporate Capital* (New York, 1959).

[11] E. J. Mishan, 'A Proposed Normalisation Procedure for Public Investment Criteria', *Economic Journal* (Dec 1967).

[12] O. Eckstein, 'A Survey of the Theory of Public Expenditure Criteria', in N.B.E.R., *Public Finances: Needs, Sources and Utilisation* (Princeton, 1961).

[13] P. D. Henderson, 'Political and Budgetary Constraints: Some Characteristics and Implications', in J. Margolis and H. Guitton (eds), *Public Economics* (London, 1969).

[14] A. Maass *et al.*, *Design of Water Resource Systems* (London, 1962).

[15] R. Turvey, 'Present Value *versus* Internal Rate of Return: An Essay in the Theory of the Third Best', *Economic Journal* (Mar 1963).

CHAPTER 8

[1] J. M. Keynes, *General Theory of Employment, Interest and Money* (London, 1935).

[2] E. O. Heady and J. L. Dillon, *Agricultural Production Functions* (Ames, Iowa, 1961).

[3] N. V. Sovani and N. Rath, *The Economics of a Multi-Purpose River Dam* (Poona, 1960).

[4] F. H. Knight, *Risk, Uncertainty and Profit* (New York, 1921).

[5] J. de V. Graaff, *Theoretical Welfare Economics* (Cambridge, 1957).

[6] Thomas Bayes, 'An Essay toward Solving a Problem in the Doctrine of Chances', *Philosophical Transactions of the Royal Society* (1763).

[7] F. P. Ramsey, 'Truth and Probability', in *The Foundations of Mathematics, and Other Logical Essays* (London, 1931).

[8] P. G. Hoel, *Introduction to Mathematical Statistics* (New York, 1962).

[9] J. von Neumann and O. Morgenstern, *The Theory of Games and Economic Behaviour* (Princeton, 1947).

[10] L. J. Savage, *The Foundations of Statistics* (New York, 1954).

[11] J. Marschak, *Three Lectures on Probability in the Social Sciences*, Cowles Commission Papers, new series, no. 82 (New York, 1954).

[12] P. Massé, *Optimal Investment Decisions* (Englewood Cliffs, N.J., 1962).

[13] J. Marschak, 'Rational Behavior, Uncertain Prospects and Measurable Utility', *Econometrica* (Apr 1950).

[14] K. J. Arrow, *Aspects of the Theory of Risk-Bearing* (Helsinki, 1965).

[15] R. D. Luce and H. Raiffa, *Games and Decisions* (New York, 1958).

[16] R. Dorfman, 'Basic Economic and Technologic Concepts', chap. 3 in A. Maass *et al.*, *Design of Water Resource Systems* (London, 1962).

[17] U.S. Government: Federal Inter-Agency River Basin Committee, Subcommittee on Benefits and Costs, *Proposed Practices for Economic Analysis of River Basin Projects* (Washington, 1950).

CHAPTER 9

[1] D. Pearce, 'The Roskill Commission and the Location of the Third London Airport', *Three Banks Review* (Sept 1970).

[2] Commission on the Third London Airport, *Papers and Proceedings*, vol. VII, parts 1 and 2 (H.M.S.O., London, 1970).

[3] Commission on the Third London Airport, *Report* (H.M.S.O., London, 1971).

[4] R. Ridker, *The Economic Costs of Air Pollution* (New York, 1966).

[5] I. Heggie, 'Are Gravity and Interactance Models a Valid Technique for Planning Regional Transport Facilities?', *Operational Research Quarterly*, XX 1 (1969).

[6] E. J. Mishan, 'What is Wrong with Roskill', *Journal of Transport Economics* (Sept 1970).

CHAPTER 10

[1] A. Maass *et al.*, *The Design of Water Resource Systems* (London, 1962).
[2] E. J. Gumbel, *Statistics of Extremes* (New York, 1958).
[3] E. C. Becker and G. E. Van Orstrand, *Hyperbolic Functions* (Washington, 1931).
[4] E. F. Renshaw, *Toward Responsible Government: An Economic Appraisal of Federal Investment in Water Resource Programs* (Chicago, 1957).

Index

Index